Society, Culture, and STEM

Society, Culture, and STEM

A Model for Student Engagement and Teacher Collaboration

Caroline R. Pryor and Rui Kang

ROWMAN & LITTLEFIELD
Lanham • Boulder • New York • London

Published by Rowman & Littlefield
An imprint of The Rowman & Littlefield Publishing Group, Inc.
4501 Forbes Boulevard, Suite 200, Lanham, Maryland 20706
www.rowman.com

86-90 Paul Street, London EC2A 4NE

Copyright © 2025 by Caroline R. Pryor and Rui Kang

All rights reserved. No part of this book may be reproduced in any form or by any electronic or mechanical means, including information storage and retrieval systems, without written permission from the publisher, except by a reviewer who may quote passages in a review.

British Library Cataloguing in Publication Information Available

Library of Congress Cataloging-in-Publication Data Available

978-1-4758-7144-9 (cloth)
978-1-4758-7145-6 (paperback)
978-1-4758-7146-3 (electronic)

∞™ The paper used in this publication meets the minimum requirements of American National Standard for Information Sciences—Permanence of Paper for Printed Library Materials, ANSI/NISO Z39.48-1992.

To my dear and loving late husband, Brandt W. Pryor, and the many students and colleagues who, over the years, have generously tried out many of the ideas in this book. To my daughter Jill Jones, who teaches high school mathematics and sews and donates quilts to anyone in need. To Rui Kang, who models dedication and hard work.

Caroline R. Pryor

To my husband, Ezekiel, who brings me love, joy, and support each day. To my wise and down-to-earth mother, Yi, whose unconditional love brightens my mood and opens my mind on my most gloomy days. To Dr. Caroline Pryor, who was a co-chair of my dissertation committee over 20 years ago and has since been a mentor, a collaborator, and a lifelong friend.

Rui Kang

Contents

Preface   xiii

Acknowledgments   xv

PART I: INTRODUCING A SOCIO-CULTURAL STEM CURRICULUM   1

1 What This Book Is About   3
    Why Integrate Socio-cultural Background with STEM Subjects?   4
    Integrating Socio-cultural Perspectives within STEM Content—An Example   5
    What about Teacher Voice and Beliefs?   6
    How Can This Book Help Teachers Develop a Socio-cultural STEM Curriculum?   6
    How to Use a Socio-cultural STEM Node in Curriculum Development   7
    The Book's Organization   8
    References   9

2 A Pedagogical Framework for a Socio-cultural STEM Curriculum   11
    A Pedagogical Framework for Socio-cultural STEM—Community Level   13
    A Pedagogical Framework for Socio-cultural STEM—School Level   15
    A Pedagogical Framework for Socio-cultural STEM—Classroom Level   19
    Summary   22
    References   22

PART II: DEVELOPING A SOCIO-CULTURAL STEM CURRICULUM — 25

3 Using Social Problems to Frame a Curriculum Theme, Essential Questions, and Goals — 27
    Key Definitions in Curriculum Development — 27
    Identifying a Problem or Challenge — 28
    Essential Questions — 29
    Using Essential Questions to Develop a Curriculum Theme — 30
    Translating a Curriculum Theme into Curriculum Goals and Topics for Units of Study — 31
    Summary — 32
    References — 32

4 A Developmental Model for a Socio-cultural STEM Curriculum — 34
    Part 1: A Framework for Curriculum Development: *Node* as a Gathering Space — 35
    A Model for Developing a Social-cultural STEM Curriculum — 36
    Phase 1: Initial Development—Identifying Problems and Essential Questions — 38
    Phase 2: Connections—Linking Perspectives on Context and Content — 39
    Phase 3: Dissemination—Collecting Feedback for a Draft Curriculum — 39
    Phase 4: Integration—Analyzing and Incorporating Participant Responses — 41
    Phase 5: Finalization—Planning and Implementing Curriculum — 41
    Phase 6: Evaluation and Reconfiguration—Reflecting on and Revising Curriculum — 42
    Evaluation of Inputs-Outputs at Each Model Phase — 43
    Part 2: Prompts for Team Discussion — 44
    Summary — 45
    References — 46

5 Resources for Generating Inputs and Outputs to Your Nodes — 47
    Resource 1: Video Inputs-Outputs — 48
    Resource 2: Students, Parents/Caregivers, and Community as Contributors — 49
    Resource 3: Media and Technology Links: Collaboration-Productivity — 50
    Summary — 51
    Additional Resources — 52
    References — 56

PART III: EXAMPLE CURRICULUM THEMES AND LESSON PLANS   57
    Lesson Plans: Ideas and Examples   57
    Reference   58

6 Tackling Local and Global Challenges with Socio-cultural STEM   59
    Sharon M. Locke and Georgia Bracey
    An Educational Imperative—Understanding Local and
        Global Challenges   59
    Overview of Lesson Plan Topics and Contexts   60
    Lesson Plans and Resources   61
        Lesson Plan 1: Renewable Energy—The Perfect Solution?   61
        Lesson Plan 2: Water Cycle   67
        Lesson Plan 3: Watersheds   73
    Expert Opinions   77
    Conclusion   79
    References   80

7 Contextualizing Socio-cultural STEM through Historical Figures and Events   81
    Whitney G. Blankenship, Anne Aydinian-Perry, Dean P. Vesperman, and Matthew T. Missias
    Overview of Lesson Plan Topics and Contexts   82
    Lesson Plans and Resources   82
        Lesson Plan 1: Computers, Counting Machines, and the
            US Census During the Gilded Age   83
        Lesson Plan 2: Typhoid Mary and Politics of Disease   88
        Lesson Plan 3: To Have and to Hold: Preservation
            Throughout the Ages   94
    Expert Opinions   101
    Conclusion   103
    References   104

8 Learning about Contributions of Diverse Cultures to Socio-cultural STEM   105
    Matthew Lindquist and Joseph Peters
    Overview of Lesson Plan Topics and Contexts   105
    Lesson Plans and Resources   106
        Lesson Plan 1: Polynesian Voyages   106
        Lesson Plan 2: Eastern Medicine   111
        Lesson Plan 3: Indigenous Ways of Knowing   117
        Lesson Plan 4: Ancient Arts, Its Cultural Significance,
            and Its Preservation   122

	Expert Opinions	126
	Conclusion	128
	References	128
9	Computer Science Education through Socio-cultural STEAM	130

Lily R. Liang, Rui Kang, and Briana Wellman

- Overview of Lesson Plan Topics and Contexts — 131
- Lesson Plans and Resources — 132
  - Lesson Plan 1: Integrating Fashion into Robotics for Broadening Participation — 132
  - Lesson Plan 2: First Amendment Rights at Lafayette Park with Minecraft Programming — 136
  - Lesson Plan 3: Intelligent Face Mask with E-Textiles — 140
  - Lesson Plan 4: Hip Hop Music with EarSketch Programming — 144
- Expert Opinions — 148
- Conclusion — 151
- References — 151

10 Building Socio-cultural Understanding through Integration of Social Science and STEM in Problem-based Lessons — 153

Barbara O'Donnell

- Overview of the Lesson Plan Topics and Contexts — 154
- Lesson Plans and Resources — 155
  - Lesson Plan 1: Collaboration in SPACE — 155
  - Lesson Plan 2: Local Renewable Energy — 160
  - Lesson Plan 3: Pollution in Our Community — 164
  - Lesson Plan 4: Taking Action — 170
- Expert Opinions — 175
- Conclusion — 176
- References — 177

11 Using Socio-cultural STEM to Investigate Moral and Ethical Issues: Teaching Bioethics — 178

Adam I. Attwood, Donna F. Short, and Philip C. Short

- Overview of Lesson Plan Topics and Contexts — 179
- Lesson Plans and Resources — 180
  - Lesson Plan 1: The Bioethics of Online Social Media — 180
  - Lesson Plan 2: Environmental Health and Housing — 184
  - Lesson Plan 3: Public Health Policy — 187
  - Lesson Plan 4: Access to Medicine for the Individual and the Community — 190
- Expert Opinions — 192
- Conclusion — 195
- References — 195

APPENDICES — 199

Appendix A: Content Domain Learning Standards and Resources	201
Appendix B: Lesson Plan Template	203
Appendix C: Sample Letter to Parents/Caregivers and Community	205
Index	207
About the Contributors	219
About the Authors	223

Preface

In our increasingly interdependent global society, a functioning and productive citizenship demands not only scientific and technological know-how but also interpersonal, communicative, and leadership skills. Contemporary socio-scientific challenges are likely to be tackled by cross-disciplinary collaborative teams rather than isolated individuals. The very nature of successful collaboration requires the incorporation of a variety of cultural funds of knowledge.

Designing curriculum that provides students the opportunity to work collaboratively in a project-based learning environment has an uneven history in U.S. public education. John Dewey (1916) emphasized the importance of the school curriculum to be relevant to the students' community and to be integrated with activities that prepare students to contribute to the society in which they live. However, the dominant challenges of world wars and disease in the twentieth century gave rise to an industrial-factory educative model that valued *single stand-alone* content knowledge production. This educative framework has remained rather steady throughout the last century, serving as a basis for the assessment frenzy of the early 2000s.

Middle school is a crucial period for developing students' competency and interests in STEM subjects. Tai et al. (2006) found that eighth-grade students who expected to enter science-related careers were much more likely to obtain baccalaureate degrees in science-related fields than students who did not have such an expectation. Students who do not expect to enter a science-related career are not likely to take advanced high school STEM courses and often believe that they are not "smart enough" to take these courses. The transmission instructional model, coupled with rigid disciplinary boundaries, can distance students from STEM learning and careers.

Often overlooked in our endeavor to enhance student engagement is *socio-cultural context* as a foundation for providing students with a relevant and rich STEM curriculum. Our students need to learn in an environment that shifts the instructional venue from single-perspective knowledge replication to a broader *socio-cultural participatory model* drawn from a community's participants—students, parents, caregivers, and community members. Reflective of the content domain connectedness suggested by organizations such as the National Council of the Social Studies and the National Research Council, this book offers a *Socio-cultural STEM Curriculum Development Model* for *teacher-teams along with participants* to develop integrative content domain curricula. We provide a step-by-step curriculum development process along with sample lesson plans and linked resources, augmented by *Node*, a "gathering space," to prompt, collect, and analyze participant input.

The importance of providing students with an understanding of the rich contributions of cultural contexts to STEM content should not be underestimated. By drawing from the perspectives of a community's participants, an integrative curriculum sends a message of our belief in the inclusion of a broad range of students' engagement in STEM subjects.

Caroline R. Pryor and Rui Kang, April 2024

REFERENCES

Dewey, J. (1916). *Democracy and education: An introduction to the philosophy of education.* MacMillan.

Tai, R. H., Liu, C. Q., Maltese, A. V., & Fan, X. (2006). Planning early for careers in science. *Educational Forum, 312,* 1143-44. https://doi.org/10.1126/SCIENCE.1128690

Acknowledgments

We wish to thank our Editorial Review Board: Matthew Campbell, Susan Foster, Cathy McNeese, and Adam Attwood for providing us with detailed feedback on drafts of this book. We also thank the many teachers who participated in graduate level courses at Southern Illinois University Edwardsville and offered their feedback about the use of integrated lessons. Special recognition is extended to Amanda Kapper, Anna Monson, and Jessica Paschedag, teachers who donated their lesson plans to Dr. O'Donnell for her interpretive adaptation here. Noted, with our thanks, in the Contributors section are the teachers and colleagues who read the lesson plan chapters and responded to the authors' interview questions.

We also thank Southern Illinois University Edwardsville and Georgia College and State University for their recognition of our efforts to enhance community outreach and student inclusion.

No manuscript could see the light of day without great editorial support. We thank our editor April Snider for her expertise and professional guidance. We are grateful to Rowman & Littlefield Publishers for their production of this book. We also appreciate the talent and hard work of Cathy McNeese, who patiently edited and formatted multiple iterations of the manuscript. Our appreciation is extended to Melanie Ethridge, whose copyediting and feedback supported our multiple writing needs. We appreciate Kacy Hochgraber, who revised a barely visible iteration of our tables and graphs and developed these for professional publication. Thank you.

Part I

INTRODUCING A SOCIO-CULTURAL STEM CURRICULUM

Chapter 1

What This Book Is About

Do you ever wonder why some middle school students are interested in STEM subjects but many others either do not connect with STEM subjects or feel left out—as though they might not even belong in STEM classes? We know from research (e.g., Tai et al., 2006) that eighth grade can be a point when students decide to enroll in advanced STEM classes in high school or to enter a science-related career. Given the breadth of American students' experiences and cultures, we wonder what curricular framework might engage *a broader range* of students in STEM content.

We know that students' prior life experience and academic skills can be a cognitive resource for learning STEM subject content (Moll et al., 1992). Making connections between these cognitive resources and STEM content, however, is often less understood by both teachers and students (Ivanitskaya et al., 2002). A student's knowledge and skills when connected with real-life environment appear to foster connections between content knowledge and the conceptual ideas foundational to content (Lee, 2007; Moser et al., 2019).

We draw here (and in chapter 2) on the work of Gay (2010), who writes that an individual's cultural fund is the knowledge and skills one needs [and learns] to function in a particular environment. These understandings are applied socially—that is, in a real-life environment that reflects a community's commonly held values and beliefs (Nisbett & Perrin, 1977). Classically, Vygotsky (1978) posited that all learning is proximal or derived from a close and familiar environment. Cultural knowledge, or our fund of social understandings, is relevant and therefore meaningful to us as it is placed in a contextual environment of specificity. Harrison (2000) writes, knowledge resides in a specified time, place, and historic space, and includes a range of factors such as geography, politics, and other environmental elements representing a culture's composition. In this book, we define the term *socio-cultural* as *one's understanding of a fund of knowledge, skills, and values as it is placed in a contextual environment.*

As we think about curriculum development, for example, a student who learns how mathematics is integral to art or music might also view mathematics as culturally relevant, that is, a place in which their own culture is acknowledged for its contribution to creative *and* academic endeavors. Small acts such as evaluating the impact of the length of a guitar string on sound wave outcomes might prompt a student to think about music as a scientific endeavor that aligns well with cultural experience. Additionally, researchers such as Nuthall (1999) suggest that integrating specific subject content, such as science and social studies (e.g., culture), is a more *natural* portrayal of actual content as students can see the application of one subject with the other. Therefore, Nuthall notes, the process of learning in an integrated curriculum can foster students' belief in a personal fit or a vision of a role for themselves within socio-scientific learning environment. Yet we found limited information about how standards-based resources could forge a connection between students' cultural experience and their engagement in STEM or what pedagogies or curricular design might foster this connection. It is our hope that the *Socio-cultural STEM Curriculum Development Model* we present in this book provides a modality for integrating students' culture and experiences into learning STEM subjects as they identify and address current socio-scientific challenges.

WHY INTEGRATE SOCIO-CULTURAL BACKGROUND WITH STEM SUBJECTS?

Problem-solving begins with the task of asking essential questions about a problem and organizing these questions into an identifiable pathway of response—a *project*. For example, a seventh-grade science class might wonder about sustaining a healthy planet. They see plastic container waste. They know that many household products do not decompose. They watch old roads and buildings destroyed and replaced with composite materials. Now students see a challenge—a multi-faceted *project* that requires both the identification of essential questions and the critical thinking skills to address these questions.

Essential questions reside in a nexus of a socio-cultural environment and the interdisciplinary content subject knowledge foundational to their resolve. Given this complexity, we suggest teacher-teams prompt students to evaluate the questions they believe essential to a problem. For example, students can determine if essential questions provide for: (a) contextual and cultural experiences, (b) connections between content domain(s) and culture, (c) additional concerns that might arise during the resolve of a project, and/or (d) global needs.

INTEGRATING SOCIO-CULTURAL PERSPECTIVES WITHIN STEM CONTENT—AN EXAMPLE

We began our work by first talking with pre-service and in-service teachers enrolled in either a social studies methods course or a curriculum development course at a metropolitan university. Our first attempt to provide teachers with a modality for integrative curriculum development began by asking teachers to coordinate learning standards across social studies and STEM subjects (see appendix A). A group of our middle school teachers had developed a science unit on the topic of weather, including a lesson on the impact of tornadoes and hurricanes and the need to rebuild a community. To connect this topic with socio-cultural understandings, one lesson in this unit was therefore designed to explore the local community and identify an essential question. Teachers wanted to extend their own thinking about essential questions and planned to incorporate students' ideas about what might be important to investigate. They prompted students to think about the roles, skills, and economic resources that might be needed and available if a weather-related event impacted their community.

What was missing in this lesson was an opportunity for students to gain a deeper understanding of *how* and *why* various community members and institutional entities might contribute to a community faced with weather-related challenges. A lesson (or series of lessons) was needed to provide students with a pathway to learn about the possible resources within their community.

To address essential questions about resources and citizen participation, students might note which businesses would donate food or supply services. They might interview residents and find out what they think they need to survive a possible intense weather experience. As students reflect on the essential questions emerging during this project, they could then begin to identify how STEM content knowledge can help resolve a specific real-world event. Still other revelations about this project might emerge during the curriculum development process.

The teachers we worked with, however, had various concerns about helping students respond to essential questions. They wondered if integrating middle school students' socio-cultural experiences would provide answers to these questions. We suggested that teachers could guide students to investigate topics closely related to the context of their problems. Encouraging students to brainstorm their ideas about an essential question provides teacher-teams and students a pathway to integrate diverse perspectives in solving a Socio-cultural STEM-related challenge.

Still, aspects of solving a problem might need further investigation. For example, the economic environment of a community might be unknown to students. What would students know about how a community might generate the funding and talent to rebuild after a tornado or what the costs are to a community for business or personal loans? Do any of our students know about the challenges of various community sectors? Do students know anyone who began to repair their own homes or businesses? How would students generate the knowledge they need to respond to these questions? It appeared to us that we might more deeply engage students in STEM if we provided opportunities for them to draw upon and apply their socio-cultural experiences as part of a problem-based approach to scientific challenges.

WHAT ABOUT TEACHER VOICE AND BELIEFS?

After each university semester of teaching this innovation, we solicited teachers' beliefs about, attitudes toward, and intentions to use a STEM-Social Studies (STEM-SS) approach in their classes in the upcoming year. This data provided us with an initial understanding of what teachers might need to align STEM with social studies (i.e., resources, examples, online links, release time). In part we found that teachers needed a better "road map," or step-by-step guidelines, for developing an integrated curriculum, as well as strategies for including a range of participants' ideas and perspectives in unit and lesson plans. We further noted from this research three main beliefs about this innovation: (1) linking a student's cultural understandings to content can engage a diverse range of students in STEM, (2) students' beliefs about where they "fit"—that is, what they believe they are "good at"—*matters* (for increasing STEM course enrollment), and (3) what others (other teachers, students, parents, communities) think is important when implementing an innovative curriculum (Pryor et al., 2016). We then included these beliefs in a curriculum development model, or roadmap, to guide teachers as they utilize students' socio-cultural experience and understandings to enhance STEM content and foundational ideas.

HOW CAN THIS BOOK HELP TEACHERS DEVELOP A SOCIO-CULTURAL STEM CURRICULUM?

We suggest that a Socio-cultural STEM integrative approach to curriculum development will establish a learning environment in which Project-based

Leaning (PBL) provides students a modality to address the essential questions inherent to solving a problem. Students in a PBL learning environment use investigatory skills to inquire about the possibilities and potential responses for solving social-scientific challenges (Pryor et al., 2022).

As you complete your readings in this book and try out the planning ideas, you might discover some of the following possible benefits for your students: (a) deep involvement in learning processes, (b) improvement in problem-solving and critical thinking, (c) increased comprehension of ecological concepts, (d) high engagement in a range of ethno-cultural perspectives, (e) increased interpersonal communication, (f) enhanced global understandings, (g) closure of gaps in student knowledge across disciplinary standards, and (h) awareness of the need to integrate multiple content domains in problem-solving.

The purpose of this book is to help you close the student-STEM engagement gap and broaden the diversity of students interested in STEM. We propose an integrated model in which STEM content and socio-cultural experience are clearly linked.

HOW TO USE A SOCIO-CULTURAL STEM NODE IN CURRICULUM DEVELOPMENT

The curriculum development process described in this book is based on the concept of a node (Smiley, 2010), a term used in computer network environments to describe connection and interaction among points of connection, [re]distribution, and expansion. Adapting the computer network definition of node, we have titled our innovation the Socio-cultural STEM Node, which we refer to simply as Node. Our iteration provides a pathway for teachers, in concert with contributions from participants (students, parents/caregivers, and community), to develop a curriculum in which local interests, experiences, and culture enhance a standards-based STEM curriculum. In chapter 4, we provide a more detailed definition of Node and suggest its use as a "gathering space" for participant inputs and a means to evaluate potential outputs (e.g., a draft of essential questions or a series of lesson plans).

The Socio-cultural STEM curriculum development process will help you create lessons that are:

- *Integrative*: Connect content across a range of domain areas
- *Expansive*: Broaden each content area
- *Personal*: Incorporate social-cultural perspectives
- *Achievement Oriented*: Produce standards-based outcomes.

THE BOOK'S ORGANIZATION

This book is organized into three parts. Part I: Introducing a Socio-cultural STEM Curriculum consists of chapters 1 and 2 and provides foundational information about the importance of teaching a Socio-cultural STEM curriculum. Part I offers an overview of what the book is about, beginning with the question: Why teach a Socio-cultural STEM curriculum? The core ideas of this integrated curricular approach are described in figure 2.1: A Pedagogical Framework for Socio-cultural STEM (in chapter 2). More specifically, in chapter 1, we present a discussion about the need to increase student engagement in the STEM subjects and engage a broader and more diverse range of students in STEM coursework. In support of these needs, a section is devoted to explaining the rationale for a Socio-cultural STEM curriculum, followed by an example project to illustrate our experiences integrating socio-cultural perspectives within STEM content. We also share our findings about teachers' beliefs related to a Socio-cultural STEM curriculum. We then explain how this book can help teachers develop a Socio-cultural STEM curriculum and what such a curriculum can achieve. We close chapter 1 with a summary of this book's organization and content. In chapter 2, we review research literature on the effects of drawing upon a wide range of content domain standards to address socio-scientific issues. Lastly, in support of developing a curriculum in which elements of socio-cultural experiences serve to contextualize content standards, we discuss the elements of our theoretical framework, portrayed in a visual model.

Part II of this book, *Developing a Socio-cultural STEM Curriculum*, consisting of chapters 3–5, offers tools for creating a socio-cultural project-based learning experience, introduces the concept of a Socio-cultural STEM Node, and includes the *Pryor-Kang Socio-cultural Curriculum Development Model*. Chapter 3 introduces an overview for designing a Socio-cultural STEM curriculum. The chapter describes how to (a) identify a socio-cultural scientific problem, (b) formulate essential questions, (c) organize essential questions into a teachable curriculum theme, (d) revisit and refine essential questions, and (e) translate a curriculum theme into goals and topics for units of study. Chapter 4 explains how to create a Socio-cultural STEM curriculum, using our adaptation of the computer term node, a nexus or crossroads of inputs and outputs (Smiley, 2010). Here, we apply the concept of Node to our curriculum model as a "gathering space" for teacher-teams to collect and evaluate socio-cultural perspectives (inputs) as a context for the development of a STEM content curriculum unit (output). In this chapter we provide a curriculum planning process for teacher-teams, *The Pryor-Kang Socio-cultural Curriculum Development Model,* and suggestions for disseminating, developing, and reconfiguring Nodes. Chapter 5 provides examples for three types of resources as inputs into Nodes followed by a range of technological platforms and content resources helpful for communicating and sharing information. Each resource entry is annotated and contains a link or a cited reference.

Part III offers six chapters, each centered on a selected curriculum theme, including a rationale for the use of the theme and example lesson plans. The author of each chapter asked teachers and professors to read their chapter and provide feedback about the potential and challenges of the theme and lesson plans. Thus, each chapter also includes a summary of teachers' and professors' beliefs about the potential of this innovation.

We sincerely hope this curriculum journey provides teacher teams an "available light" (Geertz, 2000) to incorporate socio-cultural perspectives into the learning experience of STEM content domains.

REFERENCES

Gay, G. (2010). *Culturally responsive teaching: Theory, research and practice* (2nd ed.). Teachers College Press.

Geertz, C. (2000). *Available light: Anthropological reflections on philosophical topics*. Princeton University Press.

Harrison, L. E. (2000). Introduction-why culture matters. In L. E. Harrison, & S. P. Huntington (Eds.), *Culture matters: How values shape human progress*, (pp. xviii–2). Basic Books.

Ivanitskaya, L., Clark, D., Montgomery, G., & Primeau, R. (2002). Interdisciplinary learning: Process and outcomes. *Innovative Higher Education, 27*(2), 95–111.

Lee, J. H. (2022). Building creative confidence through an interdisciplinary learning course: Changes in creative challenges and creative personal identity. *Innovations in Education and Teaching International, 59*(3), 316–25. https://doi.org/10.1080/14703297.2020.1835689.

Moll, L. C., Amanti, C., Neff, D., & Gonzalez, N. (1992). Funds of knowledge for teaching: Using a qualitative approach to connect homes and classrooms. *Theory Into Practice, 31*(2), 132–41.

Moser, K. M., Ivy, J., & Hopper, P. F. (2019). Rethinking content teaching at the middle level: An Interdisciplinary approach. *Middle School Journal, 50*(2), 17–27.

Nisbet, R., & Perrin, R. G. (1970). *The social bond*. Alfred A. Knopf.

Nuthall, G. (1999). Learning how to learn: The evolution of students' minds through the social processes and culture of the classroom. *International Journal of Educational Research, 31,* 139–256.

Pryor, B. W., Pryor, C. R., & Kang, R. (2016). Teachers' thoughts on integrating STEM into social studies instruction: Beliefs, attitudes, and behavioral decisions. *The Journal of Social Studies Research, 40*(2), 123–36. https://doi.org/10.1016/j.jssr.2015.06.005.

Pryor, B. W., Pryor, C. R., & Kang, R. (2022). *Measuring impact: Evaluating educational efficacy by beliefs, attitudes, and intentions* [Paper presentation]. American Educational Research Association (AERA).

Smiley, J. (2010). *The man who invented the computer: The biography of John Atanasoff*. Doubleday.

Tai, R. H., Liu, C. Q., Maltese, A. V., & Fan, X. (2006). Planning early for careers in science. *Educational Forum, 312*, 1143–44. https://doi.org/10.1126/SCIENCE.1128690.

Vygotsky, L. S. (1978). *Mind and society: The development of higher psychological processes*. Harvard University Press.

Chapter 2

A Pedagogical Framework for a Socio-cultural STEM Curriculum

Alvin W. Weinberg, nuclear physicist, in *Reflections on Big Science* (1965), stated:

> Our society is mission oriented. Its mission is resolution of problems arising from social, technical, and psychological conflicts and pressures. Since these problems are not generated within any single intellectual discipline, their resolution is not to be found within a single discipline.... In society, the nonspecialist and synthesizer are king. (p.145)

Echoing Weinberg, professional organizations such as the American Society for Engineering Education (ASEE), the National Council for Teachers of Mathematics (NCTM), and the National Research Council (NRC) call for an inquiry-based and interdisciplinary approach to P-12 Science, Technology, Engineering and Mathematics (STEM) education. When STEM areas are taught as divided disciplines, the knowledge developed by students tends to be fragmented and inadequate for solving complex, open-ended problems that require the coordination of multiple areas of knowledge and skills. New standards such as the Next Generation Science Standards (NGSS Lead States, 2013) and the Common Core Standards in Mathematics (CCSSM) (National Governor's Association Center for Best Practices & Council of Chief State School Officers, 2010) emphasize the connections across disciplines and especially teaching science and mathematics concepts through engineering design. However, science, math, and Career and Technical Education (CTE) are often taught in isolation, which reinforces the idea that these disciplines are distinct or unrelated to each other (Lesseig et al., 2016).

Social studies, an integrated study of social sciences and humanities, has historically carried the nation's educational mission of promoting civic competence (National Council for the Social Studies [NCSS], 2013). Despite this core mission, social studies education is not considered a priority in the current standardized testing environment. When middle and high school students receive less exposure to the importance of socio-scientific connections, many later choose not to participate in civic activities, such as national elections or global interactions, and may be unaware that their participation is crucial to the vibrancy and continuation of a democracy (Davis, 2003).

Social studies and STEM share the same goal of cultivating an engaged citizenship (Kim et al., 2020). An engaged citizenship means citizens are able to use their scientific knowledge to analyze and interpret controversial, complex, socio-scientific issues (SSI) such as genetically modified organisms (GMOs), fluoridation of water, and mask and vaccination mandates during a global pandemic. Disagreement is unavoidable in public discourse on such complex issues, and such disagreement may lead to unproductive arguments that plant deeper divisions in our society (Zummo, 2022). The NRC (2011) notes that one of the main purposes for STEM education is to equip the next generation of citizens with the necessary knowledge, skills, and dispositions to engage in productive public discussions on science-related issues and policies and to make informed personal and civic decisions. Science education reform highlights the importance of an inclusive perspective that is aimed at

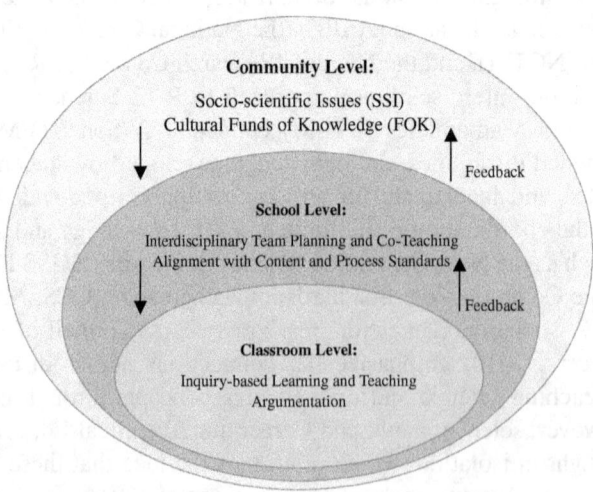

Figure 2.1 A Pedagogical Framework for Socio-cultural STEM.

increasing STEM literacy for all students, not just those who plan to pursue careers in STEM fields.

Socio-cultural STEM is an integrated approach to curriculum development that will provide a learning environment in which inquiry underscores the foundational ideas inherent in a problem. Students in this environment can use their investigatory and argumentative skills to explore the possibilities and potential resources for solving socio-scientific challenges and for developing a deeper understanding of the connections among STEM, art, history, and culture. This is an approach that encompasses multiple perspectives from students, teachers, parents/caregivers, and communities. In this chapter, we present a three-level pedagogical framework for a Socio-cultural STEM curriculum that draws from multiple theoretical perspectives and foundations (see figure 2.1).

A PEDAGOGICAL FRAMEWORK FOR SOCIO-CULTURAL STEM—COMMUNITY LEVEL

To develop a meaningful and productive curriculum outcome, we begin our work by including students and community members at the outset of the curriculum planning process. A genuine partnership with communities requires that materials are prepared *with* community partners, not *for* them (Holmes et al., 2021). Therefore, our pedagogical framework for a Socio-cultural STEM curriculum starts at the community level.

Socio-scientific Issues (SSI)

Conventional science and math curricula tend to focus on abstract, decontextualized knowledge, including laws, theories, and computations. However, such an approach does not satisfy the learner's need to know why they are learning and how learning could be used and connected with their daily lives (Klopfer & Aikenhead, 2021). Authentic science, however, often starts with a real-world problem or with students' experiences and expands the learning space from the school/classroom to the community, thus reducing the gaps between knowing and doing (Kim et al., 2020). Moreover, SSI are authentic science problems that are open-ended, ill-structured, ambiguous, and interdisciplinary (Chadwick et al., 2023). They can be problems that are close to a community—such as the lack of access to clean water or the impact of building a factory that potentially increases air and water pollution—or at a global level—such as cloning, genome projects, global warming, alternative fuel, and stem cell research. SSI usually have multiple, equally valid solutions and many ways to reach a solution (Eş & Öztürk, 2021).

Cultural Funds of Knowledge (FOK)

Gay (2010) defined culturally responsive pedagogy (CRP) as "using the cultural characteristics, experiences, and perspectives of ethnically diverse students as conduits for teaching them more effectively" (p. 106). At the heart of CRP is the concept of cultural funds of knowledge (FOK), which refers to "the historically accumulated and culturally developed bodies of knowledge and skills essential for household or individual functioning and well-being" (Moll et al., 2001, p.133). FOK encompasses a wide range of cultural assets in a local community, including history, customs, geography, visual art, dance, and music (Kim et al., 2020). FOK is built on the premise that learning is situated in social contexts in which social relations, practices, and artifacts constitute collective human experience (Klopfer & Aikenhead, 2021).

The underrepresentation of women, African Americans, Hispanic Americans, Native Americans, and people from lower socioeconomic status has been a long-time concern for the STEM field (Holmes et al., 2021). Integrating FOK is important for all students. For example, to engage Native American students in STEM learning, teachers may use STEM projects such as soil analysis and solar energy because they are familiar frames of reference as they matter to their community's survival and development (Stevens et al., 2016). Integrating dance and other art forms into STEM learning can also expand the pathway of access to STEM. In a study conducted by Solomon et al. (2022), African American girls used dance moves from krumping, stepping, and ballet as an embodied cultural resource and medium to make sense of and express their understanding of physics concepts.

Another possible way to leverage FOK is to incorporate non-western ways of knowing. Since scientific inquiry is a human behavior, people from different cultures make sense of the same elements differently. One example is the relationship between nature and culture. Western science often emphasizes the desire for control, dominance, and the overpowering of nature, whereas indigenous ways of knowing often focus on reaching harmony with nature, emphasizing connectedness and the promotion of interactivity and reciprocity (Harper, 2017). Incorporating an EthnoSTEM or non-western perspective into the conventional STEM curriculum is especially important today as our economy transitions from a profit economy to one that is sustainable (Klopfer & Aikenhead, 2021).

Engaging the Community

Local community centers, museums, zoos, aquariums, gardens, professional organizations, local businesses, and industries can all serve as potential partners for school STEM projects. A minimal level of community involvement may invite families and other community partners to be an audience for a student poster session or to participate in a field trip (De Meester et al., 2021; Stevens et al., 2016). More intensive engagement by community partners may involve community members collaborating with students during problem-solving, for example, discovering solutions together with students and sharing expertise. Sometimes, community partners can be the end users or clients of a STEM project and can provide students feedback on their initial solutions (Chiu et al., 2023). Art galleries and museum partners may serve as a cultural medium for gaining STEM knowledge as well as providing physical space for showcasing students' finished products (Kim et al., 2020).

To encourage participation from underrepresented minority groups, project materials (e.g., flyers, handouts) can be written in English and in students' home language. A translator may be provided at events that involve family and community members whose first language is not English (Steiner et al., 2019). In addition, teachers may take students outside of the classroom and into the community, but students may also reach community experts through the internet or virtual reality (Holmes et al., 2021).

A PEDAGOGICAL FRAMEWORK FOR SOCIO-CULTURAL STEM—SCHOOL LEVEL

Research has shown that student interest in mathematics and science starts to decrease in the early years of secondary school, especially for girls (Holmes et al., 2021). This finding highlights the critical need for middle school STEM education to foster long-term interest in STEM.

Middle School Learners

Middle school is an ideal period for students to learn through an integrated curriculum as their intellectual development relies on concrete, experiential learning, and an integrated curriculum is likely to support this type of learning (Senn et al., 2019). Notable educational philosophers and theorists such as John Dewey, Benjamin Bloom, William Heard Kilpatrick, and Howard Gardner all advocate for contextualizing learning in interdisciplinary problem-based or project-based learning. James Beane (1993), a leading theorist in middle school education, pointed out that real-life problems do not have clear-cut disciplinary boundaries. For example, math data are not just numbers but rather numbers that carry meaning and real impact on people's lives (Senn et al., 2019).

In *This We Believe*, the Association for Middle Level Education (AMLE, 2010) emphasizes the importance of middle school education being *responsive*, *challenging*, and *equitable*. Middle school is a critical period for not only academic and cognitive development but also physical, moral, psychological, and socio-emotional growth and the formation of social identities, including race, ethnicity, social class, gender, sexual orientation, religion, and exceptionality. A Socio-cultural STEM curriculum is *responsive* to the needs of young adolescents in this age group by offering them opportunities to solve interdisciplinary, complex, real-life application problems collaboratively with community partners. The problems or projects in a Socio-cultural STEM curriculum are typically *challenging* and do not have a single or simple answer. They require students to develop an in-depth understanding of content knowledge using higher-order cognitive skills such as analysis, interpretation, and evaluation. Moreover, as young adolescents in this age group have become more aware of the world around them and are exposed to a diverse range of perspectives and experiences, they also start to think about how their social identities may influence their position in school and society. Teachers' perspectives on what curricula to teach can be especially impactful on students in this age group, as students develop a sense of self-awareness, in part reflective of the typologies of stereotypes and biases. A Socio-cultural STEM curriculum considers students' cultural FOK as valuable assets for learning and therefore creates an *equitable* learning environment for students from diverse backgrounds (AMLE, 2010).

Benefits for Interdisciplinary Team Planning and Teaching

Team teaching can involve teachers from multiple disciplines actively teaching in close association with each other; alternatively, teachers may plan together but teach separately or co-plan and co-teach. Co-teaching is an excellent approach when a curriculum theme is selected at the beginning of the project by teacher-teams and community partners who then work together to form a community of practice (Wu et al., 2021).

Lesseig et al. (2016) report that teachers, after participating in a design challenge project, found that interdisciplinary project-based learning is a powerful experience for their students and for themselves. Teachers might initially feel frustrated and uncomfortable with open-ended projects with no identified answers. However, these researchers found that these types of projects expanded their knowledge; science and math teachers, for example, gained knowledge about the engineering design process. Teachers reported that during this collaborative work, they were less isolated and worked more collegially. Additionally, they noted that their students' perseverance increased as they faced challenging engineering design problems.

Even when implementation of wholesale interdisciplinary team teaching is not immediately possible, teachers who participated in professional development on interdisciplinary project-based learning shared that they started to (a) orchestrate more productive discourse in their classrooms, encouraging their students to provide increased levels of evidence and reasoning, (b) make problem-solving tasks more open-ended to encourage innovation and creativity, (c) provide students more opportunities to collaborate, and (d) assign additional time for students to engage in research and to practice the engineering design cycle (Lesseig et al., 2016). All of these incremental changes contribute to the full implementation of a Socio-cultural STEM curriculum.

Challenges for Interdisciplinary Team Planning and Teaching

There are challenges regarding implementing interdisciplinary project- or problem-based learning in middle and high schools. Localized projects tend to be time-consuming. There are logistical difficulties such as organizing trips outside of the classroom, which requires collaboration or coordination with other teachers and staff members. There might also be concerns about taking time away from curriculum areas that require standardized testing. Furthermore, garnering sustainable support from community and industrial partners can be difficult and create added work for teachers (Holmes et al., 2021).

It is also possible that different disciplines are not represented in an integrative curriculum in a balanced way. The value of such a curriculum may not be consistently observed in different disciplines (Hubber et al., 2022). Some teachers might struggle to find meaningful links among subjects. Math teachers in particular often note that STEM challenges do not always align with their grade-level content standards and therefore focus on covering materials on standardized math tests (Lesseig et al., 2021). Science and math teachers often acknowledge that they lack the experience in design and technology to evaluate student work appropriately (Hubber et al., 2022). Complicating issues stemming from their own skill levels is the need for teachers to find common planning time. An additional concern can be the implementation of a curriculum written around a single theme, as perceptions of content knowledge instruction can vary for different disciplinary teachers' individual classrooms.

Strategies to Overcome Challenges

To overcome the various barriers and challenges in interdisciplinary team planning or co-teaching, we recommend a whole-school approach in which

STEM projects are embedded across the curriculum and supported through ongoing teacher and community collaboration (Holmes et al., 2021). To this end, professional development workshops are necessary. In addition to support in content knowledge, pedagogical strategies, and technology, teachers also need guidance in developing techniques that facilitate argumentation around controversial SSI (Holmes et al., 2021). Since teachers might not feel confident about integrating content from different disciplines and are not given opportunities to practice integration in pre-service teacher training programs, teacher educators also need to collaborate with each other and model interdisciplinary co-planning and co-teaching in methods courses or during student teaching (De Meester et al., 2021).

Although professional development sessions typically consider implementation, it should also be noted that additional planning time needs to be allocated in order to address logistical concerns such as rearranging student schedules. Ongoing professional development support is also necessary during the collaborative process to continue to build teachers' self-efficacy in implementing interdisciplinary team planning and teaching (Lesseig et al., 2016). Lesseig et al. noted that teachers found summer institutes, follow-up sessions, and school-based meetings all contributed to the success of interdisciplinary team planning and teaching. Four elements were identified as crucial to their success: (a) a vision of integrated, problem- or project-based STEM learning, (b) teacher motivation to implement design challenges in their classrooms, (c) pedagogical tools, and (d) support for the planning and implementation process in an ongoing manner (Lesseig et al., 2016).

Two models—a multi-classroom model and an after-school model—may be used to implement team teaching and project- or problem-based learning (De Meester et al., 2021). External factors such as administrative support can make a difference in the adoption of integrative planning. For example, if your administrator wants you to focus on preparing students for standardized tests and your planning time is limited, then a multi-classroom model may not be as viable as the after-school activity model. The latter model has the advantage of allowing teachers and students from each discipline or classroom to have a common experience in an after-school setting so that teachers share ownership of the project. The downside of the extracurricular model is students' and teachers' lack of consistent available time to devote to implementation (De Meester et al., 2021). We recommend, therefore, that teacher teams develop creative forms of collaboration; for example, a social studies teacher or an expert in cultural geography each may record a video to provide the contextual knowledge needed by a science teacher or an engineering teacher to complete interdisciplinary projects.

Regardless of the model used, teachers should provide dedicated time and space to develop STEM curriculum. Content integration should be assessed so that it is not limited to a 40-minute class period. The length of class sessions needs to be determined by the teacher-team based on the needs of the projects, learning goals, and students' progress (Wu et al., 2021). "Anchor sessions" such as introductions, sharing, debriefing, and summarization may be designed to take place weekly. For example, a weekly timed block may be scheduled with students to summarize activities, debrief, and assess the learning process. Furthermore, these timeslots can be utilized to review required content knowledge related to standardized tests so that interdisciplinary lessons or projects can be used to support traditional school curricula (Wu et al., 2021). Reserving physical space to post materials to remind students of the current curriculum themes and procedures and for debriefing or bringing students and participants together for event presentations is also helpful (Wu et al., 2021).

A PEDAGOGICAL FRAMEWORK FOR SOCIO-CULTURAL STEM—CLASSROOM LEVEL

With their high cognitive demands and emphasis on real-life applications and reasoning skills, the current learning standards in science and math provide a strong rationale for an inquiry-based approach to STEM learning and teaching. For example, NGSS shifts away from a list of fragmented content standards and instead emphasizes core ideas and crosscutting concepts needed to learn science and engineering practices that meet performance expectations. The share of higher-order thinking skills on the revised Bloom's Taxonomy (Anderson & Krathwohl, 2001), including design, analyze, and evaluate, is currently prioritized over lower-level skills such as recall and define. The degree to which scientific practices and scientific content are integrated has also increased. There is a shift away from a narrow focus on a fragmented list of content standards to standards that link scientific practice (e.g., interpreting graphs and analyzing data) with scientific content (e.g., energy, chemical reactions, or genetics). A similar trend is seen in CCSSM. For example, Model with Mathematics, that is, using mathematics to represent phenomena in science, engineering, technology, and other authentic environments, is noted as one of the P-12 standards for mathematical practice (e.g., Consortium for Mathematics and Its Applications [COMAP]; Society for Industrial and Applied Mathematics [SIAM]).

A socio-cultural STEM curriculum aligns with an inquiry-based teaching approach. By virtue of its exploratory nature, an inquiry-based approach provides a rich context for learning to develop argumentation skills. Although a variety of instructional strategies and practices may be adopted when implementing a Socio-cultural STEM curriculum, we would like to highlight two key pedagogical strategies: inquiry and argumentative reasoning.

Inquiry-based Learning and Teaching

Generally speaking, inquiry-based learning and teaching involves hands-on activities that engage students in active construction of knowledge, with the teacher acting as a facilitator of learning (Chadwick et al., 2023). Inquiry-based learning and teaching provides students with opportunities to collaborate and communicate with each other. In addition, inquiry-based learning fosters a mind-body connection (Katchevich et al., 2013).

Although different inquiry approaches (e.g., structured, guided, open) may suit different learning goals, we believe that guided or open inquiry is effective in achieving the cognitive demand of a Socio-cultural STEM curriculum. We expect students to engage in a range of scientific and engineering practices as set forth in the NGSS, skills such as asking questions, collaborating with each other, developing models, carrying out investigations, analyzing and interpreting data, formulating explanations with support of empirical evidence, and communicating information.

The traditional inquiry-based mode, however, is more linear and has a more direct, obvious path to problem-solving; this path typically has only one cycle, starts with one solution, and oftentimes is confirmatory in nature. Authentic scientific inquiry into SSI, on the other hand, is flexible, cyclic, and iterative (Chiu et al., 2023). Chiu et al. outlined how to apply the *five-stage design thinking model*, proposed by the Hasso Plattner Institute of Design, to solve SSI. In the *empathize* stage students talk to target users, usually a community partner, to better understand their needs. Next, they *define* possible problems, with feedback from their teacher. Thirdly, in the *ideation* stage, at least two solutions or ideas are proposed, and students are expected to support their solutions using STEM knowledge. After the most likely solution is chosen, students enter the fourth, or *prototype,* stage during which they create a prototype for their solution. In the fifth and final stage, they can *test* their prototype with users in the community and seek feedback for improvement. The process is iterative, and students may need to redefine the problem or improve their solutions and prototypes.

Both project-based learning and problem-based learning are inquiry-oriented. Project-based learning emphasizes the need for students to produce an artifact to demonstrate their mastery of knowledge, whereas problem-based learning focuses on students presenting a solution to an authentic problem. Each type of learning can range from a few hours to several weeks. In this book, we present shorter interdisciplinary lessons centered on broad themes. The lessons typically last from a few days to one or two weeks. These lessons can be used to prepare students for a longer research project that may last 4–6 weeks, however, such as a capstone project at the end of a school year. The lessons can be used individually or together as a unit. The goal is embedding a Socio-cultural STEM curriculum as an ongoing and established instructional model rather than a short-term, one-shot implementation.

Although our focus is not on developing assessment materials, there is also a need to align inquiry-based learning with appropriate assessment approaches. Authentic assessments such as a model, a presentation, a report, or a process that can be evaluated against performance-based rubrics are compatible with a Socio-cultural STEM curriculum (Hubber et al., 2022). In addition, assessments for this curriculum may provide students opportunities to select their preferred representations in expressing their knowledge or receiving support for the development of representational fluency (e.g., visual, audio, written) (Hubber et al., 2022). Notebooks that contain students' work samples and document their progress, and reflective journals often help students develop metacognitive skills such as self-monitoring, planning, and self-assessment and are also appropriate for a Socio-cultural STEM curriculum (Lesseig et al., 2016).

Argumentation

NGSS has stressed the need for teachers to orchestrate opportunities for students to engage in scientific argumentation. Inquiry into SSI provides a rich context for developing argumentative skills as these issues are open-ended, ill-structured, and can be approached from multiple perspectives and interpretations (Chadwick et al., 2023; Katchevich et al., 2013; Klopfer & Aikenhead, 2021; Lesseig et al., 2016.)

Argumentation often refers to a type of informal reasoning that reflects practical everyday decision-making (Kolarova et al., 2013). Formal reasoning can sometimes be inflexible; it must follow a linear process and maintain a fixed premise. But argumentation allows students to change their premise or modify their initial position after they examine a variety of sources and gain a better understanding of the SSI and underlying scientific concepts (Eş & Öztürk, 2021). Argumentation is more consistent with how scientists build and refine their concepts and ideas (Katchevich et al., 2013). Due to the informal nature of argumentation, teachers need to respect students' diverse emotional and intuitive sources and not hasten to prescribe a particular mode of reasoning. Students might not start their argumentation with the rationalistic scientific mode of inquiry, but instead argue from a moral or ethical standpoint (Eş & Öztürk, 2021). However, teachers can guide students to use more rational, cognitive-based arguments based on scientific evidence as classroom discourse intensifies (Eş & Öztürk, 2021). Formulating an argument is a conceptual or cognitive process that can help deepen students' understanding of scientific concepts and improve students' communicative competence and use of scientific language (Katchevich et al., 2013).

SUMMARY

Some teachers may relate classroom-based STEM education to NGSS, CCSSM, textbooks, and standardized tests, whereas scientific literacy, or solving complex problems facing our society and leveraging STEM knowledge to make informed civic decisions, is on the fringe or belonging to a separate, informal educational setting or an after-school program (Klopfer & Aikenhead, 2021). A Socio-cultural STEM curriculum is aimed at forging a stronger link between classroom-based STEM education and students' and teachers' local and global communities. When an interdisciplinary approach is promoted as a short-term project or event, such as a STEM Day, a workshop, or a field trip, the approach might not have a long-term impact on student learning (De Meester et al., 2021). Developing scientific skills such as argumentation and reasoning cannot be achieved through on-off exploration of SSI (Chadwick et al., 2023). Long-term, sustained engagement with an inquiry-based learning process is necessary. We view a Socio-cultural STEM curriculum as a meaningful way of learning about science, technology, and society. We hope that this curriculum will be an integral or routine part of classroom-based STEM learning and teaching that addresses both content and process standards. Our goal is to generate a strong and continuous impact on students' understanding and skills.

REFERENCES

Anderson, L. W., & Krathwohl, D. R. (2001). *A taxonomy for learning, teaching and assessing: A revision of Bloom's Taxonomy of educational objectives: Complete edition.* Longman.

Association for Middle Level Education (AMLE). (2010). *This we believe: Keys to educating young adolescents.* National Middle School Association.

Beane, J. A. (1993). *A middle school curriculum: From rhetoric to reality* (2nd ed.). National Middle School Association.

Chadwick, R., McLoughlin, E., & Finlayson, O. E. (2023). Teachers' experience of inquiry into socioscientific issues in the Irish lower secondary science curriculum. *Irish Educational Studies, 42*(3), 315–37. https://doi.org/10.1080/03323315.2021.1964565.

Chiu, T. K. F., Ismailov, M., Zhou, X., Xia, Q., Au, C. K., & Chai, C. S. (2023). Using self-determination theory to explain how community-based learning fosters student interest and identity in integrated STEM education. *International Journal of Science and Science Education, 21,* S109–S130. https://doi.org/10.1007/s10763-023-10382-x.

Davis, O. L. (2003). Does democracy in education still live? *Journal of Curriculum and Supervision, 19*(1), 1–4.

De Meester, J., De Cock, M., Langie, G., & Dehaene, W. (2021). The process of designing integrated STEM learning materials: Case study towards an evidence-based model. *European Journal of STEM Education, 6*(1), 10. https://doi.org/10.20897/ejsteme/11341.

Eş, H., & Öztürk, N. (2021). An activity for transferring the multidimensional structure of SSI to middle school science courses: I discover myself in the decision-making process with SEE-STEP! *Research in Science Education, 51*, 889–910. https://doi.org/10.1007/s11165-019-09865-1.

Gay, G. (2010). *Culturally responsive teaching: Theory, research and practice* (2nd ed.). Teachers College Press.

Harper, S. G. (2017). Engaging Karen refugee students in science learning through a cross-cultural learning community. *International Journal of Science Education, 39*(3), 358–76. https://doi.org/10.1080/09500693.2017.1283547.

Holmes, K., Mackenzie, E., Berger, N., & Walker, M. (2021). Linking K-12 STEM pedagogy to local contexts: A scoping review of benefits and limitations. *Frontiers in Education, 6*, 1–10. https://doi.org/10.3389/feduc.2021.693808.

Hubber, P., Widjaja, W., & Aranda, G. (2022). Assessment of an interdisciplinary project in science and mathematics: Opportunities and challenges. *Teaching Science, 68*(1), 13–25.

Katchevich, D., Hofstein, A., & Mamlok-Naaman, R. (2013). Argumentation in the chemistry laboratory: Inquiry and confirmatory experiments. *Research in Science Education, 43*, 317–45. https://doi.org/10.1007/s11165-011-9267-9.

Kim, G., Ko, Y., & Lee, H. (2020). The effects of community-based socioscientific issues program (SSI-COMM) on promoting students' sense of place and character as citizens. *International Journal of Science and Mathematics Education, 18*, 399–418. https://doi.org/10.1007/s10763-019-09976-1.

Klopfer, L. E., & Aikenhead, G. S. (2021). Humanistic science education: The history of science and other relevant contexts. *Science Education, 106*, 490–504. https://doi.org/10.1002/sce21700.

Kolarova, T., Hadjiali, I., & Denev, I. (2013). High school students' reasoning in making decisions about socio-ethical issues of genetic engineering: Case of gene therapy. *Biotechnology, & Biotechnological Equipment, 27*(2), 3737–47. https://doi.org/10.5504/BBEQ.2012.0133.

Lesseig, K., Nelson, T. H., Slavit, D., & Seidel, R. A. (2016). Supporting middle school teachers' implementation of STEM design challenges. *School Science and Mathematics, 116*(4), 177–88.

Moll, L., Amanti, C., Neff, D., & Gonzalez, N. (1992). Funds of knowledge for teaching: Using a qualitative approach to connect homes and classrooms. *Theory into Practice, 31*(2), 132–41.

National Council for the Social Studies (NCSS). (2013). *College, career, & civic life: C3 framework for social studies state standards.*

National Governor's Association Center for Best Practices, & Council of Chief State School Officers. (2010). *Common core state standards for mathematics.*

National Research Council (NRC). (2011). *Successful K-12 STEM education: Identifying effective approaches in science, technology, engineering, and mathematics.*

NGSS Lead States. (2013). *Next generation science standards: For states, by states.* The National Academies Press.

Senn, G., McMurtrie, D., & Coleman, B. (2019). Collaboration in the middle: Teachers in interdisciplinary planning. *Current Issues in Middle Level Education, 24*(1). Retrieved from https://digitalcommons.georgiasouthern.edu/cimle/vol24/iss1/6.

Solomon, F., Champion, D., Steele, M., & Wright, T. (2022). Embodied physics: Utilizing dance resources for learning and engagement in STEM. *Journal of the Learning Sciences, 31*(1), 73–106. https://doi.org/10.1080/10508406.2021.2023543.

Steiner, A., Lemke, J., Nero, D., & McGlamery, S. (2019). STEM and community engagement: Providing preservice teachers authentic experience beyond the classroom. *Science & Children, 56*(8), 76–9.

Stevens, S., Andrade, R., & Page, M. (2016). Motivating young Native American students to pursue STEM learning through a culturally relevant science program. *Journal of Science Education, 25*, 947–60. https://doi.org/10.1007/s10956-016-9629-1.

Weinberg, A. W. (1965). *Reflections on big science.* MIT Press.

Wu, Y., Cheng, J., & Koszalka, T. A. (2021). Transdisciplinary approach in middle school: A case study of co-teaching practices in STEAM teams. *International Journal of Education in Mathematics, Science, and Technology, 9*(1), 138–62. https://doi.org/10.46328/jiemst.1017.

Zummo, L. M. (2022). Disagreement as context for science-civic learning: An analysis of discursive resources brought to bear by high school science students. *Cultural Studies of Science Education, 17*, 1115–39. https://doi.org/10.1007/s11422-022-10128-1.

Part II

DEVELOPING A SOCIO-CULTURAL STEM CURRICULUM

Chapter 3

Using Social Problems to Frame a Curriculum Theme, Essential Questions, and Goals

In this chapter we provide initial steps for integrating perspectives of teacher-teams and participants (see figure 3.1). In chapter 4, we show how these steps are used within the *Pryor-Kang Socio-cultural Curriculum Development Model*.

KEY DEFINITIONS IN CURRICULUM DEVELOPMENT

- *Curriculum Theme*: Large ideas linked together (sustainability and water conservation).
- *Curriculum Goal*: A purpose without stated achievement criteria (contribute to resource preservation).
- *Curriculum Topic*: Specific area of knowledge or skill (science and history).
- *Curriculum Unit*: Combination of subject matter content, outcomes, and socio-cultural context to demonstrate how to connect science, mathematics, history, and cultural knowledge to community efforts.
- *Participants:* Teacher-teams, students, parents/caregivers, and community.

Note: This chapter's Key Definitions are drawn from the work of Cook and Martinello (1994), Gordon et al. (2019), and Pryor and Kang (2013).

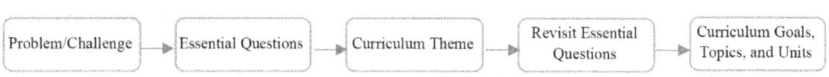

Figure 3.1 Initial Steps for Integrating Perspectives of Teacher Teams and Participants.

IDENTIFYING A PROBLEM OR CHALLENGE

Contemporary issues and ideas about how we live and work often give rise to a set of problems that we are charged to solve. As noted in chapter 2, one of the main purposes for STEM education is to equip the next generation of citizens with the necessary knowledge and skills to engage in public discussions on science-related issues and policies and make informed personal and civic decisions (National Research Council, 2011).

We wrote previously about the importance of Project-based Learning (PBL) to students' development of one such skill—problem-solving (Pryor & Kang, 2013). PBL holds immense possibilities for developing investigatory skills, such as rational thought, examination of primary sources, and envisioning the potential of ideas and products. Pedagogical practices that incorporate strategies using inquiry, critical thinking, and decision-making can help enhance students' ability to address problems (Brears et al., 2011). Moreover, Etherington (2011) notes that a learner's thinking-experiential processes are enhanced when PBL is interdisciplinary.

Each of us, however, defines problems through a lens of phenomenological experience—that is, we identify problems through the socio-cultural values and mores that surround our everyday life (Bogdan & Biklen, 2003). In this chapter, we introduce initial steps to investigating problems using a Socio-cultural STEM curriculum model process that incorporates multiple participants' perspectives in a framework of interdisciplinary project-based learning. We begin by providing an example problem and situate this problem as a *project* whose resolve requires the utilization of cross-disciplinary knowledge and investigatory skills.

In the first chapter of this book, we introduced the idea of *sustainability* as a potential problem or concern for a community. We continue to use sustainability in our example of applying the initial step of identifying a problem to planning for community participants' perspectives of this problem. In chapter 6, Sharon Locke and Georgia Bracey provide us with a rationale for students' examination of the global challenges of this topic, prompting us to remember the importance of sustainability for future generations; Locke and Bracey's detailed lesson plans offer us links to a wealth of resources.

We return here to our example of identifying the challenges that compose our problem of sustainability at the local or community level. As your team continues to explore the needs of a community, concerns such as accessibility to housing, health providers, nutrition, or transportation might emerge. You might find less is known or understood about these (and other) concerns. In chapter 1, we suggested gathering students' perspectives about a problem. Now, you might want to reach out to the parents/caregivers and members of your community as you seek insight and clarity about issues of sustainability in a community. Before you can reach out to your participants, however, as a team you will need to identify which issues you believe are central to solving a problem as well as clarify the critical components of the issue in the form of essential questions.

ESSENTIAL QUESTIONS

One problem that often arises when initially exploring the problems and challenges of sustainability concerns the physical evidence we encounter—the increasing accumulation of discarded materials such as plastic or metal items (see, e.g., Marsh & Bugusu, 2007). We are, unfortunately, familiar with how discarded items impact our environment and wonder about our ability to sustain a healthy community. We are aware of sites, often on the outskirts of a community, developed to try to retain our collected trash. Yet, the evidence of our daily habits continues to infringe on our ability to sustain our community health.

We see abandoned cars and building materials tossed onto the side of roadways. We see buildings left to deteriorate. We fill our home trash containers with plastic water bottles, food containers, and shopping bags. We hear the dialogue of concern brought forth in documentaries that explain how these and other items end up in our waterways and impact the food chain and the flora and fauna in our land spaces. We likely sense that these discarded materials cost our communities time, health, and financial stress and lessen our ability to sustain a healthy environment. In our quest to better understand these and other challenges to our community, we need to learn more about our participants' beliefs.

In part, beliefs are derived from an individual's life experience (Pryor et al., 2021). In the case of a problem or challenge such as sustainability, participant beliefs could be expressed as essential questions: "What will it cost our city, me, and my neighbors if we implement a sustainability plan?" or "What might happen if our local water supply is compromised and the health challenges of our community remain unmet?" Beliefs such as the impact of weather on a community might appear to us as outside of our control. Other concerns might appear as problems for which we can direct familiar resources, such as funding an organic food pantry. We can translate our evaluation of these beliefs (good-bad; important-not important) into categories (e.g., beliefs about access to health resources) that lead us to ask essential questions about how to solve the challenges of community sustainability.

USING ESSENTIAL QUESTIONS TO DEVELOP A CURRICULUM THEME

Much has been written about the composition of an essential question. The 2013 work of Jay McTighe and Grant Wiggins provides us insight into a definition of what might compose an essential question, but with the caveat that these attributes might not all appear in a single question. Thus, for researchers, an *essential question* can be characterized as a question that is open-ended, thought-provoking, representative of higher-order thinking and transferable ideas, and suggestive of additional questions that provide support and justification over time. Jeffrey Wilhelm (2012) defines an essential question from the perspective of how it might function to help solve a problem, phrasing his definition with attributes of functionality such as the question's relevancy to the participant, strength of endurance to the discipline, and/or potential to prompt a user to make judgments or produce a meaningful outcome.

Now, having drafted a set of essential questions, your team might want to engage students and the community in evaluating which questions they believe are central to solving the challenges of sustaining their community. As a first step to community outreach, think about which modality you and your participants will use to share information. Will you communicate online? Will you provide in-person discussions? You might begin a dialogue by sending participants an informational message: "We are planning to develop a curriculum unit for our 7th grade students about the problems and challenges on the theme of sustainability in our community. We provide here our draft of essential questions about this problem and ask if you would provide us with feedback." In preparation for participants' feedback, your team will need to decide how you will evaluate it, as well as determine if a second cycle requesting their feedback might be needed. Here are a few examples of essential questions about sustainability that could be used in a message to participants:

- What additional resources, such as housing or transportation, might help sustain our community?
- What financial issues, such as program implementation costs or tax increases, are important to consider when supporting community sustainability?
- Who in our community might contribute their knowledge or time to implement sustainability efforts?
- What community services could be eliminated or reduced so that we might better sustain our community?

Now that your team has sent a draft of essential questions to participants, reviewed participant input, and refined your list of essential questions, you will want to summarize your list of essential questions in a statement that can *guide the development of an instructional unit of study*. This statement can take the form of a *curriculum theme*. Cook and Martinello (1994) write that [curriculum] themes are large ideas that can be linked together; for example, you might link the idea of survival with environmental need. Thus, your curriculum theme might be written as: *Community Sustainability: Exploring Issues of Housing, Health, Nutrition and Transportation.*

Teachers in our graduate courses shared with us several curriculum themes they have developed:

- The Rainforest: Energy, Climate, and Community Impacts
- Renewable Energy: Designing Energy Systems, Inventions, and Human Research
- Esperanza Rising: The Great Depression and the Mathematics of Economic Change
- Prohibition: Distribution, Distillation, and Social Impacts
- Space: Climate Change, Global Warming, and the Local Environment

TRANSLATING A CURRICULUM THEME INTO CURRICULUM GOALS AND TOPICS FOR UNITS OF STUDY

Above, we noted that a curriculum theme is a statement about large ideas. As these ideas prompt us to reflect on problems and the challenges and issues inherent in these problems, it becomes necessary for us to understand how to create a process that fosters our student's ability to become problem solvers. Over time, problem-solving models have changed from the belief that a singular set of problem-solving skills can be easily transferred to multiple domains and settings (Newell & Simon, 1972). More current constructs, however, suggest that problem-solving engages various types of knowledge *within* various approaches to resolving a problem (Kirkley, 2003; Ornstein et al., 2015; Sowell, 2000). Wiggins and McTighe (2005) suggest that beginning curriculum design by first identifying our expected learning outcomes will provide clarity during our lesson implementation and increase student achievement. Thus, identifying the outcomes you envision for student learning and stating these outcomes as *curriculum goals* is a critical step.

Curriculum goals are statements of purpose often phrased as overarching end points or understandings that we plan for our students. Researchers Gordon et al. (2019) use the term *aims* to specify the general ideas that surround the purpose of a specific curriculum. Ornstein and Hunkins (2004) explain that although goals help us describe a purpose for the curriculum, they are notably written without specified outcome criteria. Your list of essential questions can help you identify the purpose you have in mind as you develop a set of curriculum goals. For example, if one of your identified essential questions regards the need to understand the relationship between a community's finances and the potential cost of sustainability efforts, your teacher-team can phrase a curriculum goal as: *Students will gain an understanding of community resources and budget priorities.*

A goal can help you generate a series of topics that enrich students' understandings, knowledge, and skills central to your curriculum theme (Gordon et al., 2019). For example, you might find it important to include topics such as the cost of staffing and supplying a food pantry or using technology to research food supplies.

SUMMARY

This chapter provides your teacher-team with ideas for identifying a socio-cultural problem or challenge, framing essential questions about this problem, translating these questions into an overriding curriculum theme, and noting goals and topics for the ensuing development of curriculum units of study. Next, in chapter 4, we present the *Pryor-Kang Socio-cultural STEM Curriculum Development Model* and describe how to link the above foundational curriculum processes to develop interdisciplinary curriculum units that are integral to the socio-cultural lives of our students.

REFERENCES

Bogdan, R. C., & Biklen, S. K. (2003). *Qualitative research for education: An introduction to theory and methods.* Allyn & Bacon.

Brears, L., MacIntyre, B., O'Sullivan, G., & North, P. (2011). Preparing teachers for the 21st century using PBL as an integrating strategy in science and technology education. *Design and Technology Education: An International Journal, 16*(1), 36–46.

Cook, G. E. &. Martinello, M. L. (1994). Topics and themes in interdisciplinary curriculum. *Middle School Journal, 25*(3), 40–44. https://doi.org/10.1080/00940771.1994.11494547.

Etherington, M. B. (2011). Investigative primary science: A problem-based learning approach. *Australian Journal of Teacher Education (Online), 36*(9), 53–74. Retrieved from https://search.informit.org/doi/10.3316/ielapa.328484780726539.

Foshay, R., & Kirkley, J. (2003). *Principles for teaching problem solving.* Plato Learning, Inc. Retrieved from https://citeseerx.ist.psu.edu/document?repid=rep1&type=pdf&doi=97f0d0f6535b7002d73a5d001b16a6964f5a8c9e.

Gordon, W. R., II., Taylor, R. T., & Oliva, P. F. (2019). *Developing the curriculum: Improved outcomes through systems approaches* (9th ed). Pearson Education.

Marsh, K., & Bugusu, B. (2007). Food packaging—roles, materials, and environmental issues. *Journal of Food Science, 72*(3), 39–55. https://doi.org/10.1111/j.1750-3841.2007.00301.x.

McTighe, J., & Wiggins, G. (2013). *Essential questions: Opening doors to student understanding.* Association for Supervision and Curriculum Design.

National Research Council (NRC). (2011). *Successful K-12 STEM education: Identifying effective approaches in science, technology, engineering, and mathematics.*

Newell, A., & Simon, H. (1972). *Human problem solving.* Prentice Hall.

Ornstein, A. C., & Hunkins, F. P. (2004). *Curriculum foundations, principles and issues* (4th ed). Pearson Education.

Ornstein, A. C., Pajak, E. F., & Ornstein, S. B. (2015). *Contemporary issues in curriculum* (6th ed). Pearson.

Pryor, C. R., & Kang, R. (2013). Project-based learning: An interdisciplinary approach for integrating social studies with STEM. In R. M. Capraro, M. M. Capraro, & J. Morgan (Eds.), *Project-based learning: An integrated science, technology, engineering, and mathematics (STEM) approach* (pp. 123–32). Sense Publishers.

Pryor, C. R., Kang, R., & Pryor, B. W. (2021). Social studies-STEM activities and resources: Enhancing the content and context for learning. In R. M. Capraro, M. M. Capraro, J. Young, & L. Barroso (Eds.), *STEM Project-based learning: Integrating engineering for a new era* (pp. 271–98). Texas Aggie Publications.

Sowell, E. J. (2000). *Curriculum: An integrative introduction* (2nd ed.). Prentice-Hall.

Wiggins, G., & McTighe (2005). *Understanding by design* (2nd ed). Association for Supervision and Curriculum Development.

Wilhelm, J. D. (2012). Essential questions. *Instructor.* Available at: http://works.bepress.com/jeffrey_wilhelm/56/.

Chapter 4

A Developmental Model for a Socio-cultural STEM Curriculum

In earlier chapters we discussed how identifying a socio-cultural problem can encourage students to think critically about how STEM subjects can be helpful in resolving challenges. We noted that inherent in these challenges are issues that concern us—that is, questions we believe are essential to resolving a problem. In this chapter we describe a multi-phase process in which participants' perspectives about a problem can be integrated into a *curriculum* of instructional *units of study*.

This chapter is composed of two parts. In Part 1 we introduce the term Node—based on the concept of a computer node where inputs are gathered and analyzed, and outputs are developed. In the context of curriculum development, a Node may be considered a rather versatile and multi-faceted concept and can be used in several ways. In this chapter, a Node functions to capture both concrete elements such as domain content or learning standards, although a Node might also contain conceptual elements such as ideas or perspectives. The contents of a Node might suggest that teachers or participants complete an action, such as developing ideas for lesson plans. Importantly, a Node can serve as a space that eases communication as we disseminate and share the progress of our developing curriculum.

To highlight our use of Node in curriculum development, we present the *Pryor-Kang Socio-cultural STEM Curriculum Development Model* as a planning process for the interaction of STEM and the disciplines of the humanities and social studies framed by a socio-cultural context for learning. Here, perspectives of teacher-teams and participants are incorporated into phases of the development process. The initial phases of the model include the topics introduced in chapter 3 (i.e., *Identifying a Problem* and *Essential Questions*), and, by extension, we then incorporate these topics in the initial phases of unit development, followed by implementation and analysis.

In Part 2, we discuss the formation and use of prompts to engage our participants with us in the development of the curriculum.

PART 1: A FRAMEWORK FOR CURRICULUM DEVELOPMENT: *NODE* AS A GATHERING SPACE

As I (CP) reviewed the curriculum themes developed by the teachers in my graduate classes, I wondered how teachers might develop lessons that would engage the interests of a broad range of students in STEM. I wondered what our students and participants—parents/caregivers or community—might think was compelling about a theme. We have long known the importance of involving parents/caregivers in our schools (e.g., Epstein & Salinas, 2004). Less is known about how to engage participants' perspectives in the actual development of the curriculum, although some suggest that it is a good idea (e.g., Dye, 2006; Gellert, 2005). I also wondered about how a teacher-team would make use of the feedback they might receive.

Little did I know that Jane Smiley's 2010 book, *The Man Who Invented the Computer,* might provide me with some answers. I was fascinated by the mathematician John Atanasoff's quest in 1936 to develop a machine that could quickly perform numerical computations, although at this early stage he had not yet thought about how a machine might store the outcome of these computations. What ensued was a long journey during which numerous mathematicians and engineers worked to develop machines that could produce both computation *and* storage. The electrical mechanisms of their experiments centered on *inputs*, information provided to the machine, and the resulting *outputs* that could be analyzed to determine the next steps toward complex mathematical computation. What these researchers were trying to learn was how to input information in a manner that would connect to a desired outcome. Eventually, however, they also wanted to learn how these outputs might be stored, and, if stored, how they could be used for future operations.

Once developed, the storage capacity—called a node—functioned not as a space with concrete dimensions, like a cardboard box, but rather *as a connection point among electrical inputs.* The connection point between an input and an output holds the potential to prompt a continual and expected application such as the output that occurs from striking the letter P on a keyboard. Alternatively, inputs could prompt unexpected outputs, such as those that result from entering a URL into a search engine. Thus, as you strike the letter P on a keyboard, an electrical storage space (a node) recognizes the input as the letter P, connects with another electrical input to prompt an action, and the letter P shows up on your computer screen. Or, if you strike the letter P *along with additional letters*, when using a search engine, designated connections will function to prompt an output, and a series of categorized information, web pages, or research results begin to appear.

Now I had an idea for a curriculum model that could function as an electrical node does—that is, a process in which the connections among input information would prompt continual interactivity. We (Caroline and Rui) drew inspiration from researchers such as Joyce Epstein, who has long reported the positive impact of caregiver and community involvement in schools on outcomes such as achievement (e.g., Epstein & Salinas, 2004). We also reflected on a range of curriculum theorists, whose foci include: (a) intentional and unintentional information (Sowell, 2000), (b) recursiveness and curriculum evaluation (Gordon et al., 2019), (c) diversity, culture, and human development (Parkay & Hass, 2000), and (d) philosophical foundations of curriculum (Ornstein & Hunkins, 2004).

The model we present highlights the integration of socio-cultural phenomena with a STEM curriculum using our concept of *Node* as a gathering space to analyze and distribute teacher-team and participants' ideas, perspectives, and resources.

We often portray our ideas about socio-cultural norms through a range of venues—our art, music, stories and experiences, thoughts and ideas, and other representations of what we think and value (Bogdan & Biklen 2003; Geertz, 2000). These experiences can capture the usefulness of STEM and enrich the lessons we provide. It is not surprising, therefore, that teachers believe that the breadth and richness of lessons that incorporate multiple content domains are likely to engage students deeply in learning targeted content (Pryor et al., 2016). The Pryor-Kang Model portrays a pathway for including these perspectives in our curriculum.

A MODEL FOR DEVELOPING A SOCIAL-CULTURAL STEM CURRICULUM

What is New and Impactful in the *Pryor-Kang Model?*

- Teacher-team integration of selected content/context
- Teacher-led outreach and participant input
- Node as gathering spaces for inputs/outputs
- Team and participant curriculum evaluation (outputs)

The Pryor-Kang Model provides for the collaborative development and analysis of a curriculum unit with suggestions for lesson planning. Underscoring this model is a process to incorporate the ideas, perspectives, resources, and evaluative feedback of teacher-teams *with* those of their students and the participants in their community. These initial steps can help you elicit and organize participant feedback (inputs) as you work with each phase of the model. First, as you begin to reach out to participants and share initial drafts of your curriculum design, think about what formats you would like participants to use when responding to you with their inputs. You might suggest formats such as videos, platform links, and in-person discussions (see chapter 5).

Participants' inputs can be categorized and then entered into a Node, such as "Essential Questions Node," "Resources Node," or "Content Information Node." Developing a set of questions about the content of each Node can help you evaluate the inputs you received. These questions can serve as prompts to help your team reflect on the importance of the inputs of a Node and identify what information is still needed. Once your team has reflected on the inputs you have received and those your team has developed, it is important to determine how these inputs align with your curriculum theme. To prompt this alignment, you might ask: "Does the input information in a Node align with our overall curriculum theme?" or "Do we have information in a Node that is not needed, or are we missing information?" In Part 2 below, we provide example prompt questions that can be useful as you evaluate your vision of an interdisciplinary Socio-cultural STEM curriculum.

In figure 4.1 we present the six phases of the Pryor-Kang Model.

Each phase of the model is noted in a rectangular box. A circle attached to each box represents a Node containing suggested teacher-team activities to help guide the completion of each phase. Note that although arrows between the phases might appear to suggest linear steps, the model is derived from a premise of interactive reflection in which the recursive use of earlier phases is encouraged. Therefore, the two-directional arrows between phases portray an emphasis on potential connections between phases, highlighting a recursive process of analysis and revision. The large arrow looped from Phase Six back to Phase One provides for reflexive evaluation and redesign of your curriculum outcomes. Sample questions your teacher-team might use to prompt inputs-outputs are found in part II.

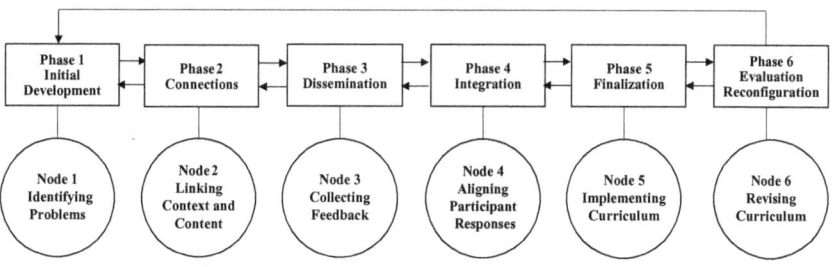

Figure 4.1 Pryor-Kang Socio-cultural STEM Curriculum Development Model.

The Pryor-Kang Model uses the concept of a Node as a gathering space for developing a curriculum unit. At first glance, a Node might appear similar to a file folder; a folder functions simply in one dimension, however, as a space that collects incoming information, whether a hard copy or an electronic file. A node in the computer environment also serves as a gathering space, albeit electronic; here inputs to the node are predetermined (as in a computer code) and prompt the node to act (such as creating the letter P) or to search among a series of connections between particular nodes and produce outputs such as websites, ideas, or photos.

In the Pryor-Kang curriculum model, a Node functions as *a flexible space* that is not dependent on a set of predetermined instructions. Given the foundational construct of input-output flexibility, the very nature of a Node, then, portends an ongoing process of formative evaluation—review, reflection, and revision.

Here we use Node to not only collect information, but also as a space for interactive analysis of ideas and questions in support of domain content information. However, this process of seeking broad participant perspectives is less dominant in the history of curriculum development. The long-standing traditionalist-linear formulation of curriculum development of Tyler (1949), for example, posits the importance of a content-driven procedure followed linearly with required steps for precise evaluation. Other models, such as that of Oliva (2005), offer a path that begins with identifying the needs of students as the basis for the specification of developing a curriculum. Gordon et al. (2019) suggest the use of learning standards as the central element of curriculum development.

The Pryor-Kang model of curriculum development is centered on a problem-solving process that draws on the socio-cultural perspectives of teacher-teams, students, and participants. The six phases of the model are presented below.

PHASE 1: INITIAL DEVELOPMENT—IDENTIFYING PROBLEMS AND ESSENTIAL QUESTIONS

Teachers might think about the development of the curriculum by first identifying a problem or challenge. To address the problem teacher-teams might initially try to determine what domain area content will be needed to resolve the problem, asking questions such as, "What learning standards will help my students bring scientific knowledge to conversations about solving these problems?" As discussed in chapter 3, however, and as presented in the Pryor-Kang Model, we suggest beginning this process by stepping back from an initial focus on domain area content and instead focus on the possible socio-cultural-scientific problems and challenges that content domains can

> **Your teacher-team:**
>
> **Input:** Identifies a series of problems
>
> **Output:** Reviews learning standards, domain content and socio-cultural perspectives to address problems
>
> Lists a scope and sequence of potential essential socio-scientific questions

Figure 4.2 NODE 1: Identifying Problems and Essential Questions.

support. In Node 1 (figure 4.2), we portray the initial teacher-team process of gathering information about the scope and sequence of questions identified as essential for the resolve of a problem.

PHASE 2: CONNECTIONS—LINKING PERSPECTIVES ON CONTEXT AND CONTENT

During these early discussions you might notice the emergence of an overriding theme that captures the essence of the questions developed in Phase 1. For example, given an essential question about the cost of sustainability projects in a community, your team might identify which math and social studies standards support students' understanding of the financial challenges of their community. Reflecting on this emerging theme, your team will then need to identify the curriculum goals and learning standards helpful in addressing a theme such as "Community Funds: Needs and Resources." In chapter 2 we discuss the importance of integrating content knowledge across domain areas as this integration has been shown to foster a student's ability to connect STEM learning with real-life applications. Node 2 (figure 4.3) shows the role of learning standards and content domains in responding to an essential question, noting that these standards will help guide a draft of the curriculum goals you develop in this phase.

PHASE 3: DISSEMINATION—COLLECTING FEEDBACK FOR A DRAFT CURRICULUM

You will now want to share your draft of curriculum goals with students and the community, asking for their input, ideas, suggested resources, and evaluation. As you think about distributing this draft, determine which community members or student groups might provide feedback to your team; think about

Your teacher-team:

Input: Identifies, analyzes and expands critical problems and essential questions from Phase 1

Output: Identifies a draft curriculum theme and list of curriculum goals

Identifies a draft list of learning standards, content and socio-cultural contexts for learning

Figure 4.3   NODE 2: Linking Perspectives on Context and Content.

Your teacher-team:

Input: Creates a draft curriculum, including goals, learning standards, content domain knowledge, pedagogical strategies, and socio-cultural context

Output: Disseminates draft curriculum for feedback

Figure 4.4   NODE 3: Collecting Feedback for a Draft Curriculum.

what student or caregiver expertise, school district resources, and cultural and social issues might have an impact on your community.

At this point, your team will have identified curriculum goals and examined learning standards, content knowledge, and community context. Offering an opportunity to review a coordinated curriculum draft can prompt additional input and analysis from your community. In part, participants might contribute ideas about the scope and sequence of potential topics for curriculum units or have ideas about resources or pedagogical strategies for lesson plans. For example, the eagle-watching activities that occur in January and early February in the Grafton and Alton, Illinois, community engagement are supported in part by volunteers who provide educational outreach to schools and the community; expert speakers also provide informational sessions. Thus, providing your curriculum draft to a range of participants could help your team organize subsequent useful unit topics such as, in the case of our eagle-watching example, weather, the science and mathematics of flight, and the exploration of a community's natural resources. The call for dissemination of your draft curriculum is found in Node 3 (figure 4.4).

A Developmental Model for a Socio-cultural STEM Curriculum   41

Your teacher-team:

Input: Evaluates and categorizes all inputs
Aligns participant socio-cultural perspectives with all inputs

Output: Incorporates participant responses into your draft curriculum

Figure 4.5   NODE 4: Analyzing and Incorporating Participant Responses.

PHASE 4: INTEGRATION—ANALYZING AND INCORPORATING PARTICIPANT RESPONSES

After disseminating your draft curriculum, review the responses you receive (inputs) and organize them into Nodes according to the type of responses you receive (e.g., Domain Content, Perspectives, Resources, or Essential Questions). As your team evaluates contributors' responses, an additional outreach to participants could be implemented. Your team might review a Node titled Resources and wonder who in your community has knowledge about the cost of recycling or what community official might speak to your class. In Node 4, we note the need to integrate a community's socio-cultural perspectives with the range of inputs you have received. For example, the recycling process might appear to some in the community as extra work or as a financial burden. As your students learn more about the topic of sustainability, they might discover that their community is not enthusiastic about a project that adds to the cost of housing or utilities. In Node 4 (figure 4.5), teacher-teams can evaluate inputs and determine how these inputs might align with a community's socio-cultural perspectives.

PHASE 5: FINALIZATION—PLANNING AND IMPLEMENTING CURRICULUM

After your teacher-team evaluates inputs gathered in Nodes 2 through 4, note how each Node category aligns with your overall curriculum goals. Are there resources in a Node that you need to meet these goals? Are other resources needed that you have not yet found? Are you planning to teach a content area such as water, for example, but need more information about how weather impacts water as a resource? Note how your Node categories relate to each other as you plan for the topics you want to include within a curriculum unit; these categories can also help you decide on the scope and sequence of potential lesson plans. Thus, you might have Node categories on

> **Your teacher-team:**
>
> **Input:** Identifies the scope and sequence of the goals of a curriculum unit
>
> **Output:** Develops a curriculum unit and lesson plans
> Implements the curriculum unit across your teacher-team

Figure 4.6 NODE 5: Planning and Implementing Curriculum.

topics such as water, velocity, and community challenges, each contributing to a curriculum unit titled "Sustainability: The Science of Supporting Community Needs."

The formation of Nodes can help you connect interdisciplinary domain content. For example, you might want to connect domain content about the science and reconstruction of landforms with the use of mapping skills taught in social studies. Additionally, you might create socio-cultural nodes about how the reconstruction of landforms, such as deforestation or the construction of dams, has impacted the sustainability of a community's access to farmland.

In chapter 5, we provide examples of resources that can help you design lessons to connect STEM content with pedagogies for problem-solving. You will find our example of an Inquiry Lesson Plan Template in appendix B. Node 5 (figure 4.6) provides for the implementation of your unit and assessment of its efficacy. Curriculum assessment models such as those presented by Sowell (2000) can be helpful evaluation tools.

PHASE 6: EVALUATION AND RECONFIGURATION— REFLECTING ON AND REVISING CURRICULUM

In Phase 6, your team will reach out to your students and community, seeking their perspectives on your newly developed curriculum unit and its recent implementation. You might want to learn about participants' thoughts on the richness of the curriculum domain content or how you used resources to support student learning. You might want to know more about students' thoughts and experiences with the pedagogies you used, such as students working in groups or the use of music or art as part of a group project. It is helpful to develop a strategy to reach out to participants using both written prepared prompts and open-ended questions to guide participant responses to your team.

> **Your teacher-team:**
>
> **Input:** Implements outreach to participants
> Reflects on implementation feedback
> Reviews curriculum goals and lesson objectives
>
> **Output:** Evaluates curriculum implementation outcomes
> Identifies needs for future implementation
> Identifies resources to support unit reconfiguration
> Reconfigures curriculum for future implementation

Figure 4.7 NODE 6: Reflecting on and Revising Curriculum.

As you have in earlier phases, organize the inputs you receive into Node categories for team reflection and analysis. For example: did you receive inputs about how a lesson plan objective was stated? Was the objective unclear? Did assessment methods align with the objective? You might create a Node category titled Lesson Objectives or Assessment Methods. Additionally, consider the socio-cultural context in which you implemented your unit. Did you receive input suggesting that students lacked the technology resources to complete an assignment? Or did you receive input suggesting that it would have been helpful if you had posted a video in a second language so parents could help students with homework?

As you review the inputs within each of your Node categories, think back to the unit curriculum goals you developed in Phases 1 and 2 and the unit goals and lesson plan learning objectives you developed in Phase 5. Reflect on these goals and objectives as you think about how you might reconfigure your unit (figure 4.7).

EVALUATION OF INPUTS-OUTPUTS AT EACH MODEL PHASE

The questions below can help your team evaluate the phases of the model.

- Did you complete each phase of the model?
- What inputs and outputs did your team receive?
- Did you categorize the inputs and outputs received into Nodes?
- How do your outputs provide for content and context domain integration?
- What are the benefits or disadvantages of an output?
- Did you need to revisit a phase?

PART 2: PROMPTS FOR TEAM DISCUSSION

There is no singular or direct path to working through the phases of the Pryor-Kang Model. Teams might have varying responses to the organization of a phase, or they might not agree on the information included in a Node. To help you determine if you want to return to a phase, we provide example discussion prompts below.

The following questions can help you organize your team's discussion before you begin to respond to questions in the prompts section:

- Do we have a draft of critical questions for our intended curriculum?
- Should we refine our outreach plan to participants for inputs or outputs?
- Do we need additional inputs/outputs for Node(s) at each phase?
- Do we need more time than originally planned to work on the phase?
- Should we refine the example discussion prompts (below) for our use?

Example Discussion Prompts by Model Phase

You might find some of the discussion prompts below useful as your team works through each phase of the model, or you might want to modify our suggestions and revise the language or positioning of these sample communication prompts.

Phase 1: Initial Development

- What problem-based focus is important to our team, students, and community?
- What essential questions guide our development of a socio-scientific curriculum?
- What learning standards, content, and socio-cultural perspectives are needed for our curriculum topic?

Phase 2: Connections

- How can the use of multiple disciplinary learning standards and content support a socio-cultural context for learning?
- What resources are available for the development of our curriculum?

Phase 3: Dissemination

- What modalities can we use to disseminate our draft curriculum?
- What modalities will we provide for participants' inputs?

Phase 4: Integration

- Do our unit goals align with our evaluation of the inputs?
- How will we determine the need for reconfiguration of a Node or additional outreach efforts?

Phase 5: Finalization

- What are the essential elements of our curricular design?
- What essential elements should be considered in the scope and sequence of lesson plans?
- What pedagogies are needed to implement the curriculum?
- How will we assess the efficacy of our curriculum?

Phase 6: Evaluation and Reconfiguration

Evaluation

- How does an output support student learning?
- Does the evidence of student learning match learning goals?
- Do participants agree/disagree on outputs as evidence of student learning?

Reconfiguration

- Which elements of our outreach plan have not been implemented or need modification?
- What elements of student learning need modification?
- What elements of socio-cultural integration could be modified to increase student STEM engagement?

SUMMARY

As we develop a middle school curriculum to provide students with a pathway to connect their personal experiences and understandings with a range of socio-scientific issues and challenges, we hope our endeavor will more deeply engage them in STEM subjects and provide opportunities to participate in greater problematic resolve. We also recognize the important role of parent/caregiver and community perspectives as they contribute to the school curriculum.

REFERENCES

Bogdan, R. C., & Biklen, S. K. (2003). *Qualitative research for education: An introduction to theories and methods*. Allyn & Bacon.

Dye, J. S. (2006). Parental involvement in curriculum matters: Parents, teachers and children working together. *Educational Research, 31*(1), 20–35. https://doi.org/10.1080/0013188890310103.

Epstein, J. L., & Salinas, K. C. (2004). Partnering with families and communities. *Educational Leadership, 61*(8), 12–18.

Geertz, C. (2000). *Available light: Anthropological reflections on philosophical topics*. Princeton University Press.

Gellert, U. (2005). Parents: Support or obstacle for curriculum innovation? *Journal of Curriculum Studies, 37*(3), 313–28. https://doi.org/10.1080/00220270412331314438.

Gordon, W. R., II, Taylor, R. T., & Oliva, P. F. (2019). *Developing the curriculum: Improved outcomes through systems approaches* (9th ed.). Pearson Education.

Oliva, P. F. (2005). *Developing the curriculum* (6th ed.). Pearson Education.

Ornstein, A. C., & Hunkins, F. P. (2004). *Curriculum foundations, principles, and issues*. Pearson Education.

Parkay, F. W., & Hass, G. (2000). *Curriculum planning: A contemporary approach* (7th ed). Allyn & Bacon.

Pryor, C. R., & Kang, R. (2013). Project-based learning: An interdisciplinary approach for integrating social studies with STEM. In R. M. Capraro, M. M. Capraro, & J. Morgan (Eds.), *Project-based learning: An integrated science, technology, engineering, and mathematics (STEM) approach* (pp. 123–32). Sense Publishers.

Pryor, B. W., Pryor, C. R., & Kang, R. (2016). Teachers' thoughts on integrating STEM into social studies instruction: Beliefs, attitudes, and behavioral decisions. *The Journal of Social Studies Research, 40*(2), 123–36. https://doi.org/10.1016/j.jssr.2015.06.005.

Pryor, C. R., Kang, R., & Pryor, B. W. (2021). Social studies-STEM activities and resources: Enhancing the content and context for learning. In R. M. Capraro, M. M. Capraro, J. Young, & L. Barroso (Eds.), *STEM Project-based learning: Integrating engineering for a new era* (pp. 271–98). Texas Aggie Publications.

Sowell, E. J. (2000). *Curriculum: An integrative introduction* (2nd ed). Prentice-Hall.

Smiley, J. (2010). *The man who invented the computer: The biography of John Atanasoff, digital pioneer*. Doubleday.

Tyler, R. W. (1949). *Basic principles of curriculum and instruction*. University of Chicago Press.

Chapter 5

Resources for Generating Inputs and Outputs to Your Nodes

This chapter describes video, participant contributions, and media/technology as example resource types for selecting inputs to include in a Node.

Resources can enrich students' understanding of lesson objectives by situating a learning objective in an informational and/or social context. A resource might refer to a historical or contemporary event that locates information in a timeframe or cultural setting, or it might be a "tool" or modality such as a media platform. The venues for locating resources are endless. Commercial materials, online podcasts, and platforms are replete with explanations about topics and are easily accessible online. Collections of materials can be found on institutional sites, such as the online materials of the Library of Congress (https://www.loc.gov/). Students and your participant community can "build their own" collection of resources and organize these in a series of Nodes. Each Node can be thought of as an output, whether or not completed with all needed inputs, and inputs to nodes can be continually accessible as an open gathering space for ideas, videos, links, and other resources.

Inasmuch as they represent a complexity of cultural nuances, such as place of origin, time frame, or geographic challenge (Bogdan & Biklen, 2003), resources can help students see how their own experiences are useful in resolving issues inherent in problems. Resources enrich and support student content domain knowledge by providing a context in which the content is applied (Sowell, 2000).

As you work through the phases of the Pryor-Kang Model in chapter 4, note the variety of resource types that contribute to the development of a Node. For example, you might have gathered a series of videos that describe geography, landforms, and math and have organized these into a Node titled Video Resources: Weather, yet you might want to find additional inputs to provide detailed information. Your teacher-teams and participants might seek information in a range of resource formats such as web links, documents, or written text. Note, however, that the recursive process of reflection and analysis on the inputs you include in a Node can appear as an output with a complete compendium of resources, or the output might prompt you to search for additional resource ideas. Below we discuss three types of resources useful as inputs to a Node: Video, Participant Contributions, and Media/Technology. A Node might include one or more resources, as in our example below, or draw from other types of resources that you locate.

RESOURCE 1: VIDEO INPUTS-OUTPUTS

Videos can be an efficient platform for sharing ideas, resources, links, and findings. Video inputs could be posted to a shared platform, providing all participants with a format for interaction and evaluation of inputs to a Node. Video inputs can serve several purposes; for example, video can serve as a modality for participants to explain or demonstrate domain content or for a teacher to introduce a content topic. Students might use videos to present their ideas, including resources they have found. You can review these video contributions and select appropriate videos for a learning community.

Pre-recorded domain content videos can prompt the need for additional research on a topic. For example, a video resource that explains the impact of water on land erosion might prompt the need to seek more information about the impact of erosion on the social and economic concerns of a community. Be certain to check your school district policy about the use of video and media images and/or the need for any participant contribution agreement forms.

Making Connections among Video Input and Nodes

In the above section we focused on the use of videos as resource inputs to a single Node to illuminate elements of a content domain area or concept. Here, we introduce a process to draw videos from *across* a series of Nodes in order to expand concepts. Your team might develop a series of Nodes in a redistribution point similar to when a teacher posts information to a network such as a website or app. As you look across the Nodes you have developed, you might notice how a video could function across Nodes.

For example, in scenario 2 below on the topic of the Civil War, you might use (or develop) a video about the impact of distance and elevation on the outcome of a battle and place this video in a Node titled Battles. You might also have created a Node titled Essential Questions and use this same video to help students draw connections between battle outcomes and essential questions about leadership and decision-making.

Note how the idea of inputs and outputs to each Node functions *flexibly*. For example, while the actual video(s) can be considered input providing background information about a unit topic, once participants reflect upon and develop their own thoughts about the ideas in the video, *their thoughts and ideas can be considered outputs*. These outputs might generate additional essential questions, prompting a team to seek additional resources.

Scenario 1: Using Ratio to Understand Historical Maps

A mathematics teacher decides to use a video to explain the basic concepts of ratio and percentage. At the same time, a social studies teacher on your team needs input for a lesson on the use of a map's compass to show the importance of ratio to historical outcomes. The math teacher's video input could be configured to target just the exact elements of the ratio needed to meet the social studies lesson objective. The social studies teacher might want the math teacher's video to focus on the concept of ratio in determining distance and less on ratio as the mathematical concept of percentage.

Scenario 2: Using Geometry to Understand a Historical Battle

A social studies teacher decides to create a video explaining General Lee's positioning at Gettysburg, as Lee had arrived late to the battle site and was unable to seek the "high ground" from which to launch his planned attack. Software products that can configure the effect of elevation and distance on battle position possibilities are available; in a self-developed video, however, a mathematics teacher can expand on these ideas. For the mathematics teacher, the video developed by a social studies teacher can highlight the importance of knowing how elevation and distance might critically influence historical outcomes.

RESOURCE 2: STUDENTS, PARENTS/CAREGIVERS, AND COMMUNITY AS CONTRIBUTORS

Students along with many contributors can help us develop a range of resource types as inputs to our curriculum (i.e., videos, mechanical devices, or photos). As you seek these contributions, note that the inputs you receive from contributors can be categorized by resource type (videos, data, or other) or by topic (using maps). Each category could become its own Node, or inputs can be organized and entirely contained as one single Node. Appendix C contains a sample letter to participants so you can explain the type of contributions you are seeking.

Here is one example of how a student's verbal explanation of the mathematical concept of geometric shapes could be used as an input into a Node; the example is drawn from a video vignette found in the 1997 landmark work of *math-e-dol-ogy*^{tm}. Although the site is no longer supported, the description below illustrates the usefulness of students' (and other participants') inputs into how ideas and thoughts contribute as resources for the development of Nodes.

In one of the vignettes in the *math-e-dol-ogy*^{tm} series, a third-grade student explains the meaning of the word "parallelogram" to another student in his class. Here, this student explains the concept of infinity underlying this mathematical shape by moving his hands in a parallel manner while explaining to another third grader that "[these lines] *never get together*" (for additional information, see Bitter & Pryor, 2002; Pryor & Bitter, 2008).

Captured on video, this student's voice, interpretation of a phenomenon, use of vocabulary, and physical portrayal can be interpreted as ideas that serve as input into a Node. The student's insights serve as an input to *his personal perspective* on the construct and function of a mathematics concept. His portrayal of his ideas, exemplified by his use of (a) select vocabulary, (b) reinforcement of a concept using hand motions, and (c) the act of collegial sharing with thoughtful and detailed explanations, represents not only math content information but also his perception of how to interact with others in a school setting. This student's response to another student's need to better understand a concept is based on his belief in the importance of sharing, a response that represents his perception of the underlying cultural norms of what it means to be a third grader.

RESOURCE 3: MEDIA AND TECHNOLOGY LINKS: COLLABORATION-PRODUCTIVITY

As you interact with your teacher-team as well as students/parents/caregivers and community, you might find these links are helpful for sharing information. The tools we present here reflect Reed's 2020 analysis of *collaborative and productivity technology*. Note, some of these links might be fee-based.

Video Tools

These tools help teachers and students interact and share ideas asynchronously by creating, editing, and communicating with videos and images. Here are a few examples:

Flip (formerly FlipGrid): https://info.flip.com/en-us.html
Classtime: https://www.classtime.com/en
VoiceThread: https://voicethread.com/

iMovie: bit.ly/42RRRmw
Movavi: bit.ly/3SQGO8b
ScreenPal: https://screenpal.com/

Conferencing Tools

The list below identifies some common conferencing tools that can help participants collaborate and communicate in real time via synchronous virtual meetings:

Zoom: https://zoom.us/
Microsoft Teams: bit.ly/42TmCar
WebEx: https://www.webex.com/
Google meet: https://meet.google.com/
Skype: https://www.skype.com/en/
Due: https://www.dueapp.com/
Slack: https://slack.com/
GoToMeeting: https://www.goto.com/meeting
Viber: bit.ly/4bMKalh

Content Domain Tools

These tools can help participants create and share content in a variety of formats and media, and work on shared documents in real time. Here are some examples:

WebQuest: bit.ly/3wpF6n1
Google Docs: https://www.google.com/docs/about/
Perusal: https://www.perusall.com/
Padlet: https://padlet.com/
Jamboard: https://jamboard.google.com/

SUMMARY

Drawing upon a range of sources and resource types as inputs into the development of a Node(s) enriches the curriculum development process. We note that Nodes function flexibly, whether as a completed space (an output) or as a continuing reflective entity with the provision for continual and open-ended reflection and contribution. The inclusion of multiple resource types in the development of a Node can illuminate the often left-behind perspectives of multiple participants central to student engagement.

ADDITIONAL RESOURCES

Scholarly Research

Applebee, A. N., Adler, M., & Flihan, S. (2007). Interdisciplinary curricula in middle and high school classrooms: Case studies of approaches to curriculum and instruction. *American Educational Research Journal, 44*(4), 1002–39.

Bell, S. (2010). Project-based learning for the 21st century: Skills for the future. *The Clearing House, 83,* 39–43.

Brears, L., MacIntyre, B., & O'Sullivan, G. (2011). Preparing teachers for the 21st century using PBL as an integrating strategy in science and technology education. *Design and Technology Education, 16*(1), 36–46.

Burris, S., & Garton, B. L. (2007). Effect of instructional strategy and critical thinking and content knowledge: Using problem-based learning in the secondary classroom. *Journal of Agricultural Education, 48*(1), 106–16.

Colley, K. (2008). Project-based science instruction: A primer—An introduction and learning cycle for implementing project-based science. *The Science Teacher, 75*(8), 23–8.

Damery, S., Walker, G., Petts, J., & Smith, G. (2008, July). *Using science to create a better place: Addressing environmental inequalities—water quality* (Report No. SC020061/SR2). Almondsbury, Bristol: Environmental Agency. Retrieved March 19, 2024 from bit.ly/490stw7.

Environmental Protection Agency. (2008, May). *Ideas for science fair projects on surface water quality topics for middle school students and teachers.* Retrieved from Environmental Protection Agency website: bit.ly/3PuToct.

Etherington, M. B. (2011). Investigative primary science: A problem-based learning approach. *Australian Journal of Teacher Education, 36*(9), 36–57.

Gallagher, S. A. (1997). Problem-based learning: Where did it come from, what does it do, and where is it going? *Journal for the Education of the Gifted, 20*(4), 332–62.

Jonassen, D. H. (1997). Instructional design models for well-structured and ill-structured problem-solving learning outcomes. *Educational Technology: Research and Development, 45*(1), 65–95.

Leonard, J. (2004). Integrating mathematics, social studies, and language arts with "A Tale of Two Cities." *Middle School Journal, 35*(3), 35–40.

Lee, M. (2007). Spark up the American Revolution with math, science, and more: An example of an integrative curriculum unit. *The Social Studies, 98*(4), 159–64.

Mercier, H., & Sperber, D. (2011). Why do humans reason? Arguments for an argumentative theory. *Behavioral and Brain Sciences, 34*(2), 57–74.

Wraga, W. G. (1993). The interdisciplinary imperative for citizenship education. *Theory and Research in Social Education, 21*(3), 201–31.

Zaslavsky, C. (1994). "Africa counts" and ethnomathematics. *For the Learning of Mathematics, 14*(2), 3–8.

Links to Content Resources

Library of Congress https//www. loc.gov

The following description is found on the LOC website: The Library of Congress, located in Washington, D.C., is the world's largest library, with nearly 110 million items in almost every language and format stored on 532 miles of bookshelves. Its collections constitute the world's most comprehensive record of human creativity and knowledge (bit.ly/4cjqOom). The site provides an educators' platform that includes lesson plans, curriculum units, and information about using primary sources with students.

Sample Links
Teachers: https://www.loc.gov/programs/teachers/about-this-program/
Digital Collections: https://www.loc.gov/collections/
Blogs: https://blogs.loc.gov/

Smithsonian Museums and Zoo https://www.si.edu/museums

The following description is found on the Smithsonian website: The Smithsonian is home to 21 museums and the National Zoo. While safeguarding and presenting our nation's treasures, our museums and zoo also support education, scholarship, and research (https://www.si.edu/museums). The Smithsonian is one of the world's foremost research centers in science, the arts, and the humanities. In addition to research pursued by the museums, the following facilities specialize in areas of inquiry spanning the globe and the farthest reaches of the universe (https://www.si.edu/researchcenters).

Sample Links
Educators: https://www.si.edu/education
Cultural Centers: https://www.si.edu/cultural-centers

National Endowment for the Humanities (NEH) https://www.neh.gov/

The following description is found on the NEH website: NEH supports research, education, preservation, and public programs in the humanities.

Sample Links
Educators: EdSITEment: https://edsitement.neh.gov/
Landmarks of American History and Culture:
https://edsitement.neh.gov/teachers-guides/landmarks-american-history-and-culture
"A More Perfect Union": America at 250: https://www.neh.gov/250

National Endowment for the Arts (NEA) https://www.arts.gov/

The following description is found on the NEA website: NEA is an independent federal agency that funds, promotes, and strengthens the creative capacity of our communities by providing all Americans with diverse opportunities for arts participation.

Sample Links
Save America's Treasures: https://www.arts.gov/initiatives/save-americas-treasures
Arts Education Partnership: https://www.arts.gov/initiative/arts-education-partnership
Art in Architecture program: https://www.arts.gov/initiatives/gsa-art-in-architecture
Independent Film & Media Arts Field-Building Initiative: bit.ly/3VqAHdM

National Science Foundation (NSF) https://www.nsf.gov/

The following description is found on the NSF website: NSF is an independent federal agency that supports science and engineering in all fifty states and U.S. territories.

Sample Links
Science Focus Areas: https://new.nsf.gov/focus-areas. Examples: Astronomy and Space, Biology, Chemistry and Materials, Computing, Diversity in STEM.
Education and Training: https://new.nsf.gov/focus-areas/education

International Society for Technology in Education (ISTE) https://www.iste.org/

The following description is found on the ISTE website: ISTE helps educators around the world use technology to solve tough problems.

Sample Links
Professional Development: https://iste.org/professional-development
STEAM in Education: https://www.iste.org/areas-of-focus/steam-education

National Council of Teachers of Mathematics (NCTM) https://www.nctm.org/

The following description is found on the NCTM website: NCTM advocates for high-quality mathematics teaching and learning for each and every student.

Sample Links
Classroom Resources: https://www.nctm.org/classroomresources/
Linking Research and Practice: bit.ly/4cl8eMw

Video Production Sites

Below is an introduction to a range of platforms that can be used to provide context for STEM or augment content for social studies as you develop a variety of Nodes for your curriculum. The following sites are a sample of interactive platforms for teachers and students to use, discuss, and assess an integrated curriculum. Note: Policies and descriptions below are derived from information provided on linked websites and are not vetted by the authors of this volume. Platform use or fee costs may vary or change.

Platform 1: Screencastify https://www.screencastify.com/ is a recording platform that provides recording, editing, and sharing of videos on Chrome. Resources for teachers to use this site are found at https://www.screencastify.com/education/resources. Open this site in the browser/tab.

Platform 2: Loom Another recording platform is Loom, found at https://www.loom.com/education. This platform, according to their website, "combines the expressiveness of *video* with the convenience of messaging, it's a new, more effective way of communicating with [others]" including student to student or student to teacher. Here, students can collaborate and respond to a video in "real time."

Platform 3: Flipgrid https://info.flipgrid.com/ Flipgrid is a Microsoft site that fosters discussions among students, especially when using video as a discussion prompt. As described on their site, "students can respond with their own video to a discussion prompt posted by a teacher. Students can watch and comment on videos from peers, with you as the educator in complete control."

Platform 4. Other commercial products may be available for recording and evaluation (e.g., Goreact.com), including the following:

DaCast. Host, monetize, and broadcast with an end-to-end live streaming solution. https://www.dacast.com/

Panopto. "Drive engagement, boost knowledge retention, and measure learning outcomes with Panopto." https://www.panopto.com/

Eduvision.TV. Eduvision notes on its webpage that it is "a media portal for the K-12 market, offering solutions for video capture, creation and publishing in a way that is cost-effective, easy and secure." https://home.mackin.com/digital/videos/eduvision/.

REFERENCES

Bitter, G. G., & Pryor, B. W. (2002). Networking the learner in professional development. In D. Watson & J. Andersen (Eds.), *Networking the learner. WCCE 2001. IFIP—The International Federation for Information Processing, 89,* 413–22. https://doi.org/10.1007/978-0-387-35596-2_41.

Bogdan, R. C., & Biklen, S. K. (2003). *Qualitative research for education: An introduction to theories and methods.* Pearson Education.

Pryor, C. R., & Bitter, G. G. (2008). Using multimedia to teach in service teachers: Impacts on learning, application, and retention. *Computers in Human Behavior, 24*(6), 2668–81. https://doi.org/10.1016/j.chb.2008.03.007.

Reed, M. (2020). *Distance learning technologies must-haves. Worldwide technologies.* Retrieved from https://www.wwt.com/article/five-technology-must-haves-distance-learning.

Sowell, E. E. (2000). *Curriculum: An integrative introduction* (2nd ed). Prentice-Hall.

Part III

EXAMPLE CURRICULUM THEMES AND LESSON PLANS

LESSON PLANS: IDEAS AND EXAMPLES

In chapters 6 through 11 we present examples of Socio-cultural STEM lesson plans.

These example plans have been developed to represent a curriculum theme, each with a teachable curricular topic. The authors of these plans utilized the *Lesson Plan Template* found in appendix B. This template is our adaptation of selected elements of the *Inquiry Design Model* developed by Grant, Lee, and Swan (2015), underscored by a charge to integrate interdisciplinary content with socio-cultural context.

As you read the chapter explanations, you will see that there is no one direct pathway to the use of the Pryor-Kang Model. Some authors' chapter discussions focus on Phase 1 of the model, planning for integration and identifying critical questions. Other authors have more deeply used Phase 2 and thereby focused their planning on aligning goals and standards with the integrative nature of content with context. Each chapter includes a narrative explaining the rationale for a selected unit topic and the learning objectives that support the goals of this topic.

Note that the authors were not yet able to try out the Input-Output outreach modality of the Pryor-Kang Model in real time. However, your teams can use the model and these example lesson plans as ideas for organizing your own planning by incorporating Input-Output outreach of participants' community knowledge, experience, cultures, and resources to better engage our students in the study and application of STEM.

REFERENCE

Grant, S. G., Lee, J., & Swan, K. (2015). *The inquiry design model*. Retrieved from http://www .c3teachers .org /wp -content /uploads /2014 /10 /IDM Assumptions C3 -Brief .pdf.

Chapter 6

Tackling Local and Global Challenges with Socio-cultural STEM

Sharon M. Locke and Georgia Bracey

AN EDUCATIONAL IMPERATIVE—UNDERSTANDING LOCAL AND GLOBAL CHALLENGES

The world is facing an unprecedented array of complex problems that will require socio-culturally informed solutions. These problems are described in the United Nations report *Transforming Our World: The 2030 Agenda for Sustainable Development*, which articulates 17 Sustainable Development Goals (SDGs) to ensure the well-being of all Earth's inhabitants and the ecosystems upon which humans depend. Sustainable development means using resources to meet the needs of the current generation without compromising the needs of future generations (Brundtland, 1987). Principles of sustainable development are related to "intergenerational justice," the idea that present generations have duties and responsibilities toward future generations (Barry, 1999). For example, as the impacts of climate change have become more visible and begun to directly impact people and communities, groups of young people have filed lawsuits alleging harm and/or violations of their rights to a healthy and clean environment (Parker et al., 2022).

Solutions to global problems are connected to solutions at the local level. For example, when international politics stand in the way of reaching an agreement on how to solve a problem, solutions at the local scale can collectively play an important role in combating the problem and creating political pressure for action at a larger scale. The world response to climate change illustrates how this can happen. Whereas international climate treaties have become mired in political agendas, cities have been able to move forward by forming global coalitions to take concrete action to lower greenhouse gas emissions and develop climate change mitigation plans (Fuhr et al., 2018).

In the United States, cities are serving at a leading edge of action, helping to counter political discord at the federal level.

Today's middle school students will become the problem solvers of tomorrow. This creates an imperative to teach students about global-scale systems and how their complexity creates challenges for scientists who seek effective solutions to problems. Hands-on learning that demonstrates solutions to small-scale problems can be the entry point for teaching global challenges. For example, SDG 6, "Ensure access to water and sanitation for all," will require the development of cost-effective systems for cleaning polluted water to make it available for drinking by populations in areas with insufficient current infrastructure. An activity that asks students to create a water filter (Lesson 2 in this chapter) conveys information about how to apply the process of natural filtration that occurs in the water cycle to help meet a personal need. With this foundational scientific understanding, students can then explore scaling up methods for water treatment to meet the needs of a community or city. Finally, integrating a socio-cultural perspective, students can examine human impacts on the water cycle and consider the various competing demands (e.g., homeowners, farmers, and industry) for a finite resource.

This chapter illustrates an approach to using socio-cultural STEM to introduce middle school-aged children to the inherent system complexity that makes solving global challenges so difficult. The lesson topics are renewable energy, the water cycle, and watersheds. These topics are especially rich for making scientific content meaningful and relevant for students, and they occur in several grade bands in the Next Generation Science Standards. Since energy, water, and ecosystems are necessary for human survival, any exploration of global and local challenges in these domains requires socio-cultural perspectives.

OVERVIEW OF LESSON PLAN TOPICS AND CONTEXTS

Renewable energy and its socio-cultural complexities are the subject of Lesson Plan 1. Increasing renewable energy sources is one solution to help curb global warming resulting from the burning of fossil fuels. Referred to as the "energy transition," replacing fossil fuels with renewable energy requires expertise and action in the realms of science, policy, and society. Renewable energy sources include solar, wind, hydro, and tidal power. Renewable energy also comes with trade-offs that lead to debates on costs and benefits for society. Renewable energy infrastructure requires large built structures that can disrupt natural systems, including dams, solar farms, and wind turbines. The conversion to electric vehicles requires ongoing research on how to build efficient rechargeable batteries. In turn, these renewable energy technologies require critical minerals such as cobalt, lithium, and nickel, leading to increased demand for mining, which has its own environmental and social costs. Lesson 1's purpose is to engage students in discovering the benefits and challenges of the coming energy transition.

Lesson Plan 2 is an exploration of the water cycle and its role in sustaining humans and shaping their cultures. "Water is life" is a central theme in the history of civilizations. Water sustains life on Earth, but it is not evenly distributed, and not all people have access to clean water to ensure their health and prosperity. Scientists project that a changing climate will further redistribute water, bringing too much to some regions and leaving others with less than before. Water stress has the potential to disrupt food systems and increase conflict between nations. The water cycle is part of our daily lives, but we rarely think about it, much less fully understand the continuous movement of water among the land, oceans, and air. Lesson Plan 2 focuses on the fate of water moving through the Earth systems and how human impacts on the water cycle affect both the individual and global society.

Lesson Plan 3 expands on the topic of water by asking students to consider watershed-scale processes and the human-environment interactions that occur within watersheds. This scientific research area is sometimes referred to as the study of socio-ecological systems. Taking a human-centered view, ecosystems provide multiple services that fulfill human needs, including provisioning of food and other resources, regulating services such as pollination and erosion control, and cultural services such as recreation and ecotourism. Different cultures, at present and throughout history, have approached watersheds and their ecosystem services using different cultural, social, and ethical lenses. Understanding these differences is important for developing solutions that take into account a diversity of perspectives and address the needs of multiple stakeholders.

LESSON PLANS AND RESOURCES

Lesson Plan 1

Title of Lesson: Renewable Energy—The Perfect Solution?

Theme:

The purpose of this lesson is to explore one type of renewable energy source (solar) within a socio-cultural context, discovering its pros and cons and examining its impacts on communities and cultures. This lesson addresses one of the UN's Sustainable Development Goals: #7 Ensure access to affordable, reliable, sustainable and modern energy for all.

Grade level: 5-9

Essential and Supporting Question(s):

Essential Question:

How can we provide enough clean, sustainable energy for everyone?

Supporting Questions:

- What is the best type of energy to use?
- What is renewable energy?
- How does renewable energy impact community and culture?
- How do humans use solar energy?
- What is passive/active solar energy?
- How did ancient communities use solar energy in constructing their homes?
- In what other ways do/did humans take advantage of the natural world (environment?) in building sustainable energy-efficient homes and communities? (cool tower [Zion National Park visitor center], water, wind, and geothermal)

Time Required: Two 90-minute blocks or equivalent.

Objective(s): *Students will be able to:*

- design, build, and evaluate a solar house.
- explain how their solar house works and how they modified it based on data.
- identify geographic locations where solar energy is most efficient (available?).
- identify pros and cons of using solar energy, including potential impacts on communities and cultures.
- explain passive solar heating.

Standards and Standards Integration:

Social Studies Standards:

- Thematic: People, places, & environment
- Disciplinary: History, Geography

Next Generation Science Standards:

- Obtain and combine information about ways individual communities use scientific ideas to protect the Earth's resources and environment. 5-ESS3-1
- Evaluate competing design solutions using a systematic process to determine how well they meet the criteria and constraints of the problem. MS-ETS1-2
- Evaluate a solution to a complex real-world problem based on prioritized criteria and trade-offs that account for a range of constraints, including cost, safety, reliability, and aesthetics, as well as possible social, cultural, and environmental impacts. HS-ETS1-3

Classroom Materials:

Pictures of solar arrays, panels; computers or laptops; large world map (or a map for each group); large index cards; string; pencils, pens, markers, colored pencils; transparency film (1 piece); cellophane tape; digital timer; cardboard; black poster paper; white poster paper; aluminum foil; and duct tape.

Socio-cultural Context:

The availability of energy has always been central to the development of societies and cultures. As the human population has grown over time, the demand for energy has accelerated. We now live in an energy-hungry world because of our dependence on technology. Although non-renewable energy sources have been sufficient for energy needs in the past, the rapid depletion of fossil fuels and concerns about their global environmental impacts have increased the urgency to develop and expand renewable energy sources.

Instructional Procedures: Solar House (~90 minutes)

Goal: Students work in groups to design and build their own solar house out of everyday items. They test their solar house, evaluate their results, and present them to the class.

1. Elicit student preconceptions and experience (10–20 minutes)
   a. Ask students what they know about solar energy.
   b. Guide the discussion to include ideas about solar power and its potential uses using pictures of solar panels, and solar-powered

devices. Address the difference between passive and active solar design:
    i. Passive: orienting a living space to take in sunlight directly for heating and designing the space (windows, roof, choice of materials) for efficient heating and cooling
    ii. Active: a collector absorbs solar radiation and transfers this energy to a living space
2. Introduce design project (15 minutes)
    a. Tell students they have been given the challenge to design a solar house. If the activity is being conducted during the cooler months, the goal is to increase and maintain the internal temperature of the house as much as possible. If this activity is being conducted during the warmer months, the goal will be to limit the temperature increase as much as possible. Explain the requirements and show possible materials.
        i. House requirements: The house must have four walls, at least four windows and two working doors, and a roof. It must be at least 15 cm. high and have an area of at least 30 cm. The design must also have a place inside for a thermometer so students can record the temperature.
        ii. Possible materials to try: This will depend on what you can gather, but show students a variety of options.
    b. Tell students they will meet as a team and discuss the problem they need to solve, develop and agree on a design for their solar house, and determine what materials they want to use. They will build, test, evaluate, and refine their design. Show a diagram of the engineering design cycle (https://www.teachengineering.org/populartopics/designprocess).
    c. Students should draw their design in their lab notebook and include the description and number of parts they plan to use. If, during construction, students decide their design needs to change, they should make a note of the changes in a new drawing in their lab notebook.
    d. Each team will test its solar house by placing the house in the sun at the orientation decided on by the team (use a compass).
    e. Students will use a thermometer to record the initial temperature inside of their house and then record the temperature every 2 minutes for 12 minutes. If time permits, they can then bring the house into the shade and record the temperature every 2 minutes for another 12 minutes. Encourage students to observe the tests of the other teams and observe how their different designs worked.
3. Groups work to design, build, test, and refine solar house (45 minutes)
4. Groups present work to class (30 minutes)

a. Each team will make a poster to help them present their solar house. These posters should include:
     i. Name/title for their house
     ii. Diagram of the solar house
     iii. Labeled components that help the solar house work
     iv. A few words about how each component helps the solar house work
  b. Each team presents their solar house, with their poster, to the group. Instructor questions may include:
     i. What was the most important feature of your solar house?
     ii. I noticed that your house has _____. Is that important for heating and cooling your house?
5. Debrief
  a. Did you succeed in creating a solar house that could increase and maintain its temperature or keep cool (depending on the time of year)? If not, why did it fail?
  b. Did you decide to revise your original design or request additional materials while in the construction phase? Why?
  c. If you could have had access to materials other than those provided, what would your team have requested? Why?
  d. Do you think that engineers have to adapt their original plans during the construction of systems or products? Why might they?
  e. If you had to do it all over again, how would your planned design change? Why?
  f. What designs or methods did you see other teams try that you thought worked well?
  g. Do you think you would have been able to complete this project more easily if you were working alone? Explain.
  h. What advantages does passive solar building designs have?
  i. What drawbacks do passive solar building designs have?

Extension:
Case Study—The Ancient Puebloan Cliff Dwellings

1. Students will read background information on the "cliff dwellers," the Ancient Puebloan culture whose structures are preserved in what is now the U.S. Southwest.
2. *Learning objective*: The student will be able to apply building techniques used by cliff dwellers to explain the building materials and directional orientation needed for passive solar design in their region.

3. *Guided discussion*: What are some of the ways that a house's location and orientation can help keep a house cool in high temperatures and warm in cold temperatures? What types of natural building materials can help insulate a home from cold and heat? What building materials would you choose to build an energy-efficient home in your neighborhood? Where would you place the windows to increase energy efficiency?

Take Action

- Students explore a map of U.S. solar potential:

  https://solargis.com/maps-and-gis-data/download/usa

Or. . .

- research solar power availability for residents in their area;
- do a cost comparison for power in their own home using different energy types;
- do an energy audit for their home.

Then. . .

- write to campus/district/local/state/national leaders to take action and/or provide suggestions for addressing the issue.
- create a public service announcement about the issue.
- share results in a school newsletter, social media post, or blog? Op/ed in local community paper?

Assessment:

Formative Assessments:

- Observation
- Discussion

Summative Assessments:

- Student posters/presentations
- Take Action activities

Socio-cultural Community Engagement:

Think about the weather/climate in your community—what is the best type of house to build there? What features could it have to use energy efficiently?

How would you advise someone thinking about building a new house? Socio-cultural community engagement is also found in the Take Action section.

Resources:

- Low energy design and renewable energy, Zion Visitor Center
  https://www.nrel.gov/docs/fy00osti/29315.pdf
- Passive solar homes, U.S. Department of Energy
  https://www.energy.gov/energysaver/passive-solar-homes
- Energy-efficient landscaping, U.S. Department of Energy
  https://www.energy.gov/energysaver/energy-efficient-landscaping

Lesson Plan 2

Title of Lesson: Water Cycle

Theme:

The purpose of this lesson is to explore the water cycle, the types of reservoirs and flows of water on Earth, and different cultural perspectives on water that influence how water is used.

This lesson addresses one of the UN's Sustainable Development Goals: #6 Ensure availability and sustainable management of water and sanitation for all.

Grade level: 5-9

Essential and Supporting Question(s):

Essential Question:

How does water affect human life?

Supporting Questions:

Where does water occur on Earth?

- What types of water occur on Earth?
- How do humans use fresh water?
- How does the water cycle determine who has access to safe drinking water?

Time Required: Three 90-minute blocks or equivalent.

Objective(s): *Students will be able to:*

- demonstrate how water moves through the environment using a model of the water cycle.

- define and demonstrate terms associated with the water cycle: evaporation, transpiration, precipitation, infiltration, percolation, condensation, sublimation.
- describe the different types of water and explain how different cultures view water.
- explain how and why access to the different types of water varies in different communities.
- design and test a water filter.
- investigate their own use of water and determine their water footprint.

Standards and Standards Integration:

Social Studies Standards

- Thematic: People, places, & environment
- Didciplinary: History, Geography

Next Generation Science Standards

- Develop a model using an example to describe ways the geosphere, biosphere, hydrosphere, and/or atmosphere interact. 5-ESS2-1
- Obtain and combine information about ways individual communities use scientific ideas to protect the Earth's resources and environment. 5-ESS3-1
- Develop a model to describe the cycling of water through Earth's systems driven by energy from the sun and the force of gravity. MS-ESS2-4
- Describe and graph the amounts and percentages of water and freshwater in various reservoirs to provide evidence about the distribution of water on Earth. 5-ESS2-2

Classroom Materials:

Students will work in groups. Teachers will need a set of these supplies for each group:
   computers or laptops; large world map (or a map for each group); Maori Case Study readings/materials.

For water cycle activity:

Water Cycle Video (https://www.youtube.com/watch?v=al-do-HGuIk); plastic shoe box or aquarium with cover; modeling clay or Play-Doh; crushed ice; Petri dish or small plastic lid; desk lamp with incandescent bulb; water; matches (optional . . . for teacher use only).

For water filter activity:

Scissors; paper towels; a glass bowl; a plastic bottle (preferably clear; a 0.5-L water bottle would work); cotton balls or coffee filter; funnels; gravel or small rocks (clean); sand (clean); activated charcoal (from other filters if possible—DO NOT USE grilling charcoal), rinse and dry before using; "impurities": dirt, glitter, food coloring, dish soap for making unclean water; water.

Socio-cultural Context:

Water sustains life. The presence of water in a geographic area has determined where the earliest human civilizations settled and/or defined seasonal migration patterns. Although many of us use water on a daily basis, we give little thought to where it comes from. Conversely, in some areas of the world, people do not have regular access to clean water and have a high awareness of sources of water. To understand where our water comes from, we must understand the water cycle, including the various reservoirs of water and how water moves and transforms over time among these reservoirs.

Instructional Procedures:
Create a model of the water cycle (~90 minutes)

Goal: Students work in groups to construct a model of the water cycle. They demonstrate their model to the class, explaining how water moves through the system (their environment).

1. Elicit student preconceptions and experience (10–20 minutes)
    a. Ask students where they have encountered water in the environment. Is it always the same? Where does it come from?
    b. Guide the discussion to prompt students to think about how and why water changes forms, locations, quantities, and temperatures.
2. Introduce activity (10 minutes)
    a. Students will create a model of a mountain and ocean landscape in their plastic shoebox.
        i. Using modeling clay, create a mountain on one side of the box. The other side of the box will be the ocean.
        ii. Add water to the shoebox until about ¼ of the mountain is under water.
    b. Students will use their model to demonstrate how water changes forms in the environment.
        i. Place the plastic lid on the shoebox.

           ii. Place the Petri dish on the lid over the mountain and fill it with ice.
           iii. Place the desk lamp next to the shoebox so the light shines over the ocean.
           iv. Observe.
       c. Students will sketch their model in a notebook, labeling where the different processes in the water cycle take place. Students should draw additional sketches as needed to show parts of the cycle that they did not observe in their model (e.g., percolation, sublimation).
   3. Groups work to build and observe a water cycle model.
       a. Adding smoke by placing a blown-out match in each shoebox may help students see the movement.
   4. Groups present work to the class.
       a. Students can show their models and notebook sketches to the class, explaining what they observed and drew.
   5. Debrief
       a. Review parts of the water cycle with the students—what did they see and not see with their models?

Make a Water Filter (~90 minutes)

Goal: Students work in groups to design and test water filters. They evaluate their results and present them to the class.

1. Elicit student preconceptions and experience (10–20 minutes)
    a. Ask students what they know about their drinking/washing water. Do they think it's clean? Safe? How do they know? How could they improve it?
    b. Guide the discussion to include ideas about where water comes from, what happens to it before they get it, water scarcity, and inequity in access.
2. Introduce activity (10 minutes)
    a. Tell students they have been given the challenge to design a water filter. They will be building a filter together in small groups using common materials and will share results.
3. Groups work to design, build, test, and refine water filters.
    a. Begin by gathering small amounts of sand, gravel, and activated charcoal. These will be the filtering materials.
    b. Use a plastic bottle to hold the filtering materials. To prepare it, cut the bottom of the bottle off, but leave as much of the bottle as possible. Remove the cap from the top (original) opening.

c. Flip the bottle over so the original opening faces down and put it into a glass or bowl so that the cut end of the bottle sticks out above the rim. The glass or bowl will catch the filtered water.
d. Place cotton balls or coffee filters in the opening of the bottle. This will be your bottom-most layer of the filter and will serve to hold the other materials in the filter. The cotton balls or coffee filters also filter out the smallest particles.
e. A 1-inch-thick layer of activated charcoal is the next layer if this material is available. This layer will also filter incredibly small particles, but it is not absolutely necessary. NOTE: Charcoal used for grilling is often too soft and will dissolve into the water. Grilling charcoal may also contain chemicals that may not be safe for human consumption. It is best to stay away from using charcoal grill briquettes.
f. Add about two inches of clean gravel or small stones as the third layer.
g. The next layer is a 3- or 4-inch layer of sand, which mimics layers of sand or sandstone.
h. Add another gravel layer at the top. Leave a little space at the top to prevent water from overflowing as you pour it into the filter.
i. To test your filter, add your impurities to a container of water and thoroughly stir it up. Pour the dirty water into the filter, being careful not to overflow the filter.
   i. What particles make it through the filters?
   ii. What color is the water after it has been through the filter?
   iii. How does the water smell? Do you think it's clean?
j. To test for detergent, soap, or other pollutants that are difficult to see, try testing the pH of the water. You can use the method of making a pH indicator with red cabbage found here: https://www.thoughtco.com/making-red-cabbage-ph-indicator-603650
k. An extension of this activity involves testing each filter material on its own with the same water and comparing them. Because adding cotton balls or a coffee filter would skew the results, you'll need to use funnels that will hold the materials instead.

4. Groups present work to class
   a. Each group should present a sample of their filtered water for visual inspection and describe the design and construction of their filter.

5. Debrief
   a. Which materials worked best (seemed to produce the cleanest water)?
   b. Why would you need to make your own water filter?

Extension:

Case Study—The Māori and the Language of Water (~90 minutes)

1. Students will read background information on the Māori people of Aotearoa, New Zealand, and their successful efforts to establish legal personhood status for the Whanganui River.
2. Learning objectives:
   a. The student will be able to explain the water-related scientific knowledge of the indigenous Māori.
   b. The student will be able to identify similarities and/or differences between their own and Māori values pertaining to water.
3. Guided discussion:
   a. Draw a diagram of the water cycle using the Māori words for the types and movement of water in your labels.
   b. How do you and/or your community value water? Are your views about water the same or different from the Māori?
   c. Are there other parts of nature that need a guardian or spokesperson? Why/why not?

Take Action

1. Students determine their water footprint (individual and/or family/household) https://www.watercalculator.org/
2. Students discuss how they can reduce their water footprint in their own living situation. They will choose three things they will do to reduce their water footprint and report back to the class in two weeks.

Assessment:

Formative Assessments:

- Observation
- Discussion

Summative Assessments:

- Student posters/presentations
- Taking Informed Action

Socio-cultural Community Engagement:

- Create a public service announcement about reducing water footprint.
- Share suggestions in a school newsletter/social media post or blog or op/ed in local community paper.

Resources:

- USGS water cycle diagrams

https://www.usgs.gov/special-topics/water-science-school/science/water-cycle-diagrams

Lesson Plan 3

Title of Lesson: Watersheds

Theme:

The purpose of this lesson is to explore how humans and landscapes interact, especially regarding safe, clean water access. This lesson addresses one of the UN's Sustainable Development Goals: #6 Ensure availability and sustainable management of water and sanitation for all.

Grade Level: 5-9

Essential and Supporting Question(s):

Essential Question:

How does human alteration of the landscape affect communities and cultures?

Supporting Questions:

- Why do humans alter the landscape?
- Who benefits from landscape alterations? Who is harmed?

Time Required: Three 90-minute blocks or equivalent.

Objective(s): *Students will be able to:*

- develop a model to describe the cycling of matter and the flow of energy among living and nonliving parts of an ecosystem.
- build a model of a watershed and use it to demonstrate how humans interact with the landscape around them.
- use data to gauge their local water quality.
- explore how other cultures manage water.

Standards and Standards Integration:

Social Studies Standards

- Thematic: People, places, & environment
- Disciplinary: History, Geography

Next Generation Science Standards

- Develop a model to describe the cycling of matter and the flow of energy among living and nonliving parts of an ecosystem. MS-LS2-3

Classroom Materials:

Pictures/diagrams of watersheds; one large piece (approx. 3' x 4') of butcher paper per group (another option is to use a 13-gal plastic garbage bag); 5–7 smaller pieces of paper per group; spray bottle for water; markers, colored pencils, crayons; cellophane tape; large plastic trays (cookie sheets?); modeling clay.

Socio-cultural Context:

Everyone lives in a watershed. The watershed type (e.g., arid versus coastal) and conditions (e.g., polluted or not polluted) influence the quality of our lives and our daily practices. In turn, our culture, religion, and belief systems can affect how we interact with the natural features in a watershed. Furthermore, watersheds are used by diverse communities and can cross boundaries, including international boundaries, meaning that there can be conflict among different users who have different needs for the services watersheds provide. The natural, built, and socio-cultural aspects of watersheds are intertwined.

Instructional Procedures:
Creating a Watershed Model (~90 minutes)

Goal: Students work in teams to create a model of a watershed, demonstrating how water flows and pools in response to the landscape.

1. Elicit student preconceptions and experience (10–20 minutes)
   a. Ask students where they typically see water in their local environment . . . do they see places where there's too much water? Too little? Does this change?
   b. Have they seen humans trying to control water? How do humans affect the water in the environment?
2. Introduce watershed model project (10 minutes)
   a. Show students examples of watersheds (maps, pictures)
   b. Students will work in groups to construct and demonstrate a model of a watershed:
      i. Crumple up several pieces of paper to create hills/mountains. Place these in the plastic tray and secure them with tape.

ii. Cover the crumpled paper with the larger sheet of paper (or plastic garbage bag), carefully molding it around the "hills" to create a landscape with various elevations.
　　　iii. Using a marker, lightly mark high points and low points on the landscape.
　　　iv. Predict where and how water will flow and collect in this landscape.
　　　v. Add a few communities to the model by carefully drawing some details on the landscape: plants, animals, houses, schools, and stores. Where will everyone build and live?
　　　vi. Gently spray water on the model to simulate rain . . . just enough to see how the water interacts with the landscape. How did the water interact with the communities?
　c. Adding a dam
　　　i. Imagine that you wish to create a lake somewhere on your landscape by blocking the flow of water. Discuss several options for the lake's location and choose one.
　　　ii. Use a small amount of modeling clay to create a dam on your landscape so that your new lake will form.
　　　iii. After constructing the dam, spray water on your model again . . . enough to see the lake take shape (you may need to carefully pour the water onto the model).
　　　iv. Note how the water flows now, especially in front of and behind the dam. How are your communities affected?
3. Groups work to build and test watershed models.
4. Groups present work to the class.
　a. Each team will make a presentation to help it share their results.

Extension:

Case Study—The Nile (~90 minutes)

1. Students will watch a video about the building of dams and then read background information on the case of the Aswan Dam.
2. Learning objectives:
　a. The student will be able to predict the impact of building a dam on river shape, flooding regime, and human use of the river.
3. Guided discussion:
　a. Compare the images of the Nile River in different seasons before and after the building of the Aswan Dam. How did the river change after the dam was built?

b. When the Aswan Dam was built, who benefited? Who experienced loss?
c. What do you think about building dams and other structures on rivers to meet human needs (such as water supply, power, transportation, and agriculture)?

Take Action

Research where the drinking water in your community comes from. Are there any threats to this water, for example, from pollution sources or excessive use? Who is responsible for protecting the sources of drinking water, and are there ways that individuals or community members/residents could get involved? Share suggestions in a school newsletter/social media post or blog or op/ed in local community paper.

Assessment:

Formative Assessments:

- Observation
- Discussion

Summative Assessments:

- Student posters/presentations
- Taking Action

Socio-cultural Community Engagement:

Socio-cultural community engagement is found in the Take Action section.

Resources:

- Drinking Water Mapping, U.S. EPA
  https://geopub.epa.gov/DWWidgetApp/
- Fueled by the Nile, NASA Earth Observatory
  https://earthobservatory.nasa.gov/images/146932/fueled-by-the-nile
- A Grand New Dam on the Nile, NASA Earth Observatory
  https://earthobservatory.nasa.gov/images/149691/a-grand-new-dam-on-the-nile

EXPERT OPINIONS

We asked a science teacher educator and a practicing science teacher to respond to a set of questions on the value of the socio-cultural STEM approach and the potential challenges of implementing a socio-cultural STEM curriculum as exemplified by the three lesson plans in this chapter. The first respondent is Dr. Jessica Krim, former professor of science education and chair of the Department of Teaching and Learning at Southern Illinois University Edwardsville and now a STEM education evaluation specialist with Goshen Education Consulting. Dr. Krim has extensive experience as a classroom science teacher and in professional development for pre-service and in-service science teachers. Our second respondent is Benjamin Scamihorn, science teacher at Roxana Senior High School in Roxana, Illinois, and instructor for the summer academy Environmental Health Investigators, which supports middle school students in completing science research projects relevant to their community. The experts' written responses were coded to identify common themes and important insights relevant to the classroom implementation of socio-cultural STEM.

Real-World Connections

The experts agreed that a socio-cultural STEM curriculum facilitates meaningful student learning by helping students make connections between the content and their own lives. The phrase "real-world" occurred several times across responses to the questions. The chapter lessons use an inquiry-based approach to explore local and global challenges, integrating hands-on activities that promote a high level of engagement and learning that can extend beyond the classroom. The holistic value of this approach was summarized by Dr. Krim:

> Adolescents are moving through physical, social-emotional, and cognitive changes. They are challenged socially by belonging to one or more friend groups, and are diving deeply into their perception of their identity. Participating in a socio-cultural STEM curriculum challenges them cognitively by demonstrating that ideas bridge, and run through groups.

Similarly, Mr. Scamihorn reflected on how socio-cultural STEM relates to his goals for teaching: "We, as teachers, hope to teach content to our students and help them understand how it applies to the real world and what they can do to help solve real world issues centered around our content." Socio-cultural

STEM is a powerful way to connect science learning to real problems in the students' community and the world. With this, students come to understand how STEM relates to their daily lives.

Learning Outcomes Beyond STEM

A second theme common to the two experts was the value of a socio-cultural STEM curriculum for generating learning outcomes that go beyond STEM content. This theme included a subtheme on the value of an interdisciplinary approach to middle-school teaching and learning. Socio-cultural STEM is an opportunity for teacher collaboration, as highlighted by Dr. Krim's comment, "incorporating case studies of locations in the U.S. and outside of the U.S. in lessons is an opportunity for social studies and science teachers to plan interdisciplinary units." Middle schools are well-suited to this type of teacher collaboration, compared to the more rigid administrative structures of many high schools. Another emergent subtheme was the benefits of the curriculum for preparing students to be engaged citizens. Mr. Scamihorn summarized this well: "This type of curriculum helps students become better citizens who know that their actions impact the world and those around them." The Take Action parts of the lesson plans encourage this extension of learning, which Dr. Krim highlighted as a benefit: "By providing even more varied socio-cultural community engagement, this curriculum has the potential to challenge all students to step out into their community and across communities as a learner, as they are preparing to become adults." The responses support the value of a socio-cultural STEM curriculum for twenty-first-century learning because it targets student understandings and skills beyond content, including interdisciplinary thinking and problem-solving.

Ethical Implications

The ethical implications of a socio-cultural STEM curriculum emerged in both responses. As a teacher educator who has argued for decolonizing education, Dr. Krim emphasized, "it is important to teach students early on that the areas being studied, whether indigenous to the United States or otherwise, are to be treated in an honorable manner." Mr. Scamihorn, on the other hand, took the perspective of a teacher (and administrators), commenting on the value of this teaching approach for students: "Administrators, just like teachers, want students to be educated in a way that allows them to make good ethical decisions in society."

The expert responses point to a potential gap and opportunity for further study of the ethical considerations of socio-cultural STEM. The comments suggest that educative materials to support teachers' classroom implementation should include ethical guidelines, as highlighted by Dr. Krim: "The curriculum can specifically instruct the teacher on how to serve as a role model when incorporating case studies, materials, or references to locations and cultures such as the Māori, the Nile, or Ancient Pueblo peoples." With this additional information, teachers would be better prepared to discuss differences across cultures and communities with their students, helping to prepare their students for perspective-taking and the ethical decision-making noted by Mr. Scamihorn.

Challenges to Implementation

Both reviewers noted potential challenges to implementation, but they did not perceive the challenges as insurmountable. The classroom teacher wondered about practical considerations such as finding and paying for the materials needed in the lessons. As he noted, even though the lessons are designed to minimize the need for materials, teachers in schools on tight budgets might still be challenged to acquire the supplies.

Both experts commented on the need for professional development workshops that would give teachers an opportunity to try out the lessons. As noted by Dr. Krim, "Teachers would need to be provided with resources and a facilitative workshop to ensure their buy-in. It would be beneficial to create a community of teachers within which they could provide support to one another."

CONCLUSION

The lessons presented in this chapter provide examples of real-world applications of STEM for solving past and present challenges. Crucially, the lessons are aligned with the Next Generation Science Standards, which enables science teachers to adhere to standards while also presenting the socio-cultural context of the STEM content. The grounding in the standards makes this a feasible teaching approach for teachers, one that can hold up to the scrutiny of school administrators. In turn, the historical and cultural context provided in the lessons showcases the meaning and relevance of the STEM content, facilitating students' ability to connect their classroom learning to their own lives. This combination is a powerful approach for equipping students to be the world's future problem-solvers and change-makers.

REFERENCES

Barry, B. (1999). Sustainability and intergenerational justice. In A. Dobson (Ed.), *Fairness and futurity: Essays on environmental sustainability and social justice* (Oxford, 1999; online edn, Oxford Academic, 1 Nov. 2003), https://doi.org/10.1093/0198294891.003.0005, accessed 25 Oct. 2023.

Brundtland, G. (1987). Our common future—Call for action. *Environmental Conservation, 14*(4), 291–94. https://doi.org/10.1017/S0376892900016805.

Fuhr, H., Hickmann, T., & Kern, K. (2018). The role of cities in multi-level climate governance: Local climate policies and the 1.5 C target. *Current Opinion in Environmental Sustainability, 30*, 1–6. https://doi.org/10.1016/j.cosust.2017.10.006.

Parker, L., Mestre, J., Jodoin, S., & Wewerinke-Singh, M. (2022). When the kids put climate change on trial: Youth-focused rights-based climate litigation around the world. *Journal of Human Rights and the Environment, 13*(1), 64–89. https://doi.org/10.4337/jhre.2022.01.03.

Chapter 7

Contextualizing Socio-cultural STEM through Historical Figures and Events

Whitney G. Blankenship, Anne Aydinian-Perry, Dean P. Vesperman, and Matthew T. Missias

The Social Studies and Science, Technology, Engineering, and Math (STEM) fields are similar in that they are both multidisciplinary, therefore including STEM-based topics within the social studies makes sense. The National Council for the Social Studies (NCSS) embodies this combination in their definition of social studies as the "integrated study of the social sciences and humanities to promote civic competence. . . . [S]ocial studies provides coordinated, systematic study drawing upon such disciplines as anthropology, archaeology, economics, geography, history, law . . . as well as appropriate content from the humanities, mathematics, and natural sciences" (Paska, 2023).

The push for students to embrace STEM subjects has its own socio-cultural context; specifically, the launch of Sputnik by the U.S.S.R. in October 1957 focused Americans' attention on the need for ongoing technological innovation if the United States was to keep up with the Soviet Union. It was known that the U.S.S.R. focused on the development of scientists and engineers, and the launch of the satellite alarmed many that the United States was losing ground to the Soviets. To address the gaps, Congress passed the National Defense Education Act (1958) a year later. Although the act focused primarily on encouraging the study of math, science, and foreign languages in higher education, emphasis on STEM subjects at the secondary level was also affected. About three years later, newly elected President John F. Kennedy (1962) told the nation, "We Choose the Moon," calling for the United States to put a man on the moon before the end of the decade. Just as the push for an increase in STEM content arose out of the unique socio-cultural factors of the time (the tense international relations with the U.S.S.R., the fear of "losing" to the Soviets, and the general fear of the spread of communism), technological developments throughout time have also been subject to their own unique contexts. The lessons developed in this chapter are designed to highlight how historical figures and events influenced the development of technologies across an array of topics.

OVERVIEW OF LESSON PLAN TOPICS AND CONTEXTS

In keeping with the focus of the chapter, we offer three lesson plans centered on the role of historical figures or events in the development of computer technologies over time. Each of the lessons is embedded within the socio-cultural context of the period and provides opportunities for students to conduct guided inquiry into the topic.

The first lesson, "Computers, Counting Machines, and the U.S. Census during the Gilded Age," explores how early inventions ultimately developed into the modern-day computer. Students conclude their inquiry with a project for taking informed action that builds upon their knowledge of the development of computers. Lesson 2 focuses on Typhoid Mary and the tensions that exist between protecting individual rights and protecting the health of community members. Students will examine the essential question: How have government policies designed to protect public health impacted individual rights? In this investigation, students begin by completing a science mystery to learn about the transmission of typhoid, then dive into media reports on Typhoid Mary and her role in spreading the disease. Students conclude their investigation with an informed action project. The final lesson takes students on a journey of food preservation throughout time. After researching historical preservation of a variety of artifacts (e.g., Egyptian mummies, amphorae, founding documents), students apply their knowledge of preservation of foodstuffs to create Global Recipe Cards.

Although each lesson addresses different topics, all lessons contain background on the specific socio-cultural contexts of the person or event to be studied. Additional resources for teacher background knowledge are also included.

LESSON PLANS AND RESOURCES

All resources listed in the lesson plans can be accessed via the link below: https://sites.google.com/view/ch6socioculturalstem/home

Key to the Standards:
NCSS-3C Framework (National Council for the Social Studies—College, Career, and Civic Life
ISTE (International Society for Technology in Education)
ITEEA-STEL (International Technology and Engineering Educators Association: Standards for Technological and Engineering Literacy)

Lesson Plan 1

Title of Lesson: Computers, Counting Machines, and the U.S. Census during the Gilded Age

Theme:

The purpose of this lesson is to explore how previous inventions led to the development of the modern computer. Counting machines were invented in the late 1880s in response to the struggle with completing the 1880 census. The development of the Hollerith Machine to help with the 1890 census slowly led to the development of the first computers in the 1950s. This lesson helps students explore this development using backward history.

Grade Level: This activity is best suited for students of the following grade levels: 7-12.

Essential and Supporting Questions:

Essential Questions: Why do we have computers?

Supporting Questions:

- SQ #1: What is a computer?
- SQ #2: What machines preceded the computer?
- SQ #3: How did a crisis lead to counting machines?

Time Required: 2 days.

Objective(s): *Students will be able to:*

1. Explain how the crisis over counting the 1880 census led to the development of counting machines.
2. Analyze the development and evolution of counting machines.
3. Create a timeline of important events related to counting machines and the development of early computers.

Standards and Standards Integration:
ITEEA STEL Standards:

STEL-1B—Explain the tools and techniques that people use to help them do things.

STEL-1D—Discuss the roles of scientists, engineers, technologists, and others who work with technology.

NCSS—C3 Framework:

D2.His.1.9–12. Evaluate how historical events and developments were shaped by unique circumstances of time and place as well as broader historical contexts.

D2.His.3.9–12. Use questions generated about individuals and groups to assess how the significance of their actions changes over time and is shaped by the historical context.

ISTE:

2. Knowledge Constructor: Students critically curate a variety of resources using digital tools to construct knowledge, produce creative artifacts, and make meaningful learning experiences for themselves and others.
    a. Students plan and employ effective research strategies to locate information and other resources for their intellectual or creative pursuits.
    b. Students evaluate the accuracy, perspective, credibility, and relevance of information, media, data, or other resources.
    c. Students curate information from digital resources using a variety of tools and methods to create collections of artifacts that demonstrate meaningful connections or conclusions.
    d. Students build knowledge by actively exploring real-world issues and problems, developing ideas and theories, and pursuing answers and solutions.

Classroom Materials: iPads or Chromebooks, large Post-it paper or butcher paper, pencils, rulers, other resources.

Socio-cultural Context:

Computers are a key cultural tool used in almost every activity in society, from learning to the creation of complex cultural artifacts. They are no longer merely computational devices used to simplify and expedite the calculation of complex mathematical equations, though they still serve this purpose in some aspects of scientific research. Over the 80 years since they first appeared around the 1940s, computers have evolved into an essential tool for the communication of culture and learning. Given the centrality of the computer and the role it plays in modern society, it is essential that students explore the origins of modern computers during the second Industrial Revolution with the development of counting machines. Starting with the development of counting machines in the 1880s, a series of inventions and innovations, driven by necessity (population growth and war), eventually led to the creation of the first computers. This lesson explores that development from the 1880s to the 1940s.

Instructional Procedures:

Day 1:

Launch—Questioning (5–7 minutes)

1. The teacher asks students a series of questions.
    a. Why is a computer called a computer?
    b. What does the word computer mean?
2. Explore both definitions of the term computer.
    a. An electronic device for storing and processing data, typically in binary form, according to instructions given to it in a variable program.
    b. A person who makes calculations, especially with a calculating machine.
    c. What do these definitions inform you about the nature of computers?
    d. What might it mean that the first definition is not about machines or technology, but humans?
3. Student-directed inquiry—History Lab (45 minutes)
    a. Inform students that, using secondary sources, they are now going to investigate the origins of computers.
    b. Break them into four groups (3 to 4 students per group). If needed, have two expert groups for each document.
    c. Assign a reading to each group.
    d. Remind groups to collect the essential data from each reading.
        i. Who is involved?
        ii. When did events occur?
        iii. Where did they occur (if mentioned)?
        iv. What happened?
        v. How did it happen?

vi. How about a question related to the science aspect of computers? For instance, what scientific issues/questions are computers trying to solve?
            e. You might want to assign roles to group members (reader, recorder, reporter).
            f. As groups are working, do one-on-one check-ins with the groups.
        4. With 5 minutes left—Exit Ticket (5 minutes)
            a. What are **three** things you learned today about computers?
            b. What are the **two** most important things you learned about computers?
            c. What is **one** question you have about computers from what you read?

Day 2:

1. Launch—Affinity map (10 minutes)
    a. On the board, create six columns. Title the columns: Who, What Happened, Cause of Change, Effect of Change, Scientific Knowledge Needed, Miscellaneous.
    b. Hand out three Post-it notes to each student.
    c. Using the exit ticket, have students write the three things they learned on Post-it notes.
    d. Students then line up and put their Post-it notes under the column they think it belongs.
    e. Discussion
        i. What patterns do you see form in the Post-it notes?
        ii. Are there any gaps you see in our research so far?
2. Have students return to their groups to finish data collection. (10 minutes)
    a. Continue with one-on-one check-ins with groups.
3. Group timeline project (30 minutes)
    a. Pick one member of each group (four people per group). You will have one person from each reading.
    b. Hand out large sheets of paper and remind students to take out necessary resources, including pencils, rulers, and other items they might use.
        i. Guide students to create their timeline starting in 1880 and ending in 1950.
    c. Inform students that they can use the ReadWriteThink Trading Card Generator to create the items they are going to attach to their timeline.

d. Using their readings, each group member should create at least three to five trading cards.
e. The teacher should visit each group as they work on their timeline.
4. Gallery Walk
   a. Post all timelines around the room.
   b. Have students walk around the room, examine, and evaluate each timeline, and write down all patterns they see in all timelines and/or if there is anything unique on a particular timeline.
5. 5-3-1 Discussion
   a. Students will write down five most important things they learned in the unit.
   b. Students then pair with another student. They will review all ten most important things and decide on the three most important things for the pair.
   c. Pairs will form a quad. The quad will review six most important things for the two pairs. They will then decide on the most important thing they learned about the origins of computers.

Day 3:

1. Entrance Ticket (How do you feel about what you have learned so far?) (5 minutes)
2. Taking informed action (50 minutes)
   Students will have several options for how they can take informed action.
   a. Investigate current contentious issues related to the U.S. Census and write a letter to the editor of a local newspaper about one issue.
   b. Write a short essay on the role of a "crisis" in providing a catalyst for innovation using examples from the 1880 Census and World War II.
   c. Investigate how technology evolves over time to meet the needs of society. Students will then create a 2-minute PSA about the evolution of the computer from human tabulation to counting machines to computers.
   d. Investigate the contributions of women and people of color in computer science . . . women of NASA, women of Google, current movements like Girls Who Code, Black Girls Who Code, CSforAll, current movements to get more students involved in computer science, and current CS offerings in their schools/districts.

Assessment:

Formative performance tasks: questioning/talk moves, student-directed inquiry, history lab, 3-2-1 exit ticket (Day 1), and affinity map (Day 2).

Summative performance tasks: small group inquiry, timeline project and gallery walk (Day 2), 5-3-1 Discussion (Day 2), and Taking Informed Action project (Day 3).

Socio-cultural Community Engagement:

Perspectives of students and other community members are included in the Taking Informed Action project. Students will use what they have learned about the evolution of counting machines into computers and their own prior knowledge to take their learning outside of the classroom. They have a choice of activities that allow them to extend their learning and apply that learning in a multi-modal project. This can then be shared, if the student chooses, with the public in several formats (see Taking Informed Action project [Day 3]).

Accommodation/Modification: (a) ability grouping, (b) modified readings for lower Lexile levels, and (c) guided reading questions or a graphic organizer for research.

Resources:

- Computer History Museum. (2023). *Exhibition: Birth of the computer.*
- International Business Machines. (n.d.) *The punch card tabulator.* IBM 100.
- Stromberg, J. (Dec. 9, 2011). Herman Hollerith's tabulating machine. *Smithsonian Magazine.*
- United States Census Bureau. (n.d.). *History: The Hollerith Machine.* Census Bureau.

Lesson Plan 2

Title of Lesson: Typhoid Mary and the Politics of Disease

Theme:

The recent pandemic provides a jumping-off point for the study of disease outbreaks across time and place. In this lesson, students will learn about Mary

Mallon (aka Typhoid Mary), the superspreader responsible for the 1906 NYC typhoid epidemic.

Grade Level: This activity is best suited for students of the following grade levels: 7–9.

Essential and Supporting Question(s):

Essential Question:

- How have government policies designed to control the spread of disease impacted individual civil rights?

Supporting Questions:

- How did government officials react to the 1906 NYC Typhoid epidemic?
- What was the role of the media in the public reaction to the typhoid epidemic?
- What was the impact of official policies on Mary Mallon?

Time Required: This lesson is designed to be taught over two 60–90-minute class periods. Time is flexible, and the lesson can be adjusted as needed to work with scheduling and time available.

Objective(s): *Students will be able to:*

- Identify and explain the historical significance of Mary Mallon (Typhoid Mary).
- Discuss the policies and actions taken by government officials in reaction to the typhoid epidemic.
- Evaluate the impact of epidemic policies on the civil rights of individuals.

Standards and Standards Integration:

NCSS Thematic Strands: Science, Technology & Society

Learners realize that both science and technology have had a profound effect on shaping human experience and the world around us.

ISTE Standards: Knowledge Constructor

1.3a Plan and employ effective research strategies to locate information and other resources for intellectual or creative pursuits.

1.3b Evaluate the accuracy, perspective, credibility and relevance of information, media, data, or other resources.

1.3d Build knowledge by actively exploring real-world issues and problems, developing ideas and theories, and pursuing answers and solutions.

Classroom Materials: Omitted.

Socio-cultural Context:

In 1906, a typhoid outbreak in NYC would ultimately end up infecting at least fifty-one people (three of whom died) over the course of two outbreaks. The job of determining the source of the infection was given to George Soper, a civil engineer and sanitation expert. Drawing on the work of John Snow during the 1856 British cholera epidemic, Soper looked for connections between typhoid victims by cross-referencing a list of wealthy individuals. Soper believed that disease could be transmitted from one person to another, a nod to Louis Pasteur's germ theory. These beliefs and methods were still very new at the turn of the twentieth century; as a result, debates over policies designed to slow the spread of disease needed to be updated to reflect this new knowledge. In the case of Mary Mallon (Typhoid Mary), her status as an asymptomatic carrier led officials to order her into isolation and quarantine against her will. Mallon's story illustrates the difficulties faced by government officials in balancing individual rights with the needs of the public, a tension that is also illustrated in the policies concerning medical inspections of immigrants on Ellis Island, the quarantine and masking during the 1918 Flu Epidemic, the quarantining of polio patients, the AIDS epidemic, and the COVID-19 pandemic.

Instructional Procedures:

Optional Day 1 or as Homework (30–40 min)

- *NOTE: The Twin Forks simulation introduces students to the methodology used by George Soper to identify Mary Mallon as the asymptomatic carrier. Students can work individually or in pairs to complete the mystery.*
    - *Tell students that they are about to embark on a medical mystery where they will have to use their critical thinking skills to determine who infected the town of Twin Forks with typhoid.*
    - *Display the opening page on the projector and direct students to the simulation website.*
    - *Tell students to click "go," which will open up the opening sequence.*

- ○ Point out the sidebar menus they can use for additional information: People, Glossary.
- ○ Students work through the mystery, collecting information and questioning individuals.
- ○ After analyzing the evidence they have collected, students submit their answers. The program will provide feedback to the student(s) if they have incorrectly identified patient zero, and they will have the opportunity to review the evidence.
- ○ Debrief game (10–15 minutes):
  - Why was it important to identify patient zero? What did students learn about how disease spreads?
  - How did students use evidence to determine patient zero? What evidence was most convincing?
  - What should the city do to keep typhoid from spreading? What problems might the city encounter in implementing these policies?

Day 1: The Case of Typhoid Mary

- Do Now: What is a superspreader event? (~5–7 minutes)
- Debrief answers.
- Introduce the story of Mary Mallon and tell students that they are going to piece together her story based on newspaper articles: about the case. (45–60 minutes)
  - ○ "Woman 'Typhoid Factory' Held as Prisoner," *The Evening World News*, April 1, 1907
  - ○ "Thrives on Typhoid," *Washington Herald*, April 7, 1907
  - ○ "Typhoid Mary Wants Liberty," *Richmond Planet*, July 10, 1909
  - ○ "Suit for $50,000 by 'Typhoid Mary,'" *The Times Dispatch*, December 4, 1911
  - ○ "Microbe Carriers," *Tacoma Times*, July 11, 1915 (in particular section on Typhoid Mary)
  - ○ "Exile for Life," *The Sun*, March 28, 1915
- Create 6 groups and assign one news article to each group.
- Give each student a copy of the Primary Source Analysis Tool. You may wish to ask students specific questions based on the LOC "How to Analyze a Newspaper" Teachers Guide.
- Student groups complete the graphic organizer for their news article.
- Groups report their findings as the teacher creates a master document. Students should record the findings of their peers on their note sheet (15–20 min).

- As students report their findings, the teacher should ask clarifying questions as needed.
- After all groups have reported on their documents, ask students to review their notes. What facts do all of the news articles agree upon? On what do they differ? What might account for those differences? How do they characterize Mary Mallon?
- Project the timeline and review the case with students. (~5 minutes)
- Formative Assessment: Exit Ticket: 3-2-1 (10–15 minutes)
  - 3 facts about Mary Mallon that appeared in most of the newspaper articles
  - 2 words to describe the media's coverage of Mallon
  - 1 connection between Mallon's story and the present

Day 2: In Her Own Words: Analyzing Mary Mallon's Letter

- Students should have access to either a print or digital copy of "In Her Own Words, Mary Mallon's Letter to the Editor."
- Students should have their graphic organizers from the previous lesson.
- Individually or in small groups, have students read and annotate Mary Mallon's letter to the editor (30–40 minutes).
- Students should highlight in the letter:
  - Evidence that contradicts the newspaper reports.
  - Evidence that supports the newspaper reports.
  - How Mary was affected by her treatment.
- Class discussion (5–10 minutes):
  - Were the actions of officials in quarantining Mary Mallon justified? What evidence supports your answer?
  - What effect do you think newspaper coverage had on officials? On the community? What evidence supports your argument?
  - When does community safety trump individual rights?

Through the examination of historical newspaper articles reporting on the typhoid outbreak and Mallon's own experiences as related in her letter to the editor, students engage in inquiry to piece together the story of "Typhoid Mary." As they work together to construct a narrative of the epidemic, students must be aware of and take into consideration:

- the adaptation of public policies as scientific knowledge advances
- the tensions between the protection of individual liberties and the protection of the public from disease
- the role of the media in shaping public policy and public opinion

Each of these questions resonates throughout history as well as contemporary society (i.e., AIDS, COVID).

Assessment:

Optional Formative Assessment: Exit Ticket:

- How did the disease spread?
- What obstacles did the investigator(s) meet as they tried to determine who was patient zero?
- 3-2-1 Exit Ticket at the end of first day (see above)

Summative Assessment—DBQ:

- Using evidence from the documents analyzed in class, students will respond to the prompt "Was the treatment of Mary Mallon by public officials and the press justified?"

Summative Assessment: Taking Informed Action:

- Students will undertake a mini-research project on one of the following historical events: the 1918 Flu epidemic, Polio & the Salk Vaccine, AIDS, or the COVID-19 Pandemic.
- After concluding their research, students will create either:
  - A podcast that chronicles the history of a chosen event, the public policies enacted as a result of the event, and an analysis of the significance of the event in terms of public health.
  - A social media campaign of 4–5 posts (e.g., Instagram/Facebook, Twitter) highlighting the public policies enacted and the pros/cons of the policy in terms of individual rights.
  - A blog investigating the causes and effects of the chosen event, as well as an analysis of the effectiveness of mediation efforts.

Socio-cultural Community Engagement:

The perspectives of students and other community members are included in the summative assessment op-ed project.

Accommodations/Modifications:

- Modify articles and other readings for a lower reading level using Rewordify.
- Provide graphic organizers for note-taking.

- Provide guided reading questions.
- Provide a detailed checklist of steps for lesson/project.

Resources:

- Access to the internet and devices for research
- Access to CANVA, PowerPoint or similar program
- Digital or print copies of documents:
  - "Woman 'Typhoid Factory,'" *The Evening World,* April 1, 1907
  - "Typhoid Mary Wants Liberty," *Richmond Planet,* July 10, 1909
  - "Suit for $50,000 by 'Typhoid Mary,'" *The Times Dispatch,* December 4, 1911
  - "Microbe Carriers," *Tacoma Times,* July 11, 1915
  - "Exile for Life," *The Sun,* March 28, 1915
  - "In Her Own Words, Mary Mallon's Letter to the Editor"

Lesson Plan 3

Title of Lesson: To Have and To Hold: Preservation Throughout the Ages

Theme:

This lesson facilitates students in rediscovering the world around them, as well as their local surroundings, through examining preservation.

Grade level: This activity is best suited for students of the following grade levels: 6-10.

Essential and Supporting Question(s):

Essential Question:

- Why do we preserve what we do?

Supporting Questions:

- What do we preserve?
- How do we preserve?
- How does geography influence preservation techniques, and how do both, in turn, influence culture?

Time Required: Three 90-minute blocks. Time is flexible, however, and should be adjusted based on student needs and abilities, student background knowledge, and period/block schedule.

Objectives: *Students will be able to:*

- Identify the types of foods that can be preserved.
- Explain how the preservation of foods is carried out in different places and eras.
- Examine how geography influences preservation techniques and how both geography and food preservation influence culture.

Standards and Standards Integration:

NCSS—C3 Framework

D2.Geo.5.6-8. Analyze the combinations of cultural and environmental characteristics that make places both similar to and different from other places.

D2.Geo.6.6-8. Explain how the physical and human characteristics of places and regions are connected to human identities and cultures.

ISTE

1.3. Knowledge Constructor

Students critically curate a variety of resources using digital tools to construct knowledge, produce creative artifacts, and make meaningful learning experiences for themselves and others.

a. Students plan and employ effective research strategies to locate information and other resources for their intellectual or creative pursuits.
b. Students evaluate the accuracy, perspective, credibility, and relevance of information, media, data, or other resources.
c. Students curate information from digital resources using a variety of tools and methods to create collections of artifacts that demonstrate meaningful connections or conclusions.
d. Students build knowledge by actively exploring real-world issues and problems, developing ideas and theories, and pursuing answers and solutions.

1.6. Creative Communicator

Students communicate clearly and express themselves creatively for a variety of purposes using the platforms, tools, styles, formats, and digital media appropriate to their goals.

a. Students choose the appropriate platforms and tools for meeting the desired objectives of their creation or communication.
b. Students create original works or responsibly repurpose or remix digital resources into new creations.

ITEEA STEL Standards

STEL-6C—Compare various technologies and how they have contributed to human progress.

STEL-8L—Interpret the accuracy of information collected.

Classroom Materials:

Possible resources for this activity may include computers or laptops, large world map, butcher paper, large index cards, string, pencils, pens, markers, and colored pencils.

Socio-cultural Context:

The preservation of food developed from the need to store food for extended periods of time to survive. As new methods of preservation were developed, human populations stabilized, which led to the development of small cities. Over time, trade routes grew, and new foods and methods of preservation were shared in geographically distant places.

Instructional Procedures:

First Block

1. Warm-up Activity—Brainstorm and Discussion (~10–20 minutes)
    - Students in the class will brainstorm answers to the following questions (either whole-class, small groups, or partners) with the goal of creating a basic class definition of preservation and its characteristics that will be added to as the lesson progresses: (a) What is "preservation"? (b) What is/has been preserved? (c) How do we do it? Students may bring up both tangible (e.g., game ball, food, photos) and intangible (e.g., memories) examples.
    - Students will next brainstorm historical examples of preservation from classes, popular culture, and/or prior knowledge. Examples may include deceased bodies, artifacts, and fossils.
    - Students will have a class conversation discussing their brainstorming responses. The teacher will facilitate the conversation and use probing questions to focus or redirect the conversation as necessary. (*Teacher Note:* Use this space to handle any misconceptions that students might have about preservation and clarify.)

    Students should exit this discussion with a class definition (10–15 words or less) of preservation similar to *"the act, process, or result of preserving something: such as (a) the activity or process of*

keeping something valued alive, intact, or free from damage or decay" (Merriam-Webster).
2. Jigsaw—Historical Preservation Investigation (~40–50 minutes)
   - In small groups (3–4 students), students read articles on one of the following topics and determine how these artifacts were preserved (i.e., containers, ingredients, climate/environment): (a) Amphorae, (b) Andean/Incan Potatoes, (c) Chinese Tombs, (d) Egyptian Mummies, (e) European Bog People, (f) Hallstatt's Man in the Salt, (g) Ötzi the Iceman, (h) The United States' Founding Documents in the National Archives. (*Teacher note:* Students might have the misconception of "scanning" to preserve these documents versus climate control of the parchment.)
   - In new groups containing one student from each topic group, group members share their document's information, identify common elements, and come to an agreement on necessary characteristics for preservation.
3. Discussion—Defining Scientific Characteristics of Physical Preservation (~30 minutes)
   - New groups will share their necessary characteristics with the class.
   - The class will refine shared characteristics into the following:
   For preservation to occur, there must be (a) a removal of moisture, (b) a removal of air/lack of oxygen, (c) the addition of chemicals (i.e., salt, sugar, acids, smoke, manufactured chemical preservatives), (d) control of temperature, and (e) control of light.

Second Block

4. Warm-up Activity—Brainstorm (~20 minutes)
   - Students in the class will brainstorm and share answers to the following questions (either whole-class, small groups, or partners): (a) Why would we preserve food? (b) When would we preserve food? (c) What preserved food do you see at snack time/lunchtime/at your place? (d) How is that food preserved? (e.g., packaging, refrigeration)
5. Visual Vocabulary—Food Preservation Terms (~20 minutes)
   - Students will create a visual vocabulary entry for the following food preservation terms: canned, cured, dried/dehydrated, frozen, fermented, pickled, and smoked.
   - Each entry consists of a *definition* (student-friendly, 10–15 words or less), an *illustration* of the definition, and a *real-life example* (use in a sentence is optional).
6. Inquiry Project—Global Preservation Recipe Cards (~50 minutes)
   - Students will create recipe card entries for an interactive global map centered on a preserved food dish.

- This can be done analogously with large maps/butcher paper, large index cards, and string, or virtually using a whiteboard/bulletin board platform such as Jamboard, Canva, and Padlet.
- Students will indicate the location (specific, national/regional cuisine), circa first appearance, preservation method/s, required ingredients, and the dish's characteristics (Was it social class specific, used, or rare ingredients?).
- Dishes should be representative of preservation techniques and global cuisine. Some examples are:
  - Canned (jams, fruits, vegetables; clay and tin containers)
  - Cured and/or smoked (salmon, sausage, beef jerky, salami, honey)
  - Dried/Dehydrated (pemmican, lutefisk, chalona)
  - Fermented (sauerkraut, kimchi, curtido/cortido, gravlax, sursild, soy sauce, nuoc mam, garum)
  - Frozen (gravlax, sursild, Clarence Birdseye & flash freezing)
  - Pickled (olives, pickles, fruits)
  - Food from students' culture
- Students will share their recipe cards on the paper or virtual map.

Third Block

7. Warm-up Activity—Gallery Walk (~30 minutes)
   - Students will read their classmates' responses and analyze them for similarities, patterns, and other information of note across the recipe cards.
   - Students will categorize gathered information by continental trends, regional trends, and preservation type trends.
   - *Teacher Note:* Prompt students to evaluate whether certain preservation methods are promoted or limited by geography (e.g., the tropics will not utilize freezing due to temperatures, coastal areas might not use dehydration due to humidity, and areas with limited wood might not use smoking due to prioritization of lumber).
8. Closure Activity—Debrief (~20–30 minutes)
   Students will debrief the lesson after the conclusion of the gallery walk. Ideally, students are sharing what they learned in the lesson, how it might counter their prior knowledge on the topic, and questions they might have on the topic or on the nature of history, geography, and/or science. Some closure activity ideas:
   - *3-2-1*: Students write down three things they learned, two things they have a question about (could be for clarification of the content or a bigger philosophical question on the topic), and one thing they want

the instructor to know. This can be shared in a whole or small group setting.
- *Whip Around*: Students share one item of interest to them (something they learned, something they are now questioning) with the whole class. Everyone participates, and no duplications.
- Now What? (How does this fit into what we are learning? Does it affect our thinking? Can we predict where we are going?)

9. Student Choice—Taking Informed Action (~30–40 minutes)
   There are several options for taking informed action in the community:
   - Students can research food waste issues (in the school/local/state/national community) and
     - write to campus/district/local/state/national leaders to take action and/or provide suggestions for addressing the issue.
     - create a public service announcement about food waste issues in the local/state/national/global community.
   - Students can research food banks/food services in their local community and investigate the role of preserved food in their work.
   - Students can further research preservation's role in specific food traditions and create a podcast/TikTok/Flipgrid/poster/other media to share this information with the local and school community.
   - Students discuss or write the answers to the following questions in a whole-group or small group setting:
     - *What* did we learn today?
     - So *What?* (relevancy, importance, usefulness)

Assessment:

Formative Assessments: Brainstorms, Jigsaw, Gallery Walk

Summative Assessments: Global Preservation Recipe Cards, Taking Informed Action

Socio-cultural Community Engagement:

Socio-cultural perspectives of parents, colleagues, and students are included in this lesson through the Food Investigation and Taking Informed Action segments of the lesson.

Accommodations/Modifications: (a) picture clues to support vocab food and techniques, (b) vocab list prepopulated, (c) sentence stems, (d) modified load, (e) mixed-level grouping, and (f) dual language dictionaries.

Resources:

Honey
Schwarcz, J. (2022, May 26). *Does honey have any value as a preservative?* McGill Office for Science and Society.

Amphorae
Jones, S. (2022, March 8). Roman boat that sank in Mediterranean 1,700 years ago gives up its treasures. *The Guardian.*
Recker, J. (2022, May 18). Ukrainian soldiers uncover fourth-century urns while digging defense trenches. *Smithsonian Magazine.*

Andean/Incan Potatoes
Allen, I. (n.d.). *Chuños.* Gastro Obscura.
Karita, J. (2013, August 20). Andean farmers freeze-dry spuds the ancient way. *AP News.*
Romero, S. (2016, August 10). A space-age food product cultivated by the Incas. *The New York Times.*

Chinese Tombs
Chaffin, C. E. (2022, January 10). *The search for immortality: The tomb of Lady Dai.* Smarthistory.
Higgins, L. (2016, December 1). Nobody knows why this ancient mummy is so well preserved. *New York Post.*
Kang, L. (2023, May 17). "Well-preserved" Han dynasty cliff tomb found in Chongqing. *Global Times.*
Ritter, M. (2023, January 18). Trove of rare tombs—some with preserved bones—unearthed in China, photos show. *Miami Herald.*

Egyptian Mummies
Anthropology Outreach Office. (n.d.). Egyptian mummies. *Smithsonian.*
Britannica Kids. (n.d.) Mummy. In *Britannica Kids Encyclopedia.*

Egyptian Mummies—Lower-level reading with illustrations
DK findout! (n.d.). *Making a mummy*
National Geographic Kids. (n.d.). *How to make a mummy!*

European Bog Bodies
Kuiper, K. (2017, December 12). nine noteworthy bog bodies (and what they tell us). *Britannica.*
Levine, J. (2017, May). Europe's famed bog bodies are starting to reveal their secrets. *Smithsonian Magazine.*
National Geographic Society. (2023, March 20). *Bog bodies.*

Hallstatt Man in the Salt
Kowarik, K., Reschreiter, H., & Loew, C. (2019). *The man in the salt.* Naturhistorisches Museum Wien.

National Archives' Charters of Freedom
National Archives Museum. (n.d.). *Founding documents in the rotunda for the charters of freedom.*

Ritzenthaler, M., & Nicholson, C. (2003, Fall). A new era begins for the charters of freedom. *Prologue Magazine, 35*(3).

Ötzi the Iceman
Britannica. (2023, February 5). *Ötzi*.
Garlinghouse, T., & Leggett, J. (2021, December 14). *Ötzi the Iceman: The famous frozen mummy*. Live Science.

EXPERT OPINIONS

The chapter authors asked several social studies and/or STEM specialists actively engaged in scholarship and having extensive experience working with preservice and in-service teachers within teacher education programs to review the lesson plans included in this chapter. Dr. Tonia Dousay is currently the Dean of the College of Education at the University of Alaska. Dr. Katherine McGaha has taught English language arts, science, and social studies as an elementary teacher in the Houston Independent School District and is formerly a teacher educator at the University of Houston. Our third expert is currently an Instructional Designer at the University of Wisconsin-River Falls. Rachelle Haroldson's background as both an instructional designer and a science teacher provides an additional lens through which to consider the chapter lessons. Dousay, McGaha, and Haroldson have worked with elementary, middle school, and high school students. As part of the review, we posed several questions to the reviewers that focused attention on the benefits of socio-cultural STEM and the challenges of implementing a socio-cultural STEM curriculum in middle schools.

Benefits of Socio-cultural STEM Curriculum

Dousay argued that although technology use is ubiquitous, many Americans are not knowledgeable regarding the development and impact of technologies on history and society. In particular, she mentioned the "general lack of historical awareness and scientific literacy surrounding the 1918 influenza pandemic during the COVID-19 pandemic. Integrated socio-cultural STEM curricula have the potential to help students close this knowledge gap."

Furthermore, it may also influence interest in STEM subjects, which in turn influences educational and career paths. McGaha agreed with Dousay, adding:

> It also shows them how the various topics they are learning are interconnected. I think it leads students to be more reflective and active individuals in their

learning rather than the passive approach of the teacher being all knowing and dispensing knowledge.

McGaha noted that she would like to think that socio-cultural STEM curricula can lead to better STEM learning outcomes, although she inquired about what the current research on the subject says. Dousay provided an answer to McGaha's query using cognitive psychology to explain. Over the long term, socio-cultural STEM curricula can improve STEM learning outcomes across knowledge and skill levels by providing students with low prior knowledge a means to make associations between new and existing knowledge. These connections then facilitate recall and retrieval. For learners with significant prior knowledge, socio-cultural STEM curricula can reinvigorate and hold their interest while also continuing to build up their knowledge base. Regardless of prior knowledge, socio-cultural STEM curricula have the capacity for sustained interest in STEM subjects.

Challenges to Implementation

One challenge of implementing socio-cultural STEM is the lack of technical knowledge. Dousay commented that "vocabulary and using terms correctly matters to teachers, and professional development will need to help them become familiar with key terms and relevant [computer] science concepts." She argued that teachers are always looking for new strategies to engage learners, and they are especially interested in transdisciplinary lessons that allow for collaboration with their peers teaching other subjects. McGaha added that teacher and student background knowledge is a barrier; it can be overcome, however, with extensive support from the district. McGaha also identified teacher support as a challenge. She noted that high-performing schools that generally do well on state assessments tend to be more receptive to new strategies and practices than low-performing schools where students are struggling to meet standards. She suggested that teachers in the latter situation may view socio-cultural STEM integration as just "one more thing" to implement without any guarantee of positive results.

In her critique of the lesson "Computers, Counting Machines, and the U.S. Census in the Gilded Age," Haroldson identified another area of concern. As social studies teachers, we focus our lessons on history primarily. However, this can lead teachers to be a bit myopic when developing socio-cultural STEM lessons. She noted that although the lesson clearly provides the reader with the historical context of the development of counting machines, the scientific problem that computers were addressing is absent. At a different point in the lesson, Haroldson recommended being very explicit about the connections between the historical context and the emergence of science and technology because of the time period. It stands to reason that our content knowledge expertise is privileged over science and technology content simply because that is what social studies teachers know best. This critique echoes Dousay's and McGaha's point about the lack of teacher expertise in technology.

The challenges to implementation are not insurmountable if teachers, administrators, districts, parents, and community members support the inclusion of socio-cultural STEM curricula. For example, teacher support is often predicated on how confident they feel about their own knowledge and understanding of a subject. Teachers should be well-versed in the vocabulary, phrases, and concepts they are teaching so that they do not risk losing credibility with students by "respond[ing] partially (at best) or incorrectly (at worst) to student questions" (T. Dousay). McGaha reiterated the need for professional development specifically focused on socio-cultural STEM integration, including a model lesson. Furthermore, she argued that teachers need access to a wide variety of resources to be successful in facilitating the development of extensive background knowledge. Dousay's and McGaha's insights regarding ongoing professional development and access to resources would also address Haroldson's issue regarding the tendency to focus on the content in which teachers have the most expertise. The lesson plans in this chapter are examples of socio-cultural STEM lessons that go beyond a mere nod to science and technology.

The second challenge comes from the introduction of creative elements into the lesson. Each of the lessons presented asks students to create an artifact. Dousay pointed out that "often educators hyperfocus on the technical aspects of creativity, ignoring the value of assessing the creativity itself" as many see assessing creativity as too subjective. Dousay recommended the adoption of the NEW (novel, effective, whole; Henriksen et al., 2015) rubric criteria "designed to help teachers assess creative artifacts."

CONCLUSION

As technology becomes ever more ubiquitous, it is vital that students understand the connections between technological developments and their ongoing effects on society. Socio-cultural STEM curricula have a role to play in this process by providing students with opportunities to study the effects of technology on a wide array of socio-cultural issues. The lessons embedded in this chapter are only a few of the ways in which socio-cultural STEM curricula can be integrated into social studies instruction.

We are now at a time when our students are truly digital natives. Beginning with Gen Z, students have never known a time when there were no smartphones, internet, or digital media. However, because they have lived in a tech-enriched society, they may have little understanding of how science and technology has influenced, and indeed changed, the way we think about the past, present, and future. Introducing socio-cultural STEM lessons is one step toward a more well-rounded view of the world around us.

REFERENCES

Henriksen, D., Mishra, P., & Mehta, R. (2015). Novel, effective, whole: Toward a new framework for evaluations of creative products. *Journal of Information Technology for Teacher Education, 23*(3), 455–78.

Kennedy, J. F. (1962). *Address at Rice University on the nation's space effort.* John F. Kennedy Presidential Museum.

National Defense Education Act, Pub. L. No. 85-864, U.S. Government Printing Office (1958). https://www.gpo.gov/fdsys/pkg/STATUTE-72/pdf/STATUTE-72-Pg1580.pdf

Paska, L. M. (2023, June 18). *Social studies: The original STEM.* National Council for the Social Studies. https://www.socialstudies.org/executive-directors-message/social-studies-original-stem.

Chapter 8

Learning about Contributions of Diverse Cultures to Socio-cultural STEM

Matthew Lindquist and Joseph Peters

Throughout time, many diverse cultures have contributed to STEM fields in various ways. Their knowledge, practices, and innovations continue to shape modern science, technology, engineering, and mathematics to this day, often laying a foundation for further scientific and technological advancements. Similarly, students come from various cultural backgrounds. Because of this, students have different ways of perceiving, interpreting, and engaging with knowledge. Lee et al. (2017) describe a form of teaching that promotes inclusivity by appreciating that individual and collective identities have an influence on learning, known as "intercultural" pedagogy, which refers to specific educational strategies and methods which should lead to the creation of a favorable space to exchange ideas, acquire knowledge of different cultural values, and create positive attitudes regarding diversity. Incorporating the contributions of diverse cultures into STEM instruction is essential for fostering inclusivity, cultural understanding, and providing a well-rounded education.

OVERVIEW OF LESSON PLAN TOPICS AND CONTEXTS

The lesson plans in this chapter highlight the diverse contributions to STEM made by various cultures. By highlighting content such as Polynesian voyages, Eastern medicine, indigenous ways of knowing, and ancient art preservation, we allow students to understand that there are cultures that have made important contributions to civilization but are not always highlighted in today's curriculum. This allows students to better explore their own cultures and the important ways that their ancestors helped shape civilization.

Polynesian voyages showcase the rich heritage, seafaring prowess, knowledge transmission, cultural exchange, and spiritual significance of the Polynesian people. The voyages fostered a sense of shared cultural practices, traditions, and language among the Polynesian people as well as allowing for the exchange of goods, resources, and ideas and fostering cultural diversity and cross-cultural interactions.

Eastern medicine encompasses the traditions, practices, beliefs, and societal context of various forms of traditional medicine found in Eastern cultures, such as Traditional Chinese Medicine (TCM), Ayurveda, and Traditional Korean Medicine (Yuan, et al., 2016). In many cultures, integration with Eastern medicine is influenced by socio-cultural factors such as attitudes toward health, access to healthcare resources, and the availability of trained practitioners to provide Eastern medicine.

Indigenous ways of knowing encompass the unique knowledge systems, epistemologies, and worldviews held by indigenous cultures around the world. These perspectives are shaped by the historical, cultural, and spiritual experiences of indigenous communities and play a crucial role in their identity, relationships, and interactions with the natural environment. Indigenous ways of knowing often promote ethical and sustainable practices that ensure the long-term well-being of both humans and the natural world.

Ancient art preservation recognizes the cultural, historical, educational, and economic value of preserving and conserving ancient artworks. It underscores the importance of protecting these treasures for future generations, ensuring the continuity of cultural traditions, and fostering a deeper understanding and appreciation of our shared human history.

LESSON PLANS AND RESOURCES

Lesson Plan 1

Title of the Lesson: Polynesian Voyages

Theme:

Polynesians perfected non-instrumental deep-sea navigation more than 3,000 years ago (Vermillion, 2021). Polynesian wayfinders, those who employ processes of orienting and traveling from place to place, migrated between more than 1,000 scattered islands across the Polynesian Triangle, bounded by Hawaii, Easter Island, and New Zealand. For the Polynesians, wayfinding represented a "deep and sacred connection to the Earth and a fluency in the planet's movements and patterns" (Vermillion, 2021, para. 2). Navigating by the sun, the Hawaiian star compass, seabirds, seaweed clumps, and other natural cues, they were able to play a crucial role in shaping the cultural identity and heritage of the Polynesian people through exploration and migration (Curriculum Research & Development Group, n.d.).

Grade Level: This lesson is best suited for students in the middle grades (6–8).

Essential and Supporting Questions:

- What tools did the Polynesian wayfinders use to navigate? Compare these to the tools that are used today, such as Long-Range Navigation (LORAN), Sound Navigation and Ranging (SONAR), and the Global Positioning System (GPS) (Perugini, 2018).
- What is the significance of Polynesian voyages in terms of exploration, settlement, and cultural exchange?

Time Required: Four class periods.

Objectives:

- Understand the significance of Polynesian voyages and their impact on the exploration and settlement of the Pacific Islands.
- Explore the navigational techniques and tools used by Polynesian voyagers.
- Analyze the cultural, social, and economic factors that influenced Polynesian voyaging.

Standards and Standards Integration:

Next Generation Science Standards (NGSS):

- ESS3. A. Natural Resources. Humans depend on Earth's land, ocean, atmosphere, and biosphere for many different resources. Minerals, fresh water, and biosphere resources are limited, and many are not renewable or replaceable over human lifetimes. These resources are distributed unevenly around the planet because of past geologic processes.
- ESS2.C. The Roles of Water in Earth's Surface Processes. The complex patterns of the changes and the movement of water in the atmosphere, determined by winds, landforms, and ocean temperatures and currents, are major determinants of local weather patterns. Variations in density due to variations in temperature and salinity drive a global pattern of interconnected ocean currents (National Research Council, 2013).

National Curriculum Standards for Social Studies:

- NSS-G.K-12.1. The World in Spatial Terms. As a result of activities in grades K-12, all students should understand how to use maps and other geographic representations, tools, and technologies to acquire, process, and report information from a spatial perspective (National Council for the Social Studies, 2010).

Common Core Math Standards. Geometry:

- Draw, construct, and describe geometrical figures and describe the relationships between them. 7.G.A.1. Solve problems involving scale drawings of geometric figures, including computing actual lengths and areas from a scale drawing, and reproducing a scale drawing at a different scale.

International Society for Technology in Education Standards:

- Students. 1.3 Knowledge Constructor. 1.3a. Students plan and employ effective research strategies to locate information and other resources for their intellectual or creative pursuits.

Classroom Materials: World map or globe, rulers, and pencils to create a scaled map, pictures or videos of traditional Polynesian canoes, diagrams or illustrations of Polynesian navigation tools (e.g., stars, waves, birds), and access to library resources or the internet for research.

Optional:

- Materials to create a homemade sextant: drinking straw, protractor, string, washer or small weight, and tape. Map or website to look up latitudes.
- Materials to make a homemade compass (refrigerator magnet, bowl of water, and a small cross section of cork). Actual compass to use as a reference.
- Materials to make a homemade sundial (paper plate, straw, marker), and a watch or clock to check accuracy.
- Materials to make a homemade star chart (ruler, a drawing compass, and a colored pencil). An online or paper star chart for comparison.
- Materials to make a homemade wave chart (graph paper, pencils). Example wave charts.

Socio-cultural Context:

Understanding the socio-cultural context of Polynesian voyagers provides insights into their seafaring achievements, social organization, and belief systems. It highlights the remarkable abilities of ancient Polynesians to navigate vast distances, adapt to new environments, and establish sustainable communities across the Pacific Ocean.

Instructional Procedures:

Day 1: Provide an Introduction to Polynesian Voyages

- Begin by engaging students in a class discussion about exploration and voyages throughout history.
- Show pictures or videos of traditional Polynesian canoes and briefly introduce the concept of Polynesian voyages. Include images of the Hōkūleʻa.
- Provide a brief overview of the geographical scope of Polynesia and its islands, using a world map or globe. Have students compare the map scale to the actual size of the Polynesian Triangle. Students will create a simple scale map of their classroom.
- Discuss the significance of Polynesian voyages in terms of exploration, settlement, and cultural exchange.

Day 2: Navigational Techniques and Tools

- Explain the navigational techniques used by Polynesian voyagers, such as celestial navigation, wave patterns, bird behavior, and star compasses. Discuss ocean currents and their role in traversing the ocean.
- Show diagrams of the navigation tools and discuss their purposes and functions.
- Divide the class into small groups and assign each group a specific navigation tool or technique to research.
- In their groups, students should gather information about their assigned topic from library resources or the internet.
- Encourage students to take notes and prepare a short presentation to share their findings.
- Optional: Research and create a homemade sextant (Space Center Houston, 2020). Locate the North Star through the straw and read the angle on the protractor. Subtract the measured angle from 90 to give you your latitude. Look up your actual latitude and compare. Why would knowing latitude be important when navigating on the ocean?
- Optional: Research and create a homemade compass. Compare its accuracy to a real compass. Why would knowing the direction of travel be important when navigating on the ocean?
- Optional: Research and create a homemade sundial. Check the accuracy with a watch. How can time be used to estimate longitude?

- Optional: Research and create a homemade star chart. Compare it to an online version. How can stars help with determining your direction of travel?
- Optional: Measure waves over a period of 12 hours and make a wave chart. Describe the crest, trough, wavelength, and amplitude. Compare the Bascom method of measuring wave height to the Hawaii scale.

Day 3: Presentations and Discussion

- Have each group present their research findings on a specific navigation tool/technique.
- Optional: If students made a homemade tool or technique, have them demonstrate its use. This allows students to be the "experts" in their classroom.

Day 4: Cultural, Social, and Economic Factors that Influenced Polynesian Voyaging

- Have students research the various aspects of Polynesian voyaging and prepare brief individual findings either as a presentation or written assignment. Areas to consider include: (a) how Polynesian voyaging knowledge was passed down through generations through oral traditions, chants, and songs, (b) canoe building and technology, (c) settlement patterns and migration, (d) religious rituals and kinship systems, (e) agricultural techniques, sustainable fishing practices, and resource management strategies, (f) artistic expressions, (g) trade and exchange networks, (h) Optional: Have students research and present on famous Polynesian navigators or voyages, such as the Hōkūleʻa's modern-day voyages, and (i) Optional: Have students explore the tenet that Polynesian voyagers reached the Americas before Columbus.

Assessment:

- The students will determine the map scale to the actual size of the Polynesian Triangle and use this technique to create a scaled map of their classroom.
- The students will work in small groups to research and present navigational techniques used by Polynesian voyagers.
- The students will prepare and present an individual report on cultural, social, and economic factors that influenced Polynesian voyaging.

Socio-cultural Community Engagement:

- Ask students if a parent or other family member is involved in water travel and if they would present to the class on their occupation.
- Contact a Navy unit to have a speaker from a historically underrepresented group discuss how they navigate and communicate on the ocean.
- If available, visit a maritime museum or a museum that has sailing artifacts.
- Contact the Polynesian Voyaging Society for information on past voyages and Moananuiākea.

Lesson Plan 2

Title of the Lesson: Eastern Medicine

Theme:

Eastern medicine, also known as traditional or alternative medicine, encompasses a wide range of healing practices that originated in various countries in East Asia, such as China, India, Japan, and Korea (Kisling & Stiegmann, 2022). It is a holistic approach to healthcare that emphasizes the balance and harmony of the mind, body, and spirit. Eastern medicine is rooted in ancient philosophies and traditions such as Traditional Chinese Medicine, Ayurveda, acupuncture, herbal medicines, and mind-body practices (Maciocia, 2015). These systems view the body as an interconnected system and focus on addressing the underlying causes of illness rather than just treating the symptoms. Eastern medicine can complement Western medicine and should be studied for its positive influences such as lifestyle, emotions, environment, and diet to restore and maintain health (Li, et al., 2020; Zhang, et al., 2019).

Grade Level: The lesson is best suited for students in the middle grades (6-8).

Essential and Supporting Questions:

- What are the five main areas of Eastern medicine and how do they support good health?
- How does Eastern medicine differ from Western medicine?
- How can Eastern medicine help you stay healthy?

Time Required: Four Class Periods

Objectives:

- Students will develop an understanding of Eastern medicine practices, including Traditional Chinese Medicine (TCM), Ayurveda, acupuncture, herbal medicine, and mind-body practices.
- Students will engage in activities to help them understand Eastern medicine principles.

Standards and Standards Integration:

Next Generation Science Standards (NGSS):

- MS. Matter and Energy in Organisms and Ecosystems.
  - MS-LS2-1. Analyze and interpret data to provide evidence for the effects of resource availability on organisms and populations of organisms in an ecosystem.

National Curriculum Standards for Social Studies:

- Culture. Social studies programs should include experiences that provide for the study of culture and cultural diversity so that the learner can: a. Explore and describe similarities and differences in the ways groups, societies, and cultures address similar human needs and concerns.

Common Core Math Standards:

- Statistics and Probability. B. Summarize and describe distributions. 6.SP.B.5 Summarize numerical data sets in relation to their context, such as describing the nature of the attribute under investigation, including how it was measured and its units of measurement.

International Society for Technology in Education Standards:

- Students. 1.1 Empowered Learner. 1.1.b. Students build networks and customize their learning environments in ways that support the learning process.

Classroom Materials: Samples of common herbs and plants used in herbal medicine, and internet access or library resources for research.

Optional: Selection of herbal teas, chart of acupuncture points and their meridian locations, graphic showing acupressure points to relieve car sickness, and exercise mats.

Socio-cultural Context:

Eastern medicine has evolved over thousands of years within specific cultural contexts, such as China, India, Japan, Korea, and other Asian countries. These traditions have been shaped by the historical, social, and cultural values of their respective societies. For example, Traditional Chinese Medicine (TCM) is deeply influenced by ancient Chinese philosophies, including Taoism and Confucianism, while Ayurveda is rooted in the cultural and spiritual traditions of India (Lemonnier, et al., 2017). Eastern medicine is often seamlessly integrated into the daily lives of individuals within its cultural context. Practices like herbal remedies, dietary guidelines, mind-body exercises, and meditation are commonly incorporated into routines and lifestyles.

Instructional Procedures:

Day 1: Overview of Eastern Medicine

- Provide an overview of the main points of Eastern medicine
  - Traditional Chinese Medicine, a comprehensive system of medicine that includes acupuncture, herbal medicine, dietary therapy, tai chi, qigong, and various mind-body practices like meditation.
  - Ayurveda, the ancient healing system from India that emphasizes the balance of body, mind, and spirit. It incorporates herbal medicine, dietary guidelines, yoga, meditation, detoxification practices, and Ayurvedic massage to promote health and prevent illness.
  - Acupuncture, a technique that involves the insertion of thin needles into specific points on the body to stimulate and balance the flow of Qi (or chi, a vital force forming part of any living entity [LeWine, 2023]. Literally meaning "breath," "vapor," or "air").
  - Herbal medicine, a fundamental aspect of Eastern medicine found in various traditions. It involves the use of medicinal plants, herbs, and natural substances to promote healing and restore balance in the body.
  - Mind-body practices, the profound connection between the mind and body and mind-body practices that play a crucial role in maintaining health and well-being. These practices include meditation, tai chi, qigong, yoga, and other breathing and movement exercises.
- Have students work in small groups to explore the main points of Eastern medicine.
- Allow time for brief presentations.

Day 2: Herbal Medicine

- Ask students if they have heard of herbal medicine or know any examples. Facilitate a brief discussion to gauge their prior knowledge and experiences.

- Show samples of common herbs and plants used in herbal medicine.
- Engage students in a discussion about the scientific basis of herbal medicine. Discuss concepts such as active compounds, pharmacological effects, and the importance of rigorous research and clinical studies.
- Assign each student a specific herb or plant used in herbal medicine, and instruct each student to research and prepare a short presentation on their assigned herb, focusing on its active compounds, traditional uses, scientific evidence (if available), and potential risks or limitations.
- Allow time for brief presentations.
- Optional: Prepare a selection of herbal teas using different herbs, such as chamomile, peppermint, ginger, or echinacea. Introduce students to the concept of herbal teas and their potential health benefits. Have students taste different teas and discuss their flavors, aromas, and any potential health effects they may have experienced. Discuss the specific properties and traditional uses of each herb used in the teas.

Day 3: Acupuncture

- Ask students if they have heard of acupuncture and what they know about it.
- Discuss the basic principles and concepts of acupuncture, such as Qi and meridians.
- Use a chart to explain acupuncture points and their locations.
- Divide students into groups and assign each a specific health condition or ailment.
- Instruct each group to research and prepare a short presentation on how acupuncture is believed to help or treat their assigned condition. They should include information on the relevant acupuncture points, potential physiological effects, and any existing scientific evidence or studies.
- Allow time for brief presentations.
- Optional: Use a chart of acupressure (or acupuncture) points to explain the twelve primary meridians (Heart, Pericardium, Lung, Spleen, Liver, Kidney, Small Intestine, Large Intestine, Triple Energizer, Stomach, Gallbladder, Bladder) (Smarterhealing.com, n.d.). Discuss how acupressure is applied (Gupta, 2021).
- Optional: Discuss how acupressure can relieve car sickness.

Day 4: Mind-Body Practices

- Explain the different types of mind-body practices, such as meditation, yoga, and deep breathing exercises, to include the benefits of mind-body

practices on physical, mental, and emotional well-being. Share scientific research that supports the effects of mind-body practices.
- Discuss the following practices in more detail.
  - Meditation: focusing the mind and achieving a state of deep relaxation and mental clarity. Various techniques include mindfulness meditation, loving-kindness meditation, and guided imagery.
  - Yoga: a combination of physical postures, breathing exercises, and meditation to improve flexibility, strength, balance, and mental well-being. Yoga promotes the integration of mind and body through a series of poses (asanas) and controlled breathing (pranayama).
  - Tai Chi: a traditional Chinese martial art that involves slow and flowing movements, deep breathing, and focused attention. Tai Chi promotes balance, flexibility, relaxation, and a sense of harmony between the mind and body (Harvard Health Publishing, 2022).
  - Qi Gong: an ancient Chinese practice that combines gentle movements, deep breathing, and focused intention to cultivate and balance the body's vital energy. Qi Gong enhances physical health, mental clarity, and emotional well-being (National Center for Complementary and Integrative Health, 2022a).
  - Progressive Muscle Relaxation: a technique that involves systematically tensing and releasing different muscle groups to promote relaxation and reduce muscle tension. Progressive muscle relaxation helps individuals become more aware of the mind-body connection and release physical and mental stress (Nunez, K., 2020a).
  - Deep Breathing Exercises: techniques such as diaphragmatic breathing or belly breathing, where the focus is on slow, deep breaths that engage the diaphragm. Deep breathing exercises help activate the body's relaxation response, reduce anxiety, and increase mental clarity (Bolen, 2023).
  - Mindfulness: involves paying attention to the present moment without judgment. Mindfulness cultivates awareness of thoughts, emotions, bodily sensations, and the surrounding environment, and practices can include mindful eating, walking, or simply observing the breath (Hoshaw, 2022).
  - Guided Imagery: involves using the power of imagination and visualization to create mental images that promote relaxation, stress reduction, and healing. Guided imagery can be done through recorded audio sessions or with the guidance of a facilitator (Nunez, 2020b).
  - Biofeedback: uses electronic sensors to measure and provide information about physiological processes, such as heart rate, muscle tension, or skin temperature. Biofeedback helps individuals become aware of their

body's responses and learn to regulate them through relaxation techniques (Mayo Clinic Staff, n.d.).
  - Music Therapy: involves using music to promote relaxation, reduce stress, and improve emotional well-being. Listening to calming music, playing musical instruments, or engaging in singing activities can have a positive impact on the mind-body connection (National Center for Complementary and Integrative Health, 2020b).
- Engage students in a short, guided meditation or deep breathing exercise to experience the effects of mind-body practice. Discuss how the experience made them feel. When possible, have students with expertise in this area facilitate the activity.
- Optional: invite a yoga instructor to facilitate a short yoga session with students.
- Optional: invite a Tai Chi instructor to facilitate a short Tai Chi session with students.

Assessment:

- The students will work in small groups to research various aspects of Eastern medicine. They will present their findings to the class.
- Individual students will research a specific herb and present their findings to the class.
- The students will engage in a mindful experience and discuss how it made them feel.

Socio-cultural Community Engagement:

- Ask students if a parent or other family member practices a form of Eastern medicine and if they would like to share the practice with the class.
- Invite practitioners or experts in Eastern medicine, such as acupuncturists, herbalists, or yoga instructors, to speak to the students.
- Organize visits to local clinics, wellness centers, or cultural centers that offer Eastern medicine services. Students can observe treatments, interact with practitioners, and gain a better understanding of the practical applications of Eastern medicine.
- Organize a traditional medicine fair within the school or community where students can showcase their research on Eastern medicine practices.
- View the "Catalysing ancient wisdom and modern science for the health of people and the planet" video from the WHO Global Centre for Traditional Medicine: https://youtu.be/wsMwFRMfe1I link.

Lesson Plan 3

Title of the Lesson: Indigenous Ways of Knowing

Theme:
Indigenous ways of knowing encompass the unique knowledge systems, beliefs, practices, and worldviews of indigenous peoples. Studying indigenous ways of knowing is essential for fostering cultural appreciation, promoting environmental sustainability, advancing social justice, and embracing diverse knowledge systems (Hornback, 2022; Nabaggala, 2021). It can lead to a more inclusive, equitable, and harmonious coexistence between indigenous peoples and the broader global community (Stairs, 1994).

Grade Level: This lesson is best suited for students in the middle grades (6–8).

Essential and Supporting Questions:

- What is an indigenous culture, and why is it important to study indigenous cultures?
- How have indigenous cultures provided knowledge related to STEM areas?
- What are some traditional practices or rituals associated with their ways of knowing?
- What technological innovations were developed by indigenous cultures?

Time Required: Four Class Periods

Objectives:

- Understand the concept of indigenous ways of knowing.
- Identify key characteristics and values of select indigenous cultures.
- Appreciate the importance of cultural diversity and respect for indigenous knowledge.
- Engage in critical thinking and reflection on the relevance of indigenous ways of knowing in contemporary society.
- Understand and appreciate the technological innovations made by indigenous cultures.

Standards and Standards Integration:

Next Generation Science Standards (NGSS):

- MS. Human Impacts. MS-ESS3-4. Construct an argument supported by evidence for how increases in human population and per-capita consumption of natural resources impact Earth's systems.

National Curriculum Standards for Social Studies:

- Culture. Social studies programs should include experiences that provide for the study of culture and cultural diversity so that the learner can: a. Explore and describe similarities and differences in the ways groups, societies, and cultures address similar human needs and concerns.

Common Core Math Standards:

- Statistics and Probability. B. Draw informal comparative inferences about two populations.

International Society for Technology in Education Standards:

- 1.7 Global Collaborator. Students use digital tools to broaden their perspectives and enrich their learning by collaborating with others and working effectively in teams locally and globally. 1.7.c. Students contribute constructively to project teams, assuming various roles and responsibilities to work effectively toward a common goal.

Classroom Materials: Videos and online resources about indigenous cultures and their ways of knowing, images or artifacts representing indigenous technologies, chart paper and markers, index cards or small pieces of paper, and art supplies (colored pencils, markers).

Socio-cultural Context:

Indigenous ways of knowing are diverse and vary across different indigenous cultures globally. Each community has its unique socio-cultural context, and their knowledge systems are shaped by their specific histories, languages, and cultural practices. Therefore, understanding and respecting the specific context of each indigenous community is crucial when engaging with indigenous ways of knowing (Barnhardt & Kawagley, 2005).

Instructional Procedures:

Day 1: Introduction to Indigenous Ways of Knowing

- Begin the lesson by engaging students in a class discussion about cultural diversity. Ask them to share their understanding of different cultures and the importance of respecting and appreciating cultural differences.
- Introduce the concept of indigenous ways of knowing. Explain that indigenous cultures have unique knowledge systems, values, and perspectives that are different from mainstream Western ways of thinking.

- Show short videos or use online resources to provide examples of indigenous cultures from different regions. Discuss key characteristics such as a deep connection to the land, oral traditions, holistic perspectives, and sustainable practices.
- Divide the class into small groups and assign each group a specific indigenous culture to research. Examples include Quechua (Peru), Māori (New Zealand), Inuit (Arctic regions), Navajo (United States), Aboriginal Australians, Maya (Mesoamerica, Guatemala), Sami (Northern Europe), Hill Tribes (Thailand), Garifuna (Belize), Kalinago (Caribbean), Maasai (Kenya/Tanzania), and Zulu (South Africa).
- Provide students with guiding questions, such as:
  - What are the main beliefs and values of this indigenous culture?
  - How do they view the natural world and their relationship with it?
  - What are some traditional practices or rituals related to their ways of knowing?
  - How have indigenous cultures helped to conserve natural resources?
- In their groups, students research their assigned indigenous culture and create posters or multimedia presentations to share their findings with the class. Encourage creativity and visual representations in their research.
- Review the posters or presentations created by the groups. Allow time for each group to present their findings, highlighting the key characteristics and values of their assigned indigenous culture. Compare and contrast indigenous practices between populations.
- Have a guest speaker from an indigenous group discuss their culture and traditions.

Day 2: Values and Reflection

- Facilitate a whole-class discussion on the values and principles that emerge from the different indigenous ways of knowing. Write these values on chart paper.
- Distribute index cards or small pieces of paper to each student. Ask them to reflect individually and write down one value or principle from indigenous ways of knowing that they find interesting or meaningful.
- Collect the index cards and shuffle them. Then, distribute them randomly among the students. Each student reads aloud the value or principle they received and briefly shares their thoughts or reactions.
- Engage students in a broader discussion about the relevance of indigenous ways of knowing in contemporary society and how these apply to everyday life. Encourage critical thinking and exploration of how these values can be applied to current social, environmental, or cultural challenges.

- Discuss how indigenous ways of knowing are used to lessen the impact of population growth on the environment.
- Optional: Have a STEM professional discuss how their indigenous culture influenced their professional work.

Day 3: Expressing Understanding

- Allow students to choose one value or principle from indigenous ways of knowing that resonates with them personally and supports an area of STEM. Consider the following:
  - Indigenous ways of knowing include a holistic perspective and can enhance scientific thinking by encouraging students to consider the broader context and interrelationships within scientific phenomena.
  - Many indigenous cultures possess extensive knowledge about the environment and natural resources.
  - Indigenous cultures have developed unique technologies and engineering practices adapted to their environments.
  - Indigenous cultures often have extensive knowledge about plants, their uses, and medicinal properties.
  - Indigenous ways of knowing often emphasize learning through direct observation, experience, and participation in cultural practices. This hands-on and experiential approach can be integrated into STEM education, encouraging students to engage in fieldwork, conduct experiments, and make firsthand observations of the natural world. It is important for students to broaden their ideas of what it means to do science beyond the typical stereotypical notions.
  - Involving local indigenous communities in STEM education initiatives can foster meaningful partnerships.
- Instruct students to create a visual representation (e.g., drawing, painting, collage) or a written reflection (poem, essay) expressing their understanding of that value or principle.
- Provide art supplies and materials for those choosing a visual representation. For written reflections, encourage students to be creative and thoughtful in their expressions.
- Once the students have completed their work, allow them to share their creations with the class. Encourage them to explain the meaning behind their chosen representation and how it connects to indigenous ways of knowing.
- Wrap up the lesson by summarizing the key takeaways and emphasizing the importance of cultural diversity and respect for indigenous people.

Day 4: Exploration of Indigenous Technologies

- Engage students in a class discussion about technology. Ask them to share their understanding of technology and examples of familiar technological innovations.
- Introduce the concept of indigenous technologies and their contributions to various fields. Show videos or use online resources to showcase examples of indigenous technologies from different cultures. Highlight the unique problem-solving approaches and sustainable practices incorporated in these technologies.
- Display images or artifacts representing indigenous technologies, and encourage students to make observations and generate questions about the technologies. Facilitate a class discussion based on their observations and questions, focusing on the functionality, materials used, and potential STEM connections.
- Optional: Divide the class into small groups and assign each group an indigenous technology to explore in-depth. In their groups, students research technology, focusing on its purpose, design principles, materials, and construction methods. Encourage them to consider the scientific and engineering concepts involved.
- Optional: Introduce a hands-on activity where students will have the opportunity to replicate or adapt an indigenous technology. Choose an indigenous technology that is feasible to recreate within the available resources and time frame.

Assessment: The students will work in small groups to research indigenous cultures and explore the relevance of indigenous ways of knowing in contemporary society, exploring indigenous cultures' extensive knowledge about the environment and natural resources, and investigating indigenous technologies and their contributions to various fields.

Socio-cultural Community Engagement:

Community engagement related to indigenous ways of knowing can take various forms, such as traditional knowledge-sharing sessions, cultural festivals and celebrations, activities such as traditional hunting, fishing, plant identification and land stewardship practices, collaborative research projects, and indigenous-led educational programs (Stinson, 2018).

Lesson Plan 4:

Title of the Lesson: Ancient Art, Its Cultural Significance, and Its Preservation

Theme:

Preserving ancient art is crucial for the sake of cultural heritage, historical documentation, artistic legacy, education, tourism, and the preservation of symbolic and spiritual significance. It shows us where we have been so we can think about where we are going (Artdaily.com, 2023). It allows us to connect with our ancestors, learn from their accomplishments, and appreciate the richness and diversity of human creativity throughout history. Ancient art offers a unique educational resource. It can be used to teach history, archaeology, anthropology, and art history. Studying ancient art helps us develop critical thinking skills, encourages creativity, and fosters an appreciation for different artistic traditions as well as connecting various cultures (USA Art News, 2021).

Grade Level: This lesson is best suited for students in the middle grades (6–8).

Essential and Supporting Questions

- How does ancient art portray culture?
- How can art help preserve cultural heritage?
- How can science and technology help preserve art?
- What skills does a conservator need to preserve art?

Time Required: Four Class Periods

Objectives:

- Understand the importance of preserving ancient art as a means of protecting heritage.
- Explore different methods and techniques used for preserving ancient art.
- Analyze the significance of ancient art in understanding past civilizations.
- Engage in a creative activity that highlights the value of ancient art preservation.

Standards and Standards Integration:

Next Generation Science Standards (NGSS):

- MS. Chemical Reactions. MS-PS1-2. Analyze and interpret data on the properties of substances before and after the substances interact to determine if a chemical reaction has occurred.

National Curriculum Standards for Social Studies:

- Geography. NSS-G.K-12.2 Places and Regions. Understand how culture and experience influence people's perceptions of places and regions.

Common Core Math Standards:

- Geometry. A. Solve real-world and mathematical problems involving area, surface area, and volume. 1. 6.G.A.1. Find the area of right triangles, other triangles, special quadrilaterals, and polygons by composing into rectangles or decomposing into triangles and other shapes; apply these techniques in the context of solving real-world and mathematical problems.

International Technology Education Association:

- Standard 6. Impact of Society on Technology. Students will develop an understanding of technology and society that includes the role of society in the development and use of technology. The use of inventions and innovations has led to changes in society and the creation of new needs and wants.

Classroom Materials: Images or replicas of ancient art pieces (sculptures, paintings, pottery; see day 1), internet access or reference books for research, art supplies, art preservation materials (e.g., adhesives, varnishes, silica gel, acrylic resins, epoxy resins, insecticides, beeswax), and preservation challenge cards.

Socio-cultural Context:

Preserving ancient art within its socio-cultural context is crucial for a comprehensive understanding and appreciation of the artwork. By considering the socio-cultural context when preserving ancient art, we can appreciate the artwork in a holistic manner, respecting its cultural significance, historical relevance, and the communities to which it belongs.

Instructional Procedures:

Day 1: Introduction to Ancient Art and Its Cultural Heritage

- Begin the lesson by asking students to share what they know about ancient art.
- Show images or replicas of various types of ancient art and discuss their origins and cultural significance: Cave Paintings, Ancient Egyptian Art, Greek Sculpture, Roman Mosaics, Chinese Terracotta Army, Mayan Hieroglyphics and Stelae, Indian Buddhist Art, and Aztec Codices.
- Engage students in a whole-class discussion using the following prompts:
  - Why do you think ancient art is important today?
  - How can ancient art help us understand different cultures?
  - What challenges could there be in preserving ancient art?
- Divide students into groups and provide each group with one image of ancient art. Instruct them to analyze the artwork and discuss its cultural context, purpose, and meaning.

Day 2: Methods of Preserving Ancient Art

- Introduce students to basic methods of preserving ancient art, such as:
  - Environmental Control (maintaining stable environmental conditions, including temperature, humidity, and lighting)
  - Cleaning and Surface Stabilization (cleaning methods, such as dry brushing or gentle surface cleaning, that remove dirt, dust, and pollutants)
  - Structural Repairs (using materials and techniques that are compatible with the original artwork)
  - Protective Enclosures (display cases that can shield artworks from dust, light exposure, and physical damage)
  - Non-Invasive Techniques (infrared imaging, ultraviolet photography, and X-ray fluorescence analysis, 3D scanning, virtual reality)
  - Consolidation Techniques (applying adhesive materials can stabilize fragile or flaking surfaces)
- Ask students to share their thoughts on the effectiveness and challenges of each method.
- Explain that students will now have an opportunity to create their own "preservation" of an ancient artwork through a creative activity. Distribute art supplies and instruct students to choose one ancient art piece from the previous day's exploration.
- Ask students to create an interpretation of the chosen artwork using their preferred medium (drawing, painting, collage).

- Allow time for students to work on their creative activity.
- Encourage students to share their artwork with the class. Ask students how they preserved the essence and significance of the original artwork. Have students explain the specific elements they preserved from the original artwork.
- Conclude the lesson with a reflective discussion, focusing on what students learned about ancient art preservation and the importance of cultural heritage.
- Optional: Supply additional art examples to preserve and have students take them home and bring them back with a homemade preservation process.

Day 3: Preserving the Art

- Have students work in small groups to discuss ways to preserve the art they created.
- Have the groups use preservation materials to implement their preservation methods.
- Have each group describe their method, the results, and if they would use a different method in the future, and why.
- Provide a sample sculpture and have students determine the total surface area so they can determine the amount of material needed to preserve the sculpture.
- Optional: Visit an art museum and discover ways the artwork is being preserved.
- Optional: Invite artists or art preservation professionals to discuss ways in which they preserve art.

Day 4: Conservation Challenges

- Present small groups of students with art challenges.
  - A portrait has a heavy coat of varnish on it. The varnish is discolored, and there may be something hidden below the varnish layer. How would the group find out if something is hidden there?
  - A sculpture is going to be lent to another museum. Before it is shipped, you need to ensure that there are no hidden cracks in it or other unseen damage. How would you find out?
  - A portrait looks good in visible light, but you suspect there is a layer of discolored varnish on the portrait. How would you find out?
  - A painting looks to be in good shape, but you want to see if there are any signs of paint loss. How would you determine if there is paint missing?

- A watercolor is in almost pristine condition, but you are interested in finding out if there were previous conservation methods employed on the watercolor. What ways could be used to determine previous conservation practices?
- Students should research the problem and discuss how they would investigate the artwork to determine which procedures are needed to meet the challenge.
- Have groups discuss their findings.
- Optional: Have students exchange challenges and see if there are differences in how they would preserve the artworks.
- Optional: Discuss what skills a conservator would need for his or her job.

Assessment:

- The students will explain (a) the cultural significance found in ancient art, (b) art preservation techniques and when various techniques should be used, and (c) the work of a conservator and techniques that they use and why they use specific techniques.

Socio-cultural Community Engagement:

Preserving ancient art involves various socio-cultural perspectives that are associated with the value, significance, and impact of preserving cultural heritage. Preserving art highlights the richness and variety of human creative expression across time and geography, fosters respect for cultural differences, encourages intercultural dialogue and community pride, and contributes to the preservation of global heritage. Preserving artworks allows societies to appreciate the mastery of techniques, craftsmanship, and artistic visions from the past and provides inspiration for contemporary artists, scholars, and the public by nurturing artistic appreciation and creativity.

EXPERT OPINIONS

A common theme across the given statements is the preservation and appreciation of cultural heritage and knowledge. In each case, there is an emphasis on recognizing and valuing traditional practices, whether it is the Polynesians' wayfinding techniques, Eastern medicine, indigenous ways of knowing, or the preservation of ancient art. These practices are seen as deeply rooted in history and hold significance in terms of cultural identity, spirituality, and the intergenerational transmission of knowledge. One reviewer, Dr. Anthony Stawiery, suggests that "this approach to STEM learning is also a welcome relief to the hard-science approach to current trends in STEM education which tend to focus on the individual tenets of science research, and less on the exploratory, critical thinking-inducing activity that is science." He continues:

> with these lessons educators also have the opportunity to benefit greatly from lessons that are likely not on topics they have explored during their formal educations and should provide them with the cultural relevant lens they need to meet the needs of a diverse group of learners.

Another reviewer, Dr. Lacey Huffling, refers to how the lessons show that "STEM is steeped in various culture traditions. . . . Students are invited to imagine not only themselves but also their ancestors as being STEM-minded. Part of increasing STEM literacy is showcasing ways that students can not only see themselves in STEM careers in the future but also experiencing ways in which STEM is used and essential for much of everyday life."

In her review, Dr. Rebecca Cooper notes that "the diversity of today's students requires an approach that is integrative." This can be accomplished by "artfully weaving STEM, socio-cultural contexts, and inquiry to provide intercultural pedagogy to center the contributions of diverse cultures to STEM fields." She suggests that while intercultural pedagogy is new to the area of science, lesson examples such as the ones in this chapter uniquely capture practices that are "deeply rooted in history and hold significance in terms of cultural identity, spirituality, and the intergenerational transmission of knowledge."

Dr. Suzanna Roman-Oliver cites in her review that "it is necessary to expose students to the scientific knowledge produced by different cultures." The notion of doing science needs to go beyond stereotypical practice and include indigenous ways of knowing. Dr. Roman-Oliver says that "The importance of this is seen in how students' ideas of what it means to do science is typically laboratory work." It is important for students "to broaden their conceptions of what it means to do science." Dr. Anthony Stawiery suggests that "what students in K-12 need most, especially in the elementary stages, is an education in doing science; being creative, curious, and critical of the information presented to them and consumed by them." A socio-cultural STEM approach can meet the need for "doing science."

In her review, Dr. Lacey Huffling cautions against the challenges associated with implementing this type of lesson; for example, "many teachers may not know as much about the cultures presented in these lessons, so the teachers will need to invest time to learn about these cultures." She further cites that "unless a teacher is committed to implementing socio-cultural lessons in their classroom, these lesson sets may be viewed as almost impossible to implement as it can feel like one more area to add in an already overcrowded curriculum." One suggestion she provides is that a "science teacher might also find they need to identify and infuse crosscutting concepts from the NGSS to justify these as three-dimensional science lessons to their districts." She also recommends that for the "Polynesian Voyages lesson teachers could connect the crosscutting concept of scale, proportion, and quantity as they could have students create a scale for the distance between islands if their classroom floor represented the ocean."

CONCLUSION

In this chapter, four sample lessons are provided for how to incorporate sociocultural perspectives into the STEM curriculum. Polynesian voyages, Eastern medicine, indigenous ways of knowing, and ancient art's cultural significance and preservation are just a few examples of how to provide a new approach to science that brings diversity into the classroom and broadens the involvement of students as they find connections to their own cultural practices. Hopefully, this approach will be a springboard for more diverse participation in STEM careers.

REFERENCES

Artdaily.com. (2023). *Why is art preservation so important?* bit.ly/3vbRmXU.
Barnhardt, R., & Kawagley, A. O. (2005). Indigenous knowledge systems and Alaska native ways of knowing. *Anthropology & Education Quarterly, 36*(1), 8–23. http://www.jstor.org/stable/3651306.
Bolen, B. (2023). How to do deep breathing exercises. *Verywellhealth*. bit.ly/3IyJByr.
Curriculum Research & Development Group. (n.d.). *Wayfinding and navigation*. University of Hawai'i, Honolulu, HI. bit.ly/4afJljH.
Gupta, S. (2021). *Acupressure*. Myupchar.com. bit.ly/4ce7c4U.
Harvard Health Publishing. (2022). *The health benefits of tai chi*. bit.ly/3IHglVX.
Hornback, P. (2022). Constructive indigenization: Educational pathways to indigenous ways of knowing and being. *The International Journal of Learner Diversity and Identities, 29*(2), 19–49. bit.ly/3PfqXz1.
Hoshaw, C. (2022). *What is mindfulness? A simple practice for greater wellbeing*. Healthline. https://www.healthline.com/health/mind-body/what-is-mindfulness.
Kisling, L A., & Stiegmann, R. A. (2022). *Alternative medicine*. bit.ly/3Tzs3Za.
Lee, A., Poch, R., Smith, A., Kelly, M. D., & Leopold, H. (2018). Intercultural pedagogy: A faculty learning cohort. *Education Sciences, 8*(4), 177. https://dx.doi.org/10.3390/educsci8040177.

Lemonnier, N., Zhou, G-B., Prasher, B., Mukerji, M., Chen, Z., Brahmachari, S., Noble, D., Auffray, C., & Sagner, M. (2017). Traditional knowledge-based medicine: A review of history, principles, and relevance in the present context of P4 systems medicine. *Progress in Preventive Medicine, 2*(7), e0011. https://doi.org/10.1097/pp9.0000000000000011.

LeWine, H. E. (2023). *Acupuncture*. Harvard Health Publishing. bit.ly/3TA6oQv.

Li, Y., Yuan, S., Jiang, J., Li, H., & Wang, Y. (2020). Systematic review and meta-analysis of effects of acupuncture on pain and function in non-specific low back pain. *Acupuncture in Medicine, 38*(4), 235–43. https://doi.org/10.1136/acupmed-2017-011622.

Maciocia, G. (2015). *The foundations of Chinese medicine. A comprehensive text* (3rd ed). Churchill Livingstone.

Mayo Clinic Staff. (n.d.). *Biofeedback*. Mayo Clinic. mayocl.in/4auriGD.

Nabaggala, J. (2021). A personal perspective on pedagogical structures and strategies that uphold Indigenous ways of knowing. *Art, Design & Communication in Higher Education, 20*(2), 129–40. https://doi.org/10.1386/adch_00035_1.

National Center for Complementary and Integrative Health. (2022a). *Qigong: What you need to know*. National Institutes of Health. bit.ly/3IBi0g0.

National Center for Complementary and Integrative Health. (2022b). *Music and health: What you need to know*. bit.ly/3IyJSRZ.

Nunez, K. (2020a). *The benefits of progressive muscle relaxation and how to do it*. Healthline. https://www.healthline.com/health/progressive-muscle-relaxation.

Nunez, K. (2020b). *The benefits of guided imagery and how to do it*. Healthline. https://www.healthline.com/health/guided-imagery.

Perugini, N. (2018). *Navigating waters before GPS: Why some mariners still refer to Loran-C*. Silver Spring, MD: NOAA Office of Coast Survey. bit.ly/49QE4PG.

Smarterhealing.com. (n.d.). *Acupuncture points guide—view all meridians*. Smarterhealing.com. bit.ly/3VcgQPx.

Space Center Houston. (2020). *Try this at home Part 3: Build a sextant*. bit.ly/4acoNsk.

Stairs, A. (1994). Indigenous ways to go to school: Exploring many visions. *Journal of Multilingual and Multicultural Development, 15*(1), 63–76. https://doi.org/10.1080/01434632.1994.9994557.

Stinson, J. (2018). *What are Indigenous and Western ways of knowing?* Canadian Research Institute for the Advancement of Women. bit.ly/4cfZo2I.

USA Art News. (2021). *Reasons why it's so important to preserve artifacts properly*. bit.ly/48OIogR.

Vermillion, S. (2021). *Polynesia's master voyagers who navigate by nature*. BBC. bbc.in/3vbRYga.

Yuan H., Ma Q., Ye L., & Piao G. (2016). The traditional medicine and modern medicine from natural products. *Molecules, 21*(5), 559. https://www.mdpi.com/1420-3049/21/5/559.

Zhang, M., Moalin, M., & Haenen, G. (2019). Connecting West and East. *International Journal of Molecular Sciences, 20*(9), Article 2333. https://doi.org/10.3390/ijms20092333.

Chapter 9

Computer Science Education through Socio-cultural STEAM

Lily R. Liang, Rui Kang, and Briana Wellman

Technological and computing skills have become increasingly relevant and essential for many careers in our modern society. In the United States (US), school systems are compelled to offer computer science (CS) education for all students and adopt CS policies, e.g., mandating the offering of CS courses, providing funds for teacher preparation, and establishing rigorous K-12 CS standards (Novak & Khan, 2022). However, providing all young children equitable opportunities to learn CS has been challenging. Female, African American, Latinx, and indigenous students have less exposure to CS education and a lower sense of belonging (Hansen & Zerbino, 2022; Novak & Khan, 2022; Wang et al., 2016). Since harnessing young children's early interests and curiosities in CS is crucial for their future academic and career decisions, inequitable opportunities to learn CS may lead to race- and gender-based gaps in economic attainment in later life (Dong et al., 2023; Hansen & Zerbino, 2022).

The contexts in which CS is taught have significant implications for the CS field to attract broader participation and to be more inclusive. Historically, CS curriculums narrowly focus on robotics, computer programming, and physics, prioritizing scientific and technical functions over social purposes, personal and cultural connections, and the need for artistic expression (Lindberg et al., 2020). The inclusion of art and design into the CS curriculum has gained ground in recent years. For example, e-textiles embed pocket-sized computers into fabric artifacts, embody rich socio-cultural contexts through sewing, quilting, knitting, weaving, and crafts, and engage a broader student population (Peppler, 2013).

Quite the contrary to the traditional view that CS and art are two vastly different careers that require very different skill sets, many careers today, such as architecture, photography, industrial design, music, and fashion design, require a skill set combining both (Master's in Data Science, 2021). Research has shown that integrating STEM, including CS, with a broad range of art forms such as visual art, dance, theater, music, and digital media has a positive impact on students' perceptions of and attitudes toward STEM and their development of critical technical concepts and communication and leadership skills (Fields & Kafai, 2023).

Socio-cultural STEAM considers learning as socially and culturally mediated (Lave & Wenger, 1991). Through the following four lessons and resources in this chapter, we hope to show how a CS-focused STEAM pedagogy has the potential to (a) help students feel connected with their peers through collaborative, creative activities, (b) help teachers build professional connections beyond their disciplinary boundaries, and (c) affirm students' socio-cultural identity by engaging local communities to create culturally relevant learning experiences (Hoffman et al., 2022).

OVERVIEW OF LESSON PLAN TOPICS AND CONTEXTS

Integrating Fashion into Robotics for Broadening Participation

Our clothes tell stories of our culture and heritage. FashionBots (Liang et al., 2019), developed by Lily Liang and her colleagues, integrates fashion as a cultural context into teaching robotics and computer programming. In this lesson, students will explore how different parts of a robot work together and how to manipulate robot movements with computer codes. They will be given opportunities to research the history, tradition, and culture of FashionBots' clothing.

First Amendment Rights at Lafayette Park with Minecraft Programming

The Lafayette Park World (Liang & Mendoza, 2023), an educational game developed by Lily Liang and her research team on the Minecraft platform, allows learners to explore Lafayette Park virtually, compete to discover women's suffrage protest signs, and build architecture through programming. This lesson plan increases awareness of gender equity, encourages civic engagement, and offers computer programming through architectural design and construction.

Intelligent Face Mask with E-Textiles

The intelligent face mask Lily Liang and a student of hers developed can display personalized light patterns and sound off alarms to maintain social distance. In this lesson, students will identify the electronic components of an intelligent mask assembled by their instructor and learn how different parts work together to generate various sound and light patterns. This lesson leverages students' experiences and knowledge of the social challenges during the COVID-19 pandemic to show the intimate connections between technology and our physical and psychological needs.

Hip Hop Music with EarSketch Programming

This lesson plan demonstrates creating music by programming with EarSketch, a software platform developed by the Georgia Institute of Technology. The immediate audio effects help students understand programming concepts such as the order of statements and loops. Students can also personalize their learning experience in computing according to their prior interests and experiences in music.

LESSON PLANS AND RESOURCES

Lesson Plan 1

Title of the Lesson: Integrating Fashion into Robotics for Broadening Participation

Theme:

Fashion embodies the rich history and tradition of a culture. It is also an artistic expression of one's identity. Affirming one's personal, social, and cultural identities plays a vital role in broadening participation in computing. Through this lesson, teachers send an inclusive message that children from diverse backgrounds belong to the computing community.

Grade Level: This activity is best suited for students of the following grade levels: 6–8.

Essential and Supporting Questions:

- How can robots be programmed to move?
- How does fashion reflect cultures and their history and tradition?

Time Required: 1.5 hours.

Objectives:

Students will be able to

1. Identify the mechanical and electrical parts of a FashionBot and understand how they work together.
2. Modify the source code of a FashionBot to manipulate its movement, for example, to turn left instead of right when sensing an obstacle in front of it.
3. Demonstrate an appreciation of the cultures FashionBots represent.

Standards and Standards Integration:

International Society for Technology in Education Standards:

1.1d Students understand the fundamental concepts of technology operations, demonstrate the ability to choose, use, and troubleshoot current technologies, and are able to transfer their knowledge to explore emerging technologies.
1.3d Students build knowledge by actively exploring real-world issues and problems, developing ideas and theories, and pursuing answers and solutions.
1.4c Students develop, test, and refine prototypes as part of a cyclical design process.
1.5c Students break problems into component parts, extract key information, and develop descriptive models to understand complex systems or facilitate problem-solving.
1.5d Students understand how automation works and use algorithmic thinking to develop a sequence of steps to create and test automated solutions.
1.6b Students create original works or responsibly repurpose or remix digital resources into new creations. (International Society for Technology in Education, 2023)

National Core Arts Standards:

Anchor Standard 1. Generate and conceptualize ideas and works.
Anchor Standard 10. Synthesize and relate knowledge and personal experience to make art.

Anchor Standard 11. Relate artistic ideas and works with societal, cultural, and historical context to deepen understanding. (National Coalition for CORE ARTS Standards, 2014)

National Curriculum Standards for Social Studies:

Theme 1: Culture and Culture Diversity.
Theme IX: Global Connections. (National Council for the Social Studies, 2010)

Classroom Materials:

For FashionBot images, videos, and assembly instructions, visit https://tinyurl.com/fashionbot-project. Materials to make a FashionBot:

- 1 chassis
- 2 Microbits (one as controller, one as receiver on the FashionBot)
- 1 Battery holder
- 4 AA Batteries
- 1 doll holder
- Multiple dolls in cultural/ethnic clothes
- 2 yards of duct tape.
- Source code (downloadable at the link above)
- A smartphone or computer to play music (optional)
- 1 disco light (optional)

Note: More than one FashionBot may be needed, depending on the class size.

Socio-cultural Context:

Like all forms of art, fashion enables us to develop our creativity, express our ideas, feelings, and experiences, and connect with communities, culture, and history. It helps us discover who we are and provides a motivating medium for learning CS concepts. In this lesson, FashionBots may wear the traditional clothing of a particular country (e.g., Mexico, Japan) or culture (e.g., African, Hispanic) during a specific historical period (e.g., Chinese Tang Dynasty).

Instructional Procedures:

1. Divide the class into small groups and have each group choose a FashionBot and research the history and tradition of its fashion, as well as the meaning, function, and social significance of a particular fashion design.

2. Have students introduce the history and meaning of FashionBots' clothes based on their research findings.
3. Demonstrate the FashionBots: Turn on music and disco lights (if available) and control the FashionBots' movements for two minutes, creating a "Wow" effect. Have students observe the demonstration of the FashionBots and predict their movements.
4. Ask students to take turns controlling the robot with the controllers.
5. Explain the robot parts and how they work together to create the movements.
6. Explain the FashionBots source code.
7. Ask students to identify a change they can make to the code for the FashionBots to move differently, e.g., backward instead of forward.
8. Have students take turns modifying the code to make the changes above, load the code on one of the FashionBots, observe how the FashionBot would move differently, and make a conclusion.
9. Optional: Demonstrate how a FashionBot automatically traces a line made with duct tape on the floor.
10. Optional: Explain how the line detector works on the FashionBot.
11. Optional: Explain the source code of line tracing.
12. Optional: Ask students to identify a change they can make to the line-tracing code, implement it, observe how the FashionBot would move differently, and make a conclusion.

Student Inquiry:

Students will have the opportunity to learn about the fashion tradition and history of a culture of their choice. Students will present their research findings when introducing their FashionBot to their classmates. Following the POE (Predict, Observe, and Experiment) model, students will first predict how different parts of the FashionBot work together and, from the source code, predict the FashionBot's movement. Then, students will observe how the instructor controls the robot's movement and manipulates its movement by modifying the source code. Finally, students will experiment with the source code and try to control and manipulate the movement of their FashionBot independently.

Assessment:

1. Ask students to describe the relationship between the source code and the movement of their FashionBot.
2. Ask students to show a change they can make to the code for the FashionBots to move differently, e.g., turn left instead of right.

3. Ask students to make a presentation about the tradition, culture, and history related to the clothing of their FashionBot.

Socio-cultural Community Engagement:

1. Host a FashionBot show at school events such as science fairs, book sales, international nights, and PTA meetings, and invite parents/caregivers, colleagues, and students to interact with the FashionBot show and with each other, asking them to provide perspectives on relationships among history, cultural identity, and fashion.
2. Invite a guest speaker, e.g., a fashion designer or a historian with knowledge of clothing and textile history, to lecture students in a class, parents at a PTA meeting, or teachers at a professional development workshop, and share personal connections with fashion.

Modification/Extension:

Although we used fashion dolls as the cultural medium for teaching computing in this lesson, other themes, such as sports, superheroes, and costume design, are possible. E-puppetry may also be used to teach various subject areas such as theater, literature, and history.

We used the low-floor and high-ceiling principles to make our lesson easy to implement while allowing students with more sophisticated knowledge about crafting and art design to dive deeper into the project (Peppler, 2013). To ease entry, the FashionBots will be assembled by the instructor so that students may focus on the programming of the robots. Students may assemble the FashionBots, however, following the instructions. Students talented in fashion design and crafting may use materials or software tools to design clothes of a culture they picked for their FashionBots.

Lesson Plan 2

Title of the Lesson: First Amendment Rights at Lafayette Park with Minecraft Programming

Theme:

This lesson integrates history, citizenship education, and computer science. It educates students about the women's suffrage movement, encourages civic engagement, and teaches computer programming through architectural design and construction in the context of a computer game. Gameplay can increase students' motivation and engagement in learning, help them develop problem-solving skills, and provide unique opportunities for collaboration and leadership.

Grade Level: This activity is best suited for students of the following grade levels: 6–8.

Essential and Supporting Questions:

- How do you program computer games?
- What were the consequences of the women's suffrage campaign of 1917–1920?
- What obstacles and controversies did the suffragists have to overcome?
- Why was Lafayette Square made the headquarters of the National Women's Party (NWP)?

Time Required: 1.5 hours.

Objectives:

Students will be able to

1. Identify programming concepts in the source code and how they work together.
2. Modify the source code of a component in the world created in Minecraft to change its shape, location, and frequency of appearance.
3. Describe the history of women's suffrage and the First Amendment rights that Lafayette Park represents.

Standards and Standards Integration:

International Society for Technology in Education Standards:

1.1d Students understand the fundamental concepts of technology operations, demonstrate the ability to choose, use, and troubleshoot current technologies, and are able to transfer their knowledge to explore emerging technologies.

1.3d Students build knowledge by actively exploring real-world issues and problems, developing ideas and theories, and pursuing answers and solutions.

1.4c Students develop, test, and refine prototypes as part of a cyclical design process.

1.5c Students break problems into component parts, extract key information, and develop descriptive models to understand complex systems or facilitate problem-solving.

1.5d Students understand how automation works and use algorithmic thinking to develop a sequence of steps to create and test automated solutions.

1.6b Students create original works or responsibly repurpose or remix digital resources into new creations. (International Society for Technology in Education, 2023)

National Curriculum Standards for Social Studies:

Theme II: Time, Continuity, and Change
Theme V: Individuals, Groups, and Institutions
Theme VI: Power, Authority, and Governance
Theme X: Civic Ideals and Practices

Classroom Materials:

- Computers can be shared among students.
- Internet access
- Minecraft Education software (needs to download; free logins for students and teachers)
- Lafayette Park World and source code examples (downloadable at https://tinyurl.com/minecraft-project-cs)

Socio-cultural Context:

In January and February 1917, women suffragists marched every day, across Lafayette Park with their banners to take up positions in front of the White House to demand that President Woodrow Wilson help them in their campaign to get all American women voting rights. Since then, Lafayette Park has become a historical site and symbol of exercising First Amendment rights. Source: https://www.nps.gov/teachers/classrooms/139layfayette.htm

Instructional Procedures:

1. Have students research the women's suffrage movement and Lafayette Park's connections to the movement.
2. Instruct students to log into their Minecraft accounts.
3. Download the Lafayette Park World and show students how to play the game.
4. Let students play the game and score by completing tasks, i.e., discovering signs, in the virtual world.
5. Encourage students to share their knowledge about the suffrage movement and explain the meanings and historical significance of the signs and sites in the virtual world.

6. Demonstrate the source code examples and explain the programming concepts in that code.
7. Ask students to identify a change they can make to a source code example, e.g., manipulate a variable that would change the location of a game component or control the number of repetitions in a loop.
8. Repeat Steps 6 and 7.

Student Inquiry:

Students will have opportunities to research the suffrage movement and its connections with Lafayette Park. Students will present their research findings as they complete tasks in the game. Following the POE (Predict, Observe, and Experiment) model, students will first predict the results of changing the value of a variable or the number of loops in the source code. Then, students will observe what happens after the instructor modifies the source code. Finally, students will experiment with changing various aspects of the source code to generate their desired results.

Assessment:

1. Ask students to recall and interpret the messages on the signs they discovered in the virtual world.
2. Ask students to identify programming concepts, such as variables, branches, and loops in the source code examples, and describe how they made a difference in the virtual world. For example, changing the value of the coordinates of a tree in the virtual world would place the tree at a different location; increasing the repetitions of a loop that builds a wall would result in a taller wall.
3. Ask students to modify the code with an intended result and execute the code to verify the result.

Socio-cultural Community Engagement:

1. Demonstrate the Lafayette Park game at school events such as science fairs, book sales, international nights, and PTA meetings, and invite parents/caregivers, colleagues, and students to interact with the game and with each other through the game, asking them to provide perspectives on the history and values the game represents.
2. Invite guest speakers to give a presentation on the women's suffrage movement to students in a class, parents/caregivers at a PTA meeting, or teachers at a professional development workshop.

3. Watch a documentary film or a movie on women's suffrage with community members knowledgeable about the movement and the history behind the park, followed by a discussion.

Modification/Extension:

This lesson was created by faculty and students in Washington, DC. Teachers may use their local historical landmarks as alternatives to Lafayette Park. Teachers may also use primary documents to emphasize the history component of this lesson.

Lesson Plan 3

Title of the Lesson: Intelligent Face Mask with E-Textiles

Theme:

E-textiles are fabric artifacts that integrate electronics, microcontrollers, and computing, generating various visual and sound effects. They embody rich socio-cultural contexts and engage a broader student population (Peppler, 2013). Research has shown that while e-textile projects engage boys and girls equally, girls tend to assume a leadership role while engaging in these projects (Peppler, 2013).

Grade Level: This activity is best suited for students of the following grade levels: 6–8.

Essential and Supporting Questions:

- How to control light and sound signals with Arduino?
- How can technology be used to solve a real-world problem created by the COVID-19 pandemic?

Time Required: 1.5 hours.

Objectives:

Students will be able to

1. Describe the relationship between the distance and the sound alert.
2. Identify the electronic components of an intelligent mask and understand how they work together.
3. Modify the source code of an intelligent mask to manipulate its output.

4. Explain the impact of the COVID-19 pandemic and describe the pros and cons of masks as a mitigation and protection policy.

Standards and Standards Integration:

International Society for Technology in Education Standards:

1.1d Students understand the fundamental concepts of technology operations, demonstrate the ability to choose, use, and troubleshoot current technologies, and are able to transfer their knowledge to explore emerging technologies.
1.3d Students build knowledge by actively exploring real-world issues and problems, developing ideas and theories, and pursuing answers and solutions.
1.4c Students develop, test, and refine prototypes as part of a cyclical design process.
1.5c Students break problems into component parts, extract key information, and develop descriptive models to understand complex systems or facilitate problem-solving.
1.5d Students understand how automation works and use algorithmic thinking to develop a sequence of steps to create and test automated solutions.
1.6b Students create original works or responsibly repurpose or remix digital resources into new creations. (International Society for Technology in Education, 2023)

National Curriculum Standards for Social Studies:

Theme VIII: Science, Technology and Society

National Core Arts Standards:

Anchor Standard 1. Generate and conceptualize ideas and works.
Anchor Standard 10. Synthesize and relate knowledge and personal experience to make art.
Anchor Standard 11. Relate artistic ideas and works with societal, cultural, and historical context to deepen understanding. (National Coalition for CORE ARTS Standards, 2014)

Classroom Materials:

- LilyPad ProtoSnap Plus (1)
- Conductive Thread (0.5 m)

- HC-SR04 ultrasonic sensor (1)
- Lithium-Ion Polymer Battery - 3.7v 100mAh (1)
- Cloth face mask (1)
- Assembly instructions (https://tinyurl.com/intelligent-mask-project)
- Source code (downloadable at the same link above)

Socio-cultural Context:

The COVID-19 global pandemic brought significant challenges to our social interactions. Facemasks, though necessary, cover the part of our body that holds rich information about our identity and emotions. Social distancing became an important safety measure during the pandemic, though maintaining it relied entirely on people's awareness. An intelligent facemask uses technology to reflect user identity, express emotions, and remind people about their distance from each other. This lesson plan leverages the students' experiences of wearing facemasks and their knowledge of the social challenges during the COVID-19 pandemic. It shows students how closely technology is related to their lives and how it can be used to meet their everyday needs.

Instructional Procedures:

1. Assemble one or more intelligent masks before class and test both the LED pattern and the social distance alert functions.
2. Wear the intelligent mask when greeting the students, with the LED lights of the mask turned on, creating a "WOW" effect.
3. Divide students into groups based on the number of computers available.
4. Have students research the impact and mitigation policies for the COVID-19 pandemic and compare COVID-19 with other pandemics in human history.
5. Have each group of students summarize their findings and share them with the class.
6. Demonstrate the social-distance alert function of the mask by getting close to a student and backing off after hearing the alert go off, and repeat with a few other students.
7. Ask students to make conjectures about what triggered the alert.
8. Explain the parts of the intelligent mask and how they work together to create light patterns or sound alerts.
9. Demonstrate the source code of the intelligent mask.

10. Ask students to identify a change they can make to the code for the intelligent mask to work differently, e.g., showing a different light pattern or sending off an alert at a shorter/longer social distance.
11. Ask students to modify the code to make the changes above, take turns loading the code onto the intelligent mask(s), observe how the mask(s) would work differently, and draw a conclusion.

Student Inquiry:

Students will have opportunities to research the impact of the COVID-19 pandemic and mitigation policies and compare COVID-19 with other major pandemics in history. Students will share their findings with the class. Following the POE (Predict, Observe, and Experiment) model, students will first predict what triggers sound alerts and different light patterns. Then, they will observe what happens after the instructor modifies a component of the source code. Finally, they will experiment with changing various aspects of the source code to generate their desired light patterns and sound alert distance.

Assessment:

1. Ask students to describe the relationship between the distance and the sound alert.
2. Ask students to identify components of the intelligent mask and describe their functions/relations.
3. Ask students to modify the code of the intelligent mask to show a different light pattern or alert at a different distance and verify the results by loading the modified code onto an intelligent mask.

Socio-cultural Community Engagement:

1. Demonstrate the intelligent mask at school events, such as science fairs, book sales, and international nights to engage parents/caregivers, colleagues, and students. Ask them to recall their personal experiences using masks during the COVID-19 pandemic or to comment on the intelligent mask.
2. Invite guest speakers to give a presentation on the global impact, mitigation policies, consequences, and controversies of the COVID-19 pandemic or other pandemics in history.

Extension/Modification:

In this lesson, we used the low-floor and high-ceiling principles to make our lesson easy to implement while allowing students with more sophisticated knowledge about crafting and art design to dive deeper into the project (Peppler, 2013). Face masks will be assembled by the teacher so that students may focus on using source code to generate different light and sound effects. Students can assemble intelligent masks under the instructor's guidance and in small groups, however, if enough e-textile supplies are available. Students with talents in crafting and art design may also be allowed to design the appearance of their face masks. Another extension could be asking students to create circuit diagrams or use e-textile supplies to implement various types of circuits.

Lesson Plan 4

Title of the Lesson: Hip Hop Music with EarSketch Programming

Theme:

There are rich connections between computational thinking and music, which makes it a unique and ideal medium to engage diverse students in computational thinking. Computational thinking, such as decomposition, patterns, abstraction, and algorithms, is related to concepts in music and can be written as code to control tempo, volume, and arrangement (Bell & Bell, 2018). Students will also have opportunities to work with their favorite instruments or music samples by their favorite artists. Hip Hop music is a type of cultural fund of knowledge that is part of a historically accumulated body of knowledge deeply connected to people, their cultural practices, and their communities (Moll & González, 2004).

Grade Level: This activity is best suited for students of the following grade levels: 6–8.

Essential and Supporting Questions:

- How do you generate music by programming?
- How does music shape our culture?

Time Required: 1.5 hours.

Objectives:

Students will be able to

1. Identify programming concepts in the source code and how they work together to produce music.
2. Modify the source code (e.g., tempo value, number of repetitions of a loop) to change how the music sounds.
3. Explain Hip Hop music's origins and key features and its connections to cultural practices and meanings.

Standards and Standards Integration:

International Society for Technology in Education Standards:

1.1d Students understand the fundamental concepts of technology operations, demonstrate the ability to choose, use, and troubleshoot current technologies, and are able to transfer their knowledge to explore emerging technologies.
1.3d Students build knowledge by actively exploring real-world issues and problems, developing ideas and theories, and pursuing answers and solutions.
1.4c Students develop, test, and refine prototypes as part of a cyclical design process.
1.5c Students break problems into component parts, extract key information, and develop descriptive models to understand complex systems or facilitate problem-solving.
1.5d Students understand how automation works and use algorithmic thinking to develop a sequence of steps to create and test automated solutions.
1.6b Students create original works or responsibly repurpose or remix digital resources into new creations. (International Society for Technology in Education, 2023)

National Curriculum Standards for Social Studies:

- Theme 1: Culture and Cultural Diversity
- Theme IV: Individual Development and Identity.

2014 Music Standards (PK-8 General Music):

Imagine:

MU:Cr1.1.6a Generate simple rhythmic, melodic, and harmonic phrases within AB and ABA forms that convey expressive intent.
MU:Cr1.1.7a Generate rhythmic, melodic, and harmonic phrases and variations over harmonic accompaniments within AB, ABA, or theme and variation forms that convey expressive intent.

MU:Cr1.1.8a Generate rhythmic, melodic, and harmonic phrases and harmonic accompaniments within expanded forms (including introductions, transitions, and codas) that convey expressive intent.

Plan and make:

MU:Cr2.1.6a Select, organize, construct, and document personal musical ideas for arrangements and compositions within AB or ABA form that demonstrate an effective beginning, middle, and ending, and convey expressive intent.

Classroom Materials:

- Computers can be shared among students.
- Internet access
- EarSketch programming platform (browser-based, no download/installation, free)
- EarSketch introduction video (on EarSketch's website https://earsketch.gatech.edu/landing/#/, click "start coding"; the video will be at the bottom right corner)
- Source code of sample Hip Hop songs (https://tinyurl.com/earsketch-project)

Socio-cultural Context:

STEM teachers have been using Hip Hop, especially rap songs and lyrics, as curricular resources to engage students. This lesson exemplifies culturally relevant computer science education that empowers students by affirming and preserving their cultural identity and heritage (Paris, 2012). In this lesson, students will have opportunities to research the history of Hip Hop music and the roles music plays in the lives of African Americans.

Instructional Procedures:

1. Have students research Hip-Hop music, its origins, key features, impacts, and personal connections.
2. Let students present their research findings to their classmates and share their ideas about the music they will create in EarSketch.
3. Divide the students into groups, ask them to log into the computers, and download an EarSketch Hip Hop music source code sample.
4. Introduce EarSketch briefly and show students how to play music by running a downloaded source code sample.

5. Let students play the music samples.
6. Demonstrate the source code of the music and explain the programming concepts, such as variables, loops, and branches.
7. Ask students to identify a change they can make to the code, e.g., the tempo value or the number of repetitions in a loop.
8. Encourage students to make connections between the EarSketch music and their research findings on Hip Hop music.

Student Inquiry:

Students will have opportunities to research Hip-Hop music, its origin, features, function, and impact, and make personal connections. Students will share their research findings as they play the music produced in EarSketch. Following the POE (Predict, Observe, and Experiment) model, students will first predict the results of changing the value of a variable or the number of loops in the source code. Then, students will observe what happens after the instructor modifies the source code. Finally, students will experiment with changing various aspects of the source code to generate their desired rhythm, and tempo.

Assessment:

1. Ask students to describe the music they explored and their favorite genre of music.
2. Ask students to identify programming concepts, such as variables, branches, and loops in the source code, and describe how they made a difference in a piece of music. For example, how increasing the value of a variable would change the tempo or how the number of repetitions of a loop would make the music sound different.
3. Ask students to modify the code of a piece of music with an intended result and execute the code to verify the result.

Socio-cultural Community Engagement:

1. Demonstrate EarSketch music at school events such as science fairs, book sales, international nights, and PTA meetings, and invite parents/caregivers, colleagues, and students to interact with the songs and with each other, asking them to provide perspectives on the history and values that the Hip Hop music/songs represent.
2. Invite a Hip Hop musician to give a performance to students in a class, parents at a PTA meeting, or teachers at a professional development workshop, and share personal connections with the music.

3. Watch a documentary film on the roles of music in history or a movie about a musician, and conduct a discussion among students.
4. Repeat the above exercises with other popular music genres in the community.

Modification/Extension:

Although Hip Hop music is used as a context in this lesson to illustrate the integration of computer science and music, teachers may choose other types of music that are personally meaningful and relevant to their students as alternatives, such as Ragtime, Jazz, and other folk music worldwide.

EXPERT OPINIONS

We invited three computer science and information technology educators to review the lesson plans of this chapter and provide feedback. George Dimitoglou is currently an associate professor in the Department of Computer Science and Information Technology at Hood College in the state of Maryland. His area of expertise includes software engineering and cybersecurity. He has extensive experience working with K-12 students and teachers on curriculum development and implementation. Onyinye Ukeneru-Steve and Daniel Scott are high school Career and Technology Education (CTE) teachers in the District of Columbia Public Schools (DCPS), specializing in information technology. Both have years of teaching experience and have taught at the middle school level. Ukeneru-Steve is also a DCPS Teaching Ambassador responsible for interviewing elementary, middle, and high school CTE teacher applicants. We conducted individual interviews with each of them. Below is a summary of their responses.

Benefits of a Socio-cultural STEM Curriculum

Enhance Student Engagement. All three educators noticed the authenticity and real-world connections of a socio-cultural curriculum. For example, Dimitoglou argued that socio-cultural STEM is crucial for forging "an authentic connection between students and STEM subjects" and inspiring students to pursue STEM careers. He also noted that a socio-cultural STEM curriculum provides a richer experience to students, "offers greater opportunity for participation across varying student interests," and "triggers curious minds." Scott and Dimitoglou both believe that the lesson plans in the chapter require a student-centered, active pedagogy that they appreciate. Scott related the lesson plans to problem-based learning and hands-on inquiry. Dimitoglou pointed out that integrating art and computer science makes a socio-cultural curriculum "more real" and more engaging to students, and such a curriculum helps students visualize the effects of their codes. Ukeneru-Steve reflected that her students often found computer science abstract, hard to learn, and challenging. She found that a socio-cultural STEM curriculum shows students "how they can implement what they have learned" and makes computer science more concrete. In a way, a socio-cultural curriculum "enhances student engagement by meeting their interests and needs."

Broadening Participation. All three educators noted that the lesson plans in this chapter embrace diverse cultural perspectives and have the potential to broaden participation in STEM. Dimitoglou observed that artistic expression is "a seemingly across-the-board interest for young students" and a common thread in all the lesson plans in the chapter. He believes that such a curriculum fosters a sense of belonging and "is bound to increase inclusivity across race, gender, and ethnicity." Ukeneru-Steve pointed out that "culture is key to students' education and success," and a socio-cultural curriculum "reflects the differences in the classroom." Mr. Scott argues that a socio-cultural curriculum "promotes equity in education" because it allows each student to apply their strengths and points of view to STEM learning.

The Interdisciplinary Approach. All three educators commented on the interdisciplinary nature of a socio-cultural STEM curriculum. For example, Ukeneru-Steve used the phrase "blended learning" to describe how a socio-cultural STEM curriculum allows students to "understand, model, and analyze the world around them." She was also excited about the potential opportunity to collaborate with her colleagues in the art and math departments, stating, "One teacher alone will not be able to do the whole thing from beginning to end." Scott noted that real-life applications often require an interdisciplinary approach. Echoing the other two educators, Dimitoglou argued:

> Computer science is almost by nature interdisciplinary in its application to different domains, and the socio-cultural STEM approach "fits" well in enhancing CS education.... The collaborative and creative nature of socio-cultural STEM/STEAM activities can enhance students' understanding and engagement with STEM topics.

Implementation Considerations

Support of Teachers, Parents/Caregivers, and Administrators. All three educators believe that a socio-cultural curriculum has the support of various stakeholders, including teachers, parents/caregivers, and administrators. For example, Dimitoglou stated, "I would be surprised if there were teachers not supporting this curriculum. Its expected benefits would be obvious." Ukeneru-Steve also believes that the lesson plans in this chapter will be well received by teachers because they provide "clear, effective strategies for teaching all learners, as well as strategies for effective classroom management and community-building." Moreover, Scott believes that teachers will support a socio-cultural curriculum because "it helps create critical thinkers," increases science literacy, and "enables the next generation to be innovators." When it comes to administrative support, Dimitoglou commented that "administrators care about each and every outcome discussed in this chapter." Both Scott and Ukeneru-Steve argued that administrators are likely to support this curriculum because it aligns with workforce opportunities and helps students "easily transition from middle school to high school" (Ukeneru-Steve). In terms of support from parents/caregivers, Ukeneru-Steve believes that a socio-cultural STEM curriculum will be supported by parents/caregivers and the community they represent. Dimitoglou shared that "the principles, outcomes, and opportunities behind offering this curriculum would most definitely resonate with . . . the K-12 extended community," and a socio-cultural STEM curriculum would be seen "as an added-value educational contribution to the existing school program that may lead to tangible interest and skills for STEM-related careers."

Challenges. All three educators brought up teacher training when asked, "What kind of assistance do you think teachers will need to effectively implement a socio-cultural STEM curriculum?" Both Ukeneru-Steve and Scott observed that teachers assigned to teach computer science courses often do not have computer science degrees, making professional development particularly important to ensure the successful implementation of a socio-cultural STEM curriculum. Besides content knowledge, Ukeneru-Steve commented that teachers would also "need a clear vision of the best practices" for "how the classroom should be built to ensure the students meet the set goal." Moreover, Dimitoglou pointed out the importance of providing teachers with the cultural contexts and implications underlying a socio-cultural curriculum in addition to showing teachers "how the code works." Besides teacher training, Dimitoglou believes that time is another concern for implementing a sociocultural STEM curriculum: "The challenge I foresee is how to fit this rich curricular experience in the already fairly packed middle school curriculum." "How much of it can they actually implement?" and "What existing activity they may need to replace?" He also offered some suggestions based on his experience working with school districts. One strategy he used was to first find a couple of teachers who showed interest in the new curriculum and pilot the implementation. He explained that the pilot programs could be very small sometimes, but the teachers in the pilot programs often were able to take the curriculum to their colleagues. Finally, Dimitoglou emphasized that answering the question: "What type of resources would be required to implement the curriculum?" would be critical in gaining administrative support. He pointed out that teachers' development days, technical support provided by teaching assistants, and software installation are some of the most common resources that are needed. Both Scott and Dimitoglou emphasized the importance of testing an activity using a student account to ensure students are not blocked from using certain content or features.

CONCLUSION

In this chapter, we provide four lesson plans to show how effective computer science education can be achieved through a socio-cultural STEM/STEAM curriculum. By integrating fashion into robotics, incorporating citizenship education into Minecraft programming, using programming to create music on EarSketch, and applying e-textiles to meet the significant social and psychological challenges of a pandemic, we demonstrate an interdisciplinary approach to STEM education based on diverse cultural perspectives and artistic expressions. We believe that our curricular approach will broaden participation in STEM and inspire more students to pursue STEM careers. As pointed out by the reviewers of this chapter, implementing such a curriculum requires resources, administrative support, and teacher professional development, and teachers may face challenges such as limited time and an already packed curriculum. However, we believe that the abundant benefits of a socio-cultural STEM curriculum are evident and that such a curriculum will flourish in K-12 computer science classrooms with the support of teachers, administrators, parents/caregivers, and local communities.

REFERENCES

Bell, J., & Bell, T. (2018). Integrating computational thinking with a music education context. *Informatics in Education*, *17*(2), 151–66. https://eric.ed.gov/?id=EJ1195661.

Dong, J., Choi, K., Yu, S., Lee, Y., Kim, J., Vajir, D., Haines, C., Newbill, P. L., Wyatt, A., Upthegrove, T., & Jeon, M. (2023). A child-robot musical theater after-school program for promoting STEAM education: A case study and guidelines. *International Journal of Human-Computer Interaction*. https://doi.org/10.1080/10447318.2023.2189814.

Fields, D., & Kafai, Y. (2023). Supporting and sustaining equitable STEAM activities in high school classrooms: Understanding computer science teachers' needs and practices when implementing an E-textiles curriculum to forge connections across communities. *Sustainability, 15*(11), 8468. https://doi.org/10.3390/su15118468.

Hahn, K. H. Y., & Bhaduri, G. (2021). Mask up: Exploring cross-cultural influences on mask-making behavior during COVID-19 pandemic. *Clothing and Textiles Research Journal, 39*(4), 297–313. https://doi.org/10.1177/0887302X211012747.

Hansen, M., & Zerbino, N. (2022, April 11). *Exploring the state of computer science education amid rapid policy expansion*. Brookings. https://www.brookings.edu/articles/exploring-the-state-of-computer-science-education-amid-rapid-policy-expansion/.

Hoffman, D. L., Leong, P., Ka'aloa, R. P. H., & Paek, S. (2022). Teachers' perspectives on culturally-relevant computing: Principles and processes. *TechTrends, 66*, 423–35. https://doi.org/10.1007/s11528-022-00733-w.

Lave, J., & Wenger, E. (1991). *Situated learning: Legitimate peripheral participation*. Cambridge University Press. https://doi.org/10.1017/CBO9780511815355.

Liang, L., Enamorado, J., Jia, Y., & Wellman, B. (2019, October 25). *Integrating fashion into robotics for broadening participation*. Consortium for Computing Sciences in Colleges Eastern Region (CCSC Eastern), Robert Morris University in Moon Township, PA, United States.

Liang, L., & Mendoza, C. S. (2023, October 20). *Developing socio-cultural computing for broadening participation with Lafayette Park Minecraft World*. Consortium for Computing Sciences in Colleges Eastern Region (CCSC Eastern), Bay Atlantic University, Washington, DC, United States.

Lindberg, L., Fields, D. A., & Kafai, Y. (2020). STEAM maker education: Conceal/reveal of personal, artistic, and computational dimensions in high school student projects. *Frontier Education, 5*. https://doi.org/10.3389/feduc.2020.00051.

Master's in Data Science. (2021, June 14). *Skills and tools for careers that bridge computer science and art*. bit.ly/49VKY5W.

Moll, L., Gonzalez, N. (2004). Engaging life: A funds of knowledge approach to multicultural education. In J. Banks & C. McGee Banks (Eds.), *Handbook of research on multicultural education* (2nd ed.) (pp. 699–715). Jossey-Bass.

Novak, E., & Khan, J. (2022). A research-practice partnership approach for co-designing a culturally responsive computer science curriculum for upper elementary students. *TechTrends, 66*, 527–38. https://doi.org/10.1007/s11528-022-00730-z.

Paris, D. (2012). Culturally sustaining pedagogy: A needed change in stance, terminology, and practice. *Educational Researcher, 41*(3), 93–7. https://doi.org/10.3102/0013189X12441244.

Peppler, K. (2013). STEAM-powered computing education: Using E-textiles to integrate the arts and STEM. *Computer, 46*, 38–43. https://doi.org/10.1109/MC.2013.257https://doi.ieeecomputersociety.org/10.1109/MC.2013.257.

Wang, J., Hong, H., Ravitz, J., & Moghadam, S. H. (2016). Landscape of K-12 computer science education in the US: Perceptions, access, and barriers. *Proceedings of the 47th ACM Technical Symposium on Computer Science* (pp. 645–50). Memphis, TN. https://doi.org/10.1145/2839509.2844628.

Chapter 10

Building Socio-cultural Understanding through Integration of Social Science and STEM in Problem-based Lessons

Barbara O'Donnell

In this chapter, lessons integrate social science's C3 Framework's Inquiry Arc and cross-cutting science concepts, which include Ecosystems: Interactions, Energy and Dynamics, Earth's Place in the Universe, Earth Systems, Earth and Human Activity, Engineering Design, and Matter and Energy in Organisms and Ecosystems. These lessons also require students to use English language arts and technological practices to research and present their learning. Integration is intended to help students see content through many lenses so they can attain meaningful learning goals (Beck & Parker, 2022). Throughout these lessons, students will experience the power of collaboration, use inquiry skills to learn about the physical and socio-cultural environment, find a voice to make change, and take part in the community in which they live. These social learning experiences follow the tenets of Vygotsky's (1978) socio-cultural approach to cognitive development, specifically the Zone of Proximal Development, More Knowledgeable Other, and language development.

In these lessons, students will exercise the social science skills of inquiring, identifying diverse perspectives, analyzing sources, making hypotheses leading to claims, supporting claims with evidence, communicating ideas and insights, and acting on these claims and ideas to advocate for change. Students will use a science-based design thinking protocol (d.school, 2010) in which they *empathize, define, ideate, prototype,* and *test* to creatively solve problems. Students will also make sense of the content of lessons by using visible thinking strategies (VTS) (Ritchhart et al., 2011). These language development strategies help students understand content through systematic processes that ask them to identify central concepts, find relationships between concepts, question viability, and make conjectures. All of these lessons create a culture of thinking (Ritchhart, 2015) wherein students' individual and group thinking is valued and visible to others. In this culture, students are encouraged to research to find their perspectives, evaluate sources, voice ideas, and advocate based on these ideas. The following lessons require students to utilize voices from peers, parents, and the community. These experiences foster students' learning and growth in twenty-first-century skills (AACTE, 2010).

OVERVIEW OF THE LESSON PLAN TOPICS AND CONTEXTS

Collaboration in Space (Lesson 1) focuses on the International Space Station's (ISS) history, scientific accomplishments, and its international partnership between countries. Students will uncover and examine the power of collaboration to overcome differences in current political settings. This lesson requires students to work collaboratively, analyze data, make and support claims, and present their findings. The lesson was developed from a thematic unit on space and a socio-cultural themed lesson designed by graduate student Anna Monson.

Local Renewable Energy (Lesson 2) can be taught as a stand-alone community-based lesson or it can augment a science unit on energy that includes lessons on such concepts as potential and kinetic energy, the six main forms of energy, types of energy transfer, and the Law of Conservation of Energy. The goal of this lesson is to engage students to use socio-cultural theory experiences to find their stance on renewable energy, engage in inquiry based on community needs, and use their learning to promote renewable energy in their community. Amanda Kapper, a graduate student, created the initial design of this socio-cultural lesson.

Pollution in Our Community (Lesson 3) spotlights the civic responsibility of keeping our planet healthy by investigating past and current issues surrounding pollution. Students will use design thinking to build an understanding of the results of pollution, diverse viewpoints on addressing the problem, and potential solutions to keep our planet healthy. Undergraduate student Jessica Paschedag inspired this lesson and the Taking Action lesson.

Taking Action (Lesson 4) concentrates on taking civic responsibility within the community. Students will assess the needs of their community in terms of recycling, investigate community resources, and find ways to promote recycling. They will collaborate to build productive relationships and become aware of the power of their voice in social change. The advocacy process involved in this lesson can be adapted to other topics and concepts.

LESSON PLANS AND RESOURCES

Lesson Plan 1

Title of the Lesson: Collaboration in SPACE

Theme: The theme of this lesson is to examine how people collaborate to study our world and solve its problems. By studying how countries have contributed to space exploration, students learn about diverse cultures and how they intermingle to create a space for collaboration.

Grade Level: This lesson is best suited for 5th or 6th grade.

Essential and Supporting Questions:

- How can collaboration create a better Earth?
- Why do we need an International Space Station (ISS)?
- What is the mission of the ISS?
- Who participates in the creation, building, and continuing work on the ISS?
- Why is it important for countries to work together?
- How can work conducted on the ISS help our planet?
- Is the cost of the ISS worth it?

Time Required: This lesson extends over four class periods.

Objectives: *Students will be able to:*

- Analyze how the ISS has impacted the United States (US) and the rest of the world.
- Work collaboratively to develop claims from sources concerning creation, collaboration, and continuing work on the ISS.
- Investigate and write about how the United States uses the ISS resources to preserve our planet.

Standards and Standards Integration:

National Council for the Social Studies (NCSS)—C3 Framework:

- D2.Geo.12.3-5. Explain how natural and human-made catastrophic events in one place affect people living in other places.
- D2.His.16.3-5. Use evidence to develop a claim about the past.

156   Chapter 10

- D3.1.3-5. Gather relevant information from multiple sources while using the origin, structure, and context to guide the selection.
- D4.2.3-5. Construct explanations using reasoning, correct sequences, examples, and details with relevant information and data.

Next Generation Science Standard (NGSS):

- 5-ESS3-1. Earth and Human Activity: Obtain and combine information about ways individual communities use scientific ideas to protect the Earth's resources and environment.

Classroom Materials: Chromebook, online storage file for each group, WebQuest worksheet, exit tickets, pencils and other writing tools, chart paper with markers, and Smartboard or projector to show the video, display directions, and make the concept map. In addition:

Video: https://youtu.be/OyaXBrttBFQ
Instruction sheets: International Space Station WebQuest and Exit Ticket

Socio-cultural Context:

Historically, the International Space Station (ISS) took ten years and thirty missions to assemble. It is a scientific and engineering collaboration among five space agencies representing fifteen countries. It began in 1984 with President Ronald Reagan's State of the Union Address, where he directed NASA to build an international space station. After construction, the first segments were launched in 1998 from Russia, followed by a U.S.-built component. The first crew consisted of one American, Bill Shepherd, and two cosmonauts. In November 2000, they spent four months completing tasks to ensure that there would be a continued human presence in space. In 2001, a U.S. laboratory module was added for experimental studies, and this was followed by European and Japanese labs in 2008. Since 2000's Expedition 1, the ISS has had continuous human occupancy, with a total of 258 people visiting the station. For a more complete timeline of the ISS, the following website can be accessed: https://www.issnationallab.org/about/iss-timeline/

Instructional Procedures and Student Inquiry:
Day 1
Opening (10 minutes): Begin the lesson with a short question and answer session which serves as a pre-assessment for the lesson: Describe what you know about space travel. How long do you think that people (astronauts)

have been traveling in space? Why do astronauts go into space? Is the United States the only country that sends astronauts into space? Why do you think that?

Use the Smartboard or chart paper to record answers. Remind students that all ideas are accepted regardless of correctness. Answers will be reviewed at the end of the 2-day lesson.

Introduction to the International Space Station (10–15 minutes): Preview the video about the ISS by posting and asking the following questions:

- What do you know about the ISS? Why would we need a space station? In what ways would it help us here on Earth?
- Students watch the video about the ISS: https://youtu.be/OyaXBrttBFQ. When the video ends, start the Think-Pair-Share process: Why would we need a space station? In what ways would it help us here on Earth? Answer these two questions on their own and then turn to their partners to compare answers.

Student-led Investigation of Historical Facts (25 minutes): Forming student groups of three, students in each group have duties: recorder, leader, and monitor. The recorder keeps a log of all the information found using the WebQuest document, the leader directs the inquiry and helps other group members focus on the task at hand, and the monitor is the liaison to the teacher and will present their group's work. Explain to the students that they need to have a basic understanding of the history of the ISS before investigating its work. They will use the following websites and the WebQuest document to build this basic understanding: go.nasa.gov/4cf8JYi, bit.ly/49QPNxw, and bit.ly/3wRnZuB.

Closing: What Do We Know Now? (15 minutes)

- Pull all groups together to review what they know after this informational investigation. Ask the monitors of each group's answers to present their WebQuest answers. Recorders will save their work in their online folder.
- Conclude by asking this question: Do we need to have an ISS? What makes you think that? Students answer this question on an exit ticket.

Day 2

Opening (5–10 minutes):

Students recall some of the surprising facts learned in the previous class.

Building a Concept Map for Investigations (20 minutes): Generate-Sort-Connect-Elaborate Activity in stages:

1. **Generate** a list of items that come to mind when you think of the ISS. (Some examples might be astronauts, countries, Earth, experiments, collaboration, living in space, history of the ISS, cost, women in space, scientists, benefits, and current missions).
2. **Sort** these items into categories according to their importance and place them on a concept map with more relevant items closer to the center. Items related to each relevant item are added to the map. This can be done on a whiteboard or by using an online app such as Canva.
3. **Connect** items with lines. These lines are used to show that the items are relevant to each other in some way. As this is being done, record why they are relevant.
4. **Elaborate** on any items by adding innovative ideas that expand upon or add to the topic.

Student-led Investigation (25 minutes): Each group will investigate one of the main topics using the same websites used in the last class, plus the following videos:
NASA Science Casts: Keeping an Eye on Earth: bit.ly/43cuqo3
NASA Science Casts: Observing Change over Time: bit.ly/49MEGpt

- *Questions:* What types of experiments would you expect astronauts to do? In what ways can the ISS help us understand changes on Earth? How can work conducted on the ISS help our planet and the rest of the solar system? Why is it important for countries to work together? Is the cost of the ISS worth it? Explain the pros and cons of this expenditure.
- Students are placed into new groups. Each group is given a question above that will help them dig deeper into the effects of the ISS on the following day. They will use the concept map as a guide for their investigation. Remind students that their answers are claims that need to be supported with evidence.
- Each group needs to plan its investigation for the following day and decide on group member roles (10 minutes).

Day 3
Opening (10 minutes): Before the inquiry starts, display the concept map. As students enter the class, they sit in their inquiry groups.
Procedure (45 minutes): Review the connections from the previous day and ask the students if they have any more connections or additions (elaboration) to the map. Remind each group of the question they are investigating during this class. Monitor the progress of the groups to determine when the student-led investigation time can be closed. Remind them that they need to examine the connections between categories.

Day 4
Opening (10 minutes): Putting It All Together: As students enter the class, they sit in their inquiry groups. "Yesterday, you investigated a question related to a category on the concept map; now it is time to share what you learned so we can see the whole picture of the ISS. You will have 10 minutes to prepare answers to your questions and their connections to other categories on the concept map. You will have 5 minutes to present."

What Did You Learn? Presentations (25 minutes): Each group presents what they learned by making and supporting their claims and talking about the connections between the categories. "Now we need to think beyond our current questions and categories to a larger question: In what ways does collaboration create a better Earth? How does the ISS illustrate this?" Talk in your groups to answer this question and prepare to share your ideas and insights.

Seeing the Bigger Picture (25 minutes): Groups present their collaboration ideas. To close the 4-day lesson, students will complete an exit ticket based on the visible thinking strategy: I used to think . . . Now I think . . . (5 minutes).

Assessment:
Formative Assessment: teacher observation of group work, planning, and roles and responsibilities, Day 1 exit ticket, WebQuest document.
Summative Assessment: inquiry skills, presentation of category answers and connections, final exit ticket: I used to think . . . Now, I think . . .

Socio-cultural Community Engagement:
Prior to this lesson, the teacher will email the parents with a brief overview of the lesson, which includes ways for families to connect the content to home through discussions, educational websites, and articles that students can explore with their families.

Accommodations and Modifications:

- Websites are chosen for this age group with the intent that the content is relevant, more succinct, has videos with closed captioning, and is easier to navigate: bit.ly/49QPNxw and bit.ly/3wRnZuB
- NASA websites can be added for students needing a challenge.
- Readers struggling with website text can watch the videos on both websites. English learners can opt for text translations.
- All directions, activities, vocabulary, and questions will be shared on the Smartboard and read aloud. These will be reviewed at the start of the next lesson phase.
- Although this is planned for 4 days, it may be extended to another day for further investigation and presentation preparation.

Resources:

National Aeronautics and Space Administration (2021). *NASA explores earth's connections.*
Retrieved from https://youtu.be/WCMsdz8wMQc

National Aeronautics and Space Administration (April 30, 2023). *Spot the station.*
Retrieved from https://spotthestation.nasa.gov/sightings/index.cfm

National Aeronautics and Space Administration (March 5, 2020). *Humans in space.* Retrieved from https://www.nasa.gov/topics/humans-in-space

National Aeronautics and Space Administration (August 27, 2023). *International Space Station.*
Retrieved from go.nasa.gov/4ceD89q

National Aeronautics and Space Administration. (n.d.). *First 8K video from space.* Retrieved
from https://youtu.be/7k2uKb9vCOI

National Aeronautics and Space Administration (August 30, 2023). *NASA History.* Retrieved
from https://www.nasa.gov/topics/history/index.html

Lesson Plan 2

Title of the Lesson: Local Renewable Energy

Theme: Renewable energy is key in preserving our quality of life and paving the way to a sustainable world. Without energy, life would not be possible. Energy is more than turning on a light or using an appliance. It is needed by all living beings to function, grow, and develop.

Grade Level: The target audience for this lesson is 6th grade students.

Essential and Supporting Questions:

- How can we effectively safeguard our environment?
- Who oversees making changes in our local area?
- What can an individual or group do to conserve energy?
- What options does our community have for renewable energy?
- How can we make our community aware of the energy situation?
- What is the downside to adopting renewable energy system?

Time Required: This lesson extends over 4–6 days.

Objectives: *Students will be able to:*

- Recall their knowledge of renewable resources from previous lessons.
- Use the Visible Thinking Strategy of Think-Puzzle-Explore to capture their ideas about what local/statewide renewable resources are in the community.
- Investigate the roles and responsibilities of local organizations in terms of energy usage and production.
- Examine what other communities are doing to use renewable resources.
- Investigate ways to build civic awareness and action for renewable energy.
- Work collaboratively to create a renewable energy presentation which utilizes supported claims to educate the community and local organizations.

Standards and Standards Integration:

National Council for the Social Studies (NCSS)—C3 framework:

- D1.5.6-8. Determine the kinds of sources that will be helpful in answering compelling and supporting questions, taking into consideration multiple points of view represented in the sources.
- D2.Civ.1.6-8. Distinguish the powers and responsibilities of citizens, political parties, interest groups, and the media in a variety of governmental and nongovernmental contexts.
- D2.Civ.6.6-8. Describe the roles of political, civil, and economic organizations in shaping people's lives.
- D2.Geo.5.6-8. Analyze the combinations of cultural and environmental characteristics that make places both similar to and different from other places.

Next Generation Science Standards (NGSS):

- MS-LS2-4. Construct an argument supported by empirical evidence that changes to physical or biological components of an ecosystem affect populations.
- MS-ESS3-3. Apply scientific principles to design a method for monitoring and minimizing a human impact on the environment.

Classroom Materials: Printed copy of Think-Puzzle-Explore sheet for students, video introducing renewable energy: https://youtu.be/1kUE0BZtTRc, Chromebooks, APPARTS strategy for analyzing sources (Author, Place and time, Prior knowledge, Audience, Reason, The main idea, Significance), local websites, newspapers, guest speakers as needed, and whiteboard or chart paper for brainstorming.

Socio-cultural Context:

Renewable energy is energy derived from natural sources. These sources are replaced at a higher rate than they are used. For example, sunlight and wind are constantly being replenished. Fossil fuels such as coal, oil, and gas are non-renewable because they take hundreds of years to form. These fuels also cause harmful greenhouse gases. Some examples of renewable energy are solar energy, wind energy, geothermal energy, hydropower, ocean energy, and bioenergy. Science tells us that fossil fuels are the largest contributor to global climate change, with 75 percent of global greenhouse gas emissions and 90 percent of carbon dioxide emissions. The following arguments support using renewable energy: its sources are everywhere on Earth; it is cheaper and healthier; it creates jobs; and it makes economic sense. To preserve the environment, the local community must assess its needs and develop plans to create and use energy that is clean. This lesson focuses specifically on the local level.

Instructional Procedures and Student Inquiry:

Day 1

Opening: (10–20 minutes): *Questions based on earlier lessons:*

- What is the difference between potential and kinetic energy? Describe the six main forms of energy. How is energy transferred from object to object?
- How can energy be renewed? Can energy be conserved? How can we increase the efficiency of energy?

Exploration of Our Prior Knowledge (20 minutes): Use the Think-Puzzle-Explore VTS to record thoughts about renewable resources found in our local community.

Using the template, answer the following questions: What do you think you know about renewable energy? What questions or puzzles do you have about renewable energy? How might you explore your puzzles about renewable energy?

After completing the VTS individually, students will share their answers in a group. Once the group discussion is completed, the following video by National Geographic will be shown: https://youtu.be/1kUE0BZtTRc. Students can then make changes to their VTS.

Making a To-Do List (20–30 minutes): "If we want to pursue an increase in renewable energy in our community, what do we need to do?" Students brainstorm ideas, such as:

- Learn more about the community: resources, officials, duties, energy providers.
- Find out what options might be available for renewable energy.
- Investigate what other communities are doing in terms of renewable energy.
- Ask community members why renewable energy might matter to them in a survey.
- Investigate the downsides of renewable energy.
- Determine what might happen if renewable energy is not pursued.
- Seek out allies who will help you persuade the community to invest in renewable energy. These ideas need to be recorded on the Smartboard for future use.

Closing (10–20 minutes): Once the To Do List is created, students are welcome to choose which area they want to investigate. Students collaborate in teams to build an inquiry plan so that all members have a task to do.

Day 2 (1–3 class periods):

The inquiry process that students follow will include identifying diverse perspectives, analyzing sources using APPARTS, corroborating sources, making claims, and supporting their claims. This portion of the lesson will take a few class periods. The teacher will need to monitor group progress and provide resources (guest speakers from the community, energy providers, websites, contact information) as needed. The goal of this presentation is to show how something the community already does can be converted to using renewable energy and to argue why it would be a better, sustainable option.

Day 3 (60+ minutes):

Once groups are ready, the information will be shared with the entire class; each group will present their findings, resources, and surveys to the class. Based on this information, student groups will create a presentation, podcast, or speech to present an idea of how we, as a community, can use local renewable energy sources to help the local environment. They will act as though this will be presented to the local government and/or community groups.

Day 4 (60+ minutes):

To close the lesson, students will present their inquiries to their classmates and/or other interested individuals. Their presentations should include the inquiry process (diverse perspectives, analysis and corroboration of sources, claims with support), findings, resources used, and insights into what can be accomplished locally to support renewable energy.

Assessment:

Formative Assessment: Observation of student answers, participation, written work, and discussion, Think-Puzzle-Explore VTS, APPARTS strategy for analyzing sources (Author, Place and time, Prior knowledge, Audience, Reason, The main idea, Significance), and surveys and other documents within their group investigation documents.
Summative Assessment: Oral and written presentations.

Socio-cultural Community Engagement:

The community will be engaged in many ways. As students explore their chosen inquiry, they will ask family, friends, community members, and business owners for information about their ideas on renewable energy and the effect it might have on their lives. Students will also investigate websites that represent various perspectives on the issue. They will use this information to present projects to fellow classmates, parents, local community members, and other interested parties with the intent that changes will be made.

Accommodations and Modifications:

- Directions for creating a slideshow presentation and/or formatting a speech
- Group members could be assigned specific jobs within their group
- Additional discussions of prior knowledge might need to be provided
- Information on building and conducting a survey may need to be provided
- Google Translate can be utilized for English language learners

Resources:

Hierl, W. (2018). *APPARTS strategy: Origins and implementation.* Retrieved from bit.ly/3wPDNOd

National Geographic Society (n.d.). *Renewable energy 101.* Retrieved from https://youtu.be/1kUE0BZtTRc

Project Zero (2023). *PZ's Thinking Routines Toolbox.* Retrieved from http://www.pz.harvard.edu/thinking-routines

United Nations (2023). *Climate action.* Retrieved from bit.ly/3TumgE9

Lesson Plan 3

Title of the Lesson: Pollution in Our Community

Theme: This activity centers on the civic responsibility of recycling. Students will look at a variety of primary sources, discussing different viewpoints on the pollution problem. Students will follow the design thinking process of empathizing, designing, ideating, prototyping, and testing in order to plan a Take Action project.

Grade Level: This lesson is best suited for students in the 7th grade.

Essential and Supporting Questions:

- What can we do to keep our planet healthy?
- Who is responsible for taking care of our community?
- How can we reduce pollution?
- What can we do to conserve and recycle to reduce the effects of pollution?
- What should governments do to protect the planet?
- What if we decide not to recycle?
- Is recycling even worth the trouble?
- Are recycled goods actually being recycled?

Time Required: This lesson extends over 5 to 6 class sessions.

Objectives: *Students will be able to:*

- Analyze primary sources for audience, context, perspectives, purpose, and significance.
- Evaluate the credibility of arguments and explanations about recycling.
- Collaborate to identify differing viewpoints using reasoning, examples, and details.
- Analyze their abilities and resources to act based on historical and present-day movements promoting the common good.
- Make claims based on multiple forms of evidence, yet understand that there may be limitations to their findings.

Standards and Standards Integration:

National Council for the Social Studies Standards (NCSS)—C3 Framework:

- D1.5.6-8. Determine the kinds of sources that will be helpful in answering compelling and supporting questions, taking into consideration multiple points of view represented in the sources.
- D2.Civ.1.6-8. Distinguish the powers and responsibilities of citizens, political parties, interest groups, and the media in a variety of governmental and nongovernmental contexts.

- D2.Civ.14.6-8. Compare historical and contemporary means of changing societies and promoting the common good.
- D4.7.6-8. Assess their individual and collective capacities to take action to address local, regional, and global problems, taking into account a range of possible levers of power, strategies, and potential outcomes.

Next Generation Science Standards (NGSS):

- MS-ESS3-3. Apply scientific principles to design a method for monitoring and minimizing a human impact on the environment.
- MS-ETS1-1. Define the criteria and constraints of a design problem with sufficient precision to ensure a successful solution, taking into account relevant scientific principles and potential impacts on people and the natural environment that may limit possible solutions.

Classroom Materials: Typed script for all primary sources that are in audio format, printed copies of primary sources and scripts for those in audio format, printed copies of Analysis Tool with Source Fields, printed copies of I used to think . . . Now I think VTS, screen projector for presentation of primary sources, The Crying Indian commercial: bit.ly/3wTrm49.

Socio-cultural Context:
Pollution has been an ongoing issue for many years. In the spring of 1970, Senator Gaylord Nelson created Earth Day, where many people gathered to peacefully protest and clean polluted areas to force the issue of pollution onto the national agenda. In December 1970, Congress authorized the creation of the U.S. Environmental Protection Agency (EPA). In the following 10 years, many legislative acts were enacted into law, including the Clean Air Act and the Clean Water Act. Later legislation was introduced to alter the Clean Water Act to give industries the ability to regulate themselves. Keep America Beautiful has released various Public Service Announcements on Earth Day, including the Crying Indian (1971) and Back by Popular Neglect (1998). Cartoonist Herbert Block has had several editorial cartoons published in the Washington Post. Architect Michael Reynolds has developed self-sustaining homes, called Earthships, using garbage across the world.

Instructional Procedures and Student Inquiry:

Day 1: Opening (10–15 minutes): Begin the open-discussion lesson by asking students the following questions: What does it mean to recycle? What is recyclable? How do you know if an item can be recycled? How do the people you know recycle?

Investigating the Problem (30 minutes): Review a commercial that was made in 1971 and aired on Earth Day that year. Students are now working in groups of three or four to answer the following questions: What are the messages behind this commercial? List at least 3. Who are the polluters depicted in the commercial? Why do we allow pollution? Who has the power to control pollution? Can a single person make a difference?

Call groups together to discuss answers to the questions. To close this section of the lesson, repeat the final words of the commercial, "People start pollution, people can stop it." Ask the whole group to define the meaning of this sentence and what actions we can take.

Closing (5 minutes): Ask students if they have any questions they would like to investigate. Record these questions on the Smartboard for future use.

Day 2: Opening (10 minutes): Start with the statement at the end of the commercial: "People start pollution, people can stop it." Review what it means. "To help our environment, we need to figure out what we as citizens can do. Let's use Design Thinking to help us." Remind students of the basic stages of this process:

- **Empathize**—consider others' needs and local influences, not just solve the problem.
- **Define**—define the problem and create a meaningful and actionable problem statement.
- **Ideate**—encourage innovation through brainstorming.
- **Prototype**—identify and develop the best solution through multiple iterations.
- **Test**—evaluate prototypes and consider improvements.

Available at: https://www.nsta.org/science-and-children/science-and-children-januaryfebruary-2022/design-thinking

Student groups will record their work for each phase of the Design Thinking process.

Empathize (40 minutes): To better understand the problem, we will be analyzing primary sources using the Analysis Tool with Source Fields from the Library of Congress. Each group will receive a primary source to analyze.

- "There goes the entire neighborhood"—Herblock February 20, 1973
- "We can even improve on turning things over to the states—we can let the industries regulate themselves"—Herblock May 19, 1995
- Photos of marine debris taken by Emily Hackett at a New Jersey beach

- Albatross photo by Chris Jordan
- A recording of a CBS News Special on Earth Day by Walter Cronkite
- Text of House Bill 6745

Groups share their primary source and analysis tool responses with the entire class. Then, students are asked, "What is the big takeaway from these sources?"

Day 3: Define (25 minutes): After a review of the primary source activity, students will start defining the problem. Review the documents, photos, or cartoons while they are projected on the Smartboard. Use the ideas generated from the question, "What is the big takeaway from these sources?" to define the problem. Student groups reconvene to brainstorm questions that they would like to explore that will address the pollution problem. Each group will share their question(s). We will look for commonalities and areas of interest in the questions to create an overarching essential question and supporting questions that will be addressed in our inquiries.

Ideate (25 minutes): Using the question(s) they generated, groups will brainstorm ideas to address the supporting questions which will ultimately provide information that will answer the overarching essential question. These ideas might include the following topics: civic responsibilities (government, individuals, businesses, industry), educating the population, ways to reduce littering, effective recycling and efforts.

Day 4: Prototype (50 minutes): Now that we have generated questions to answer, students are now ready to brainstorm possibilities, investigate, and propose answers to their assigned question. They should also consider the diverse viewpoints around their questions. They will use a mind map based on "Circle of Viewpoints" to show that they are thinking about the questions from many vantage points. Students will use the following websites for inquiries:

- https://www.epa.gov/recycle
- https://www.epa.gov/landfills
- https://www.epa.gov/p2/what-you-can-do-about-pollution-prevention
- https://illinoisrecycles.org/
- https://cleanoceanaction.org/issues-campaigns/marine-debris

Add a local government site to see the roles and responsibilities of elected officials in your community. They will also use these articles: bit.ly/3v8dNNx, bit.ly/3TgSNft, bit.ly/3Ti9bfZ.

Students should also interview or survey their family members, community members, city officials, and business owners to learn about their practices in recycling, limiting waste, and conservation.

Closing: Students start preparations to present their inquiry process, various viewpoints, potential answers based on supported claims, and any new questions they have the next day.

Day 5: Test (50 minutes): Student groups present their prototypes to the whole group.

Students will evaluate the information they have from each group. They will determine the following: Are the supporting questions answered? Is further research needed? Are all viewpoints included? Is there any content missing? Are we able to address the essential question?

If more research is needed, an extra class period could be scheduled.

Closing: End this part of the lesson with an Exit Ticket: I used to think . . . Now, I think . . .

Assessment:

Formative Assessment: Teacher observation of student participation in discussions, group collaborations, and activities, Circle of Viewpoints VTS, Library of Congress Primary Source Analysis Tool; *and* interview and/or survey results.

Summative Assessment: Design Thinking planning document, I used to think . . . Now I think . . .

Accommodations and Modifications:

- If students are struggling with the primary source analysis tool, the teacher can demonstrate the process using a primary source with the whole group.
- Videos have closed captioning, or a text of the video will be available.
- Text-to-speech will be available for students who need assistance with writing or typing.
- Primary sources may be altered using the Library of Congress guidelines.
- Google Translate can be used to support English language learners.

Socio-cultural Community Engagement:

Students will be inquiring about home and community practices of conservation and recycling through surveys or interviews. They will examine historical and current practices in their community, their country, and the world. Guest speakers from the community and utility providers can be invited to talk with students.

Resources:

Barrett-Zahn, E. (January/February 2022). *Design thinking*. Retrieved from bit.ly/4at51cf

Block, H. (February 20, 1973). There goes the entire neighborhood. [Cartoon] *Washington Post*. Retrieved from https://loc.gov/pictures/resource/hlb.08163/

Block, H. (May 19, 1995). We can even improve on turning things over to the states—we can let the industries regulate themselves. [Cartoon] *Washington Post*. Retrieved from https://loc.gov/pictures/resource/hlb.13030/

Clean Ocean Action. (n.d.). *EPA announces national strategy to prevent plastic pollution*. Retrieved from https://cleanoceanaction.org/issues-campaigns/marine-debris

Clean Water for All Act. H.R.6745 (2020). https://www.congress.gov/bill/116th-congress/house-bill/6745/text

Coffeekid99. (May 1, 2007). *The crying Indian —full commercial—keep America beautiful*. Retrieved from bit.ly/3wTrm49

EarthWeek 1970. (April 11, 2010). *Earth Day 1970 Part 1: Intro (CBS News with Walter Cronkite (April 22, 1970)*. [Video]. Retrieved from bit.ly/3VhK2EU

Hackett, E. (2023). *Marine debris photos. CleanOceanAction.org*. Retrieved from bit.ly/49LQCrq

Illinois Recycling Association (August 2023). *Promoting waste reduction, reuse, and recycling*. Retrieved from https://illinoisrecycles.org/

Jordan, C. (2023). Albatross. (U.S. Fish and Wildlife). *National Geographic*. Retrieved from bit.ly/3Ti9bfZ

KabmanKAB (May 25, 2007). *1998 crying indian "back by popular neglect."* [Video]. Retrieved from bit.ly/4cekZIH

Library of Congress (2023). *Teacher's guides and analysis tool*. Retrieved from bit.ly/3PlJudk

National Geographic (May 20, 2022). *A whopping 91 percent of plastic isn't recycled*. Retrieved from bit.ly/3v8dNNx

National Geographic (May 20, 2022). *The world's plastic pollution crisis explained*. Retrieved from bit.ly/3TgSNft

National Geographic (May 20, 2022). *Great Pacific Garbage Patch*. Retrieved from bit.ly/3Ti9bfZ

Lesson Plan 4

Title of the Lesson: Taking Action

Theme: This activity centers on the civic responsibility of recycling and calls students to act. The lesson is a continuation of the lesson "Pollution in Our Community" or it can be modified and used as a culminating lesson for a different topic.

Grade Level: The target audience for this lesson is 7th grade students.

Essential and Supporting Questions:

- What can we do to keep our planet healthy?
- Can 7th graders create change?
- What are the recycling processes?
- What can we do to reduce the effects of pollution?
- How can we get people to hear our message and join our cause?

Time Required: This lesson will extend over 5 class periods.

Objectives: *Students will be able to:*

- Choose and evaluate sources that will support arguments that promote change.
- Identify and practice skills that will assist them in promoting change.
- Identify ways in which individuals and groups can use their skills to make changes that address environmental problems.
- Propose and develop plans (Plan of Action) to address an identified problem.
- Enact their Take Action plan.

Standards and Standards Integration:

National Council for the Social Studies (NCSS—C3 Framework):

- D1.5.6-8. Determine the kinds of sources that will be helpful in answering compelling and supporting questions, taking into consideration multiple points of view represented in the sources.
- D2.Civ.14.6-8. Compare historical and contemporary means of changing societies and promoting the common good.
- D4.7.6-8. Assess their individual and collective capacities to take action to address local, regional, and global problems, taking into account a range of possible levers of power, strategies, and potential outcomes.

Next Generation Science Standard (NGSS):

- 5-ESS3-1. Obtain and combine information about ways individual communities use scientific ideas to protect the Earth's resources and environment.

Classroom Materials: Printed copies of 3-2-1 VTS, Chromebooks to research websites, view videos, and search for information, APPARTS strategy for analyzing sources (Author, Place and time, Prior knowledge, Audience, Reason, The main idea, Significance), laptop and screen projector for presentation of materials, and various art materials to create posters, infomercials, and other visuals.

Socio-cultural Context:

Pollution takes on many forms: air pollution, carbon emissions, plastic and toxic waste, water pollution, and noise pollution. Some of these affect the immediate area in which students live. Students need to be aware of the dangers, potential solutions to immediate problems, and the actions they can take. Many organizations have been created to combat the destruction of the environment: United Nations' Community Action against Plastic Waste (CAPWs), Community Action Works, National Institute of Environmental Health Sciences, Environmental Consortium, World Resource Institute, Green America, and, of course, the United States Environmental Protection Agency, to name a few. These organizations offer support in determining present and future risks to people and the environment, providing statistical information to support claims, building action plans, offering policy support, and immediate actions that can make a difference.

Instructional Procedures:

Day 1: (1 class period)

Opening (15–20 minutes): Start by asking students to individually complete a 3-2-1 VTS. "Based on what we have learned in our study on Pollution in Our Community, list three things you learned, two things that you want to know more about, and one question that you still have." After they have completed the VTS, they will share with a neighbor. Students come back to the whole group. Call on students to share.

Determining Community Needs (25 minutes): What is the biggest environmental problem in the community? In the state? In our country? How do we go about addressing this problem? What additional information do we need to know? Are we considering both pros and cons of recycling? If so, how?

Students work in their design thinking groups to formulate answers. They will need to reference the Circle of Viewpoints they constructed in the Pollution in Our Community lesson. They then return to the whole group to share their ideas and determine if they are considering all viewpoints. Roundtable discussion strategies can be used to voice their ideas. After sharing, the teacher asks the groups to think about the feasibility of producing solutions that can be acted upon. The teacher then asks them to brainstorm areas of recycling, upcycling, and actions they can take that the class considers important to the community. Some potential topics are:

(a) recycling plastic, (b) recycling paper/litter, (c) recycling household hazardous waste, (d) upcycling instead of disposal, and (e) how to manage recycling efforts.

Closing (15 minutes): Students choose their group. These groups can be based on the answers to the earlier questions, specifically what they still need to know. Groups are formed, and the roles of the group members are determined (leader, recorder, monitor, and materials manager).

Day 2: Learning About the Work of Others (1 or 2 class periods)

Each group will explore recycling through researching websites, videos, and documents within their groups (see resource list of potential websites, videos, and documents). The inquiry process that students follow includes identifying diverse perspectives, analyzing sources using APPARTS, corroborating sources, making claims, and supporting their claims. Students will need 1 or 2 class periods to consume the information. After inquiries have concluded, each group will present what they learned to the whole group. Students will then identify cross-cutting themes that will be used in the Take Action lesson plan.

Day 3: Take Action (1 or 2 Class Periods)

Students will now think about what they can do as informed citizens (Plan of Action) to protect the environment. Groups will use what they learned during this lesson's inquiry section and any cross-cutting ideas presented by their peers. Students will choose the format for their Take Action project. These projects might include:

- Making a podcast, radio broadcast, or infomercial about their group's topic
- Creating a graphic novel about their topic
- Preparing presentations for other classes in the school and local community groups
- Leading a cleanup effort in their community
- Volunteering in recycling efforts
- Starting a recycling campaign/program

Day 4 (variable times)

Projects are enacted.

Assessment:

Formative Assessment: Teacher observations of discussions, presentations, group collaboration, 3-2-1 VTS, APPARTS documentation, and presentation of inquiry findings.

Summative Assessment: enactment of Take Action Project.

Accommodations/Modifications:

- Videos have closed captioning, or a text of the video will be available.
- Audiotapes of online articles will be available.
- Text-to-speech will be available for students who need assistance with writing or typing.

Socio-cultural Community Engagement:

Students will be designing and presenting their Take Action projects. These can be presented to other students, the faculty and administration of their school building, parents, and community groups.

Resources for Inquiries:

Recycling Plastic
The Story of Plastic Trailer https://youtu.be/37PDwW0c1so?si=WMn3HPDIjuDQU4ju
Solving Plastic Ep.1 https://youtu.be/rxDjEqGLK-s?si=Z-_fT6WZDbCxf5XF
Solving Plastic Ep.2 https://youtu.be/_L723Eu9UUI?si=ItZkpQ5cAfO6D2_Q
Solving Plastic Ep.3 https://youtu.be/P3eBeLTT4IY?si=JnxqISQ81MYzze6L
Solving Plastic Ep.4 https://youtu.be/0JzPwKoeWf8?si=mldk20sNaeqJD8Sc
Solving Plastic Story: True Solutions: https://youtu.be/xSMwV0nzb8M?si= -nDC6bUXmWMZ8WZY
Recycling and Waste https://www.treehugger.com/recycling-and-waste-4846074

Recycling Paper/litter
What paper products are recyclable? https://www.afandpa.org/whats-recyclable
Everything you need to know about paper recycling bit.ly/48St17j
How to recycle paper at home https://www.recycling.com/paper-recycling/
How is paper recycled? https://www.recyclenow.com/how-to-recycle/paper-recycling
Recycling and Waste https://www.treehugger.com/recycling-and-waste-4846074

Recycling Household Hazardous Waste
Hazardous waste recycling https://www.recyclenow.com/how-to-recycle/paper-recycling
Household Hazardous Waste https://www.epa.gov/hw/household-hazardous-waste-hhw
Household Hazardous Waste Disposal bit.ly/4cqZsNh
Recycling and Waste https://www.treehugger.com/recycling-and-waste-4846074

Upcycling
What is upcycling? https://www.treehugger.com/what-is-upcycling-5116081
What is upcycling? https://www.habitat.org/stories/what-is-upcycling
What is upcycling, and how it's good for the Earth https://www.rd.com/article/upcycling/

How to start and manage a recycling effort:
How to Start recycling at your school bit.ly/3TgjdxX
Recycling with us bit.ly/3PijGi8
How to Set Up a Recycling Program bit.ly/3Tzl6Gv

Other Resources:
American Forest & Paper Association (2023). *What paper products are recyclable?* Retrieved from https://www.afandpa.org/whats-recyclable

Habitat for Humanity (2023). *What is upcycling?*
Retrieved from bit.ly/3PfEQNO

Illinois Environmental Protection Agency (2023). *Household hazardous wastes.* Retrieved from bit.ly/4cqZsNh

Recycling.com (2023). *How to recycle paper?* Retrieved from https://www.recycling.com/paper-recycling/

Saint Louis City Recycles (2023). *Resources.*
Retrieved from bit.ly/3Txwq6T

Sukalich, K. (2023). *Everything you need to know about paper recycling.* Earth911.com. Retrieved from bit.ly/48St17j

Taubenfeld, E. (2023). *What is upcycling and how it's good for the Earth?* Reader's Digest.
Retrieved from https://www.rd.com/article/upcycling/

The Story of Stuff Project. (n.d.). *The story of plastic.* Retrieved from https://www.storyofstuff.org/

The Waste and Resources Action Programme. (n.d.). *How is paper recycled?* Retrieved from https://www.recyclenow.com/how-to-recycle/paper-recycling

Treehugger sustainability for all. (n.d.). *Recycling and waste.*
Retrieved from https://www.treehugger.com/recycling-and-waste-4846074

EXPERT OPINIONS

In addition to my ideas and those of the students who inspired these lessons, I called on two experts in the field of STEM and Social Sciences integration to share their thoughts on a socio-cultural-STEM integrative approach to curriculum development, Dr. Michael E. Karpyn and Nicholas Simmons. After reviewing the lesson plans, these experts provided answers to many questions that addressed the benefits, challenges, and implementation of socio-cultural understanding into middle level curriculum.

Benefits of Socio-cultural Integration in Social Sciences and STEM Curriculum

Michael Karpyn states that the integration of STEM issues, the social sciences, and civic education creates a richer educational experience. Specifically, these lessons enhance civic responsibilities, competencies, and thinking skills. Nicholas Simmons believes these lessons will promote student learning, allow students to exercise their thinking skills, see real-world events, and experience problems "that will challenge them to see through a different lens of learning." He also believes that this will "allow teachers to be more creative and adaptive to new learning standards."

Another point reviewers made concerned the idea that a socio-cultural STEM curriculum might lead to improved STEM learning outcomes. Simmons states that student learning increases in other fields through "inquiry-based strategies, discussion-based learning, comprehension skills, leadership, and organization skills." He suggests that students would receive more resources for problem-based projects, which allows them to see diverse perspectives and challenge their thinking.

Challenges of Socio-cultural Integration in Social Sciences and STEM Curriculum

According to Karpyn, teachers need to have cross-curricular understanding to implement these lessons. Social Science teachers need to understand the scientific concepts and content as well as design thinking processes, whereas science teachers need to understand the social science content and its inquiry skills, such as finding primary sources, building essential questions, and analyzing primary sources and diverse perspectives. This means that teachers will need to collaborate and teach lessons that support learning in other classrooms. For example, the local renewable energy lesson in a social science classroom would need to be scheduled in conjunction with or after lessons in energy in the science classroom. Karpyn adds that the curriculum at the middle level usually includes ancient history and U.S. History. Teachers may need to find ways to include these lessons within the U.S. History curriculum through civics and government.

Simmons is also an advocate of content integration and community involvement, and as such, he worked for two years to advocate for and implement integrative curricular changes. He concluded that it would take time and support from colleagues, administration, and the community. He suggests starting with a few lessons so that colleagues and the administration will "see how beneficial, engaging, and creative the process is and change their minds."

CONCLUSION

The world around us is changing rapidly. Middle school students need to be prepared to think about the challenges ahead. Socio-cultural theory suggests that students thrive in a culture of thinking (Ritchhart, 2015; Vygotsky, 1978) where teachers have elevated expectations, and engage and empower students, making students' thinking visible (Ritchhart et al., 2011). Using inquiry, allowing students to voice ideas and choose tasks, collaborating to build community connections, exposing diverse perspectives, and advocating for change allows students to become informed, active citizens in their community.

REFERENCES

American Association of Colleges of Teacher Education (AACTE). (September, 2010). *21st century knowledge and skills in educator preparation.* Retrieved from https://files.eric.ed.gov/fulltext/ED519336.pdf.

Beck, T. A. & Parker, W. C. (2022). *Social studies in the elementary school* (16th ed.). Pearson.

d.school. (2010). *An introduction to design thinking: Process guide.* Hasso Plattner Institute of Design. Stanford University.

Ritchhart, R. (2015). *Creating a culture of thinking: The eight forces we must master to truly transform our schools.* Jossey-Bass.

Ritchhart, R., Church, M., & Morrison, K. (2011). *Making thinking visible: How to promote engagement, understanding, and independence for all learners.* Jossey-Bass.

Vygotsky, L. S. (1978). *Mind in society: The development of higher psychological processes.* Harvard University Press.

Chapter 11

Using Socio-cultural STEM to Investigate Moral and Ethical Issues

Teaching Bioethics

Adam I. Attwood,
Donna F. Short, and Philip C. Short

The theme of this chapter centers on the topic of bioethics. Ethics, as a social studies concept, is connected here with the concept of applied bioethics in biochemical sciences. Discussion-based approaches are emphasized in this chapter's analysis of why and how to teach bioethics in the middle school classroom. This interdisciplinary approach explains how integrating social studies and science standards can be used in topics that address bioethics for middle school students. These content areas can provide students with an introductory understanding of how social media, environmental health and housing, public health policy, and medicine affect their lives and the lives of their families.

There has been a gap in addressing bioethics in secondary school science and social studies; bioethics was not listed as a concept of study in the National Research Council of the National Academies' (2012) *A Framework for K-12 Science Education: Practices, Crosscutting Concepts, and Core Ideas*. There have been calls for providing teaching and learning opportunities about bioethics for students in secondary schools (Araújo et al., 2017; Gutierez, 2015). Moreover, the National Council for the Social Studies' (NCSS, 2013) *The College, Career, and Civic Life (C3) Framework for Social Studies State Standards* does address ethics from both a humanities and social science perspective. Therefore, an interdisciplinary collaboration across science and social studies education can help to address the wide-ranging implications of bioethics in secondary schools.

OVERVIEW OF LESSON PLAN TOPICS AND CONTEXTS

Middle school students typically have ready access to a vast amount of entertainment media, much of which interfaces with social media. The sociocultural context of adolescence, then, is one influenced by popular entertainment films, television series, and online social media influencers. Despite this influence, it appears that students enter middle school having never heard of bioethics; it becomes important therefore to establish a historical context for learning in ways that interface with students' present contextual experiences. This [bioethics] contextualization process, Petersen (2013) suggests, is the application of a "sociology of bio-knowledge," in which practical implications of bioethics are discussed more than the foci of theoretical principles. For example, the *Jurassic Park* series has six films from the first in 1993 to the sixth in 2022, demonstrating the continued interest in American popular culture in the scientific concepts of genetics, genetic modification, and cloning. These films provide fictional, yet visceral, examples of some of the potential results of what could happen after reanimating and modifying dinosaur DNA. Given the popularity of these biochemical concepts, there could be additional discussions of the ethical implications of how commercial companies—such as the one in the first two *Jurassic Park* movies—might implement genetic manipulation on prehistoric or ancient DNA and what bioethical review process companies should use prior to performing experiments (Attwood, 2021).

Popular culture venues such as movies can be an entry point for generating student interest in discussing ethics and its relationship to science-related topics. Movies—such as *Erin Brockovich* (Soderbergh et al., 2000), based on the non-fiction, real-life events in advocating for protecting drinking water from pollution, and the 2017 movie *The Immortal Life of Henrietta Lacks,* based on Skloot's (2010) non-fiction book about the real-life events of the ethics of medical and research consent—can highlight public health ethics issues in engaging ways to promote discussion.

One teaching approach might focus on a discussion-based format in which students read a common set of articles, view relevant videos, and then develop responses to a set of questions using a range of sources. Using these responses, students could then discuss bioethics in a Socratic seminar format (Attwood, 2021), using, in part, a preparation assignment that introduces a bioethical framework, such as an adaptation of Pavarini et al.'s (2021) "design bioethics." Here, middle school students are given the opportunity to interact with an introduction to bioethical inquiry that practices active listening, synthesizing multiple sources from social studies and science, and integrating these content areas for an informed discussion of bioethics.

In practice, the Socratic seminar format, a popular approach to social studies education, provides students with opportunities to develop critical thinking skills valued in both social studies and science, such as raising good questions, gathering relevant information from multiple sources to further areas of inquiry, and developing information literacy. The Socratic seminar format also helps develop essential scientific and engineering practices, such as evaluating competing design solutions, constructing explanations, and predicting patterns.

The Next Generation Science Standards (NGSS Leads States, 2013), the NCSS's (2013) National Curriculum Standards for Social Studies, and the C3 Framework are all central to the teaching of bioethics. According to NGSS, ecosystems and biodiversity are important disciplinary core ideas for middle school students. Bioethics is not only directly related to these core content ideas but also is an ideal topic exemplifying connections between societal issues and science and technology. This connectedness is seen in Theme 8: Science, Technology, and Society of the NCSS standards, which requires teachers to draw upon several scholarly fields, including physical science, social science, and humanities.

The lesson plans presented in this chapter address a sample of issues that may be taught using interdisciplinary connections between science and social studies. Here, students are encouraged to see connections between a scientific concept and sociocultural context clues, noticing, for example why a concept may have differing perspectives or what these perspectives might mean for their civic responsibilities. Hahn and Inhorn's (2009) "case illustrations" (p. vii) portray the possibilities of social studies, such as anthropological evaluation methods that can help students understand and discuss public health issues.

LESSON PLANS AND RESOURCES

Lesson Plan 1

Title of Lesson: The Bioethics of Online Social Media

Theme:
This lesson is relevant to bioethics because of the prevalence of online social media in the lives of most students today, particularly due to the effect on the social cognitive development of youth (Attwood, 2020; Stieger & Wunderl, 2022). The NGSS standard that addresses "ecosystem services" is used broadly here to apply ecological systems theory (Bronfenbrenner, 2005) as a framework to address interconnected issues of physiological effects of events

and social interactions on people individually and across and within groups. Online social media is part of people's microsystem and macrosystem and, as such, is an influential part of the sociocultural ecosystem.

Grade Level:
This activity is best designed for students in grade levels: 7–8.

Essential and Supporting Questions:

- What is online social media? (Knowledge)
- How often do you use online social media, and how does it make you feel? (Health and Physiological Cognition)
- How does online social media affect socialization? (Social Cognition)
- Why does online social media affect political discourse individually and in groups? (Social Cognition and Civics)
- What are the civics implications of online social media for how it is or is not regulated? How should online social media be regulated? (Civics)

Time Required:
1 class period (block schedule) or 2 class periods on a shorter schedule.

Objectives: *Students will be able to*:

- define online social media.
- identify how online social media makes them feel and how often they engage with online social media.
- describe how online social media may affect socialization.
- explain why online social media affects political discourse.
- explain an implication of how online social media affects civics.
- explain a way in which online social media is or could be regulated.

Standards and Standards Integration:

- NCSS: D2.Civ.6.6-8. Describe the roles of political, civil, and economic organizations in shaping people's lives.
- NCSS: D3.1.6-8. Gather relevant information from multiple sources while using the origin, authority, structure, context, and corroborative value of the sources to guide the selection.
- NGSS: MS-LS2-5. Evaluate competing design solutions for maintaining biodiversity and ecosystem services.

Classroom Materials:
Computers with internet connectivity, presentation software, and a projector.

Socio-cultural Context:
While online social media originated in the 1990s, it did not become widely used until the smartphone became popular in 2007. Given this relatively recent timeline, studies of online social media use and its effects on individual and group physiological and mental health have increased substantially, although there have been differing conclusions about its use (Friesen & Lowe, 2012). Online social media has been demonstrated to have benefits for learning while also presenting challenges to behaviors such as socialization (Reid & Weigle, 2014; Uhls et al., 2017). It is perhaps not surprising that what might be viewed as inconclusive results of the aggregate of these studies, we note here that as with any tool, online social media use may vary, and may be used for a range of purposes; therefore it is not perhaps the tool—online social media—that is the problem, but instead it might be that the use of that tool interferes in ethical behaviors. Learning about online social media can help students understand how to use this tool responsibly and avoid the dangers or at least mitigate the risks of online social media usage.

Discussing online social media's potential effects is important for understanding how scientific processes are mediated by social constructs. The usage of online social media and its intersection of that usage with bioethics affect how people think about digital civics and its relationship to individual and group behavior. There have been substantial legislative efforts to regulate online social media usage (Asher-Schapiro, 2022; Kern, 2022). Developing an informed view of its use is important for students to practice.

Instructional Procedures:

1. Entry Task:
   a. Students watch a video on the topic of online social media from adolescents' perspectives (e.g., https://youtu.be/ottnH427Fr8) and answer these four questions for the Entry Task discussion: What is online social media? How can it affect people emotionally (part of physiological health)? What is a benefit? What is a risk? (5 minutes)
   b. Think-pair-share activity (5 minutes). Teacher explains physiological health and the potential effects of online social media.
2. Main Activity:
   a. Teacher gives students a copy of an article about online social media socialization and civics. The teacher reads aloud to the

whole class if modification is necessary. Screen readers may be used for the digital version. (The source can be modified by the teacher to shorten it, if necessary: pewrsr.ch/49x2i1d.) Answer the following questions: How do the authors discuss online social media's effect or potential effects on how you socialize? Do you use online social media the way the authors observed, or is there a difference between what they observed and how you use it? If there is a difference, why might that be? How does online social media affect feelings? How do the experiences the authors discuss affect the way you think online social media should or should not be regulated? (30 minutes)
   b. Introduce an example of state legislation regarding online social media usage regulation (e.g., reut.rs/4bRjsIx). The teacher reads this aloud with the article on the screen.
   c. Exit Task: Do you agree that regulation will help control political discourse and make it less extreme? Whole group discussion. (15 minutes)

Assessment:

Formative Assessment: Students write responses to an Entry Task question, the Main Activity questions, and the Exit Task question. These can be in students' paper or digital notebook and can be reviewed by the teacher. Any of these tasks could also be considered part of summative assessment.

Socio-cultural Community Engagement:

An additional question could be posed in which students are asked to consider how their family or local community is affected by online social media. A question could be posed that asks students to estimate how much time their family spends on online social media or what modality they use to get news. Students can use Edpuzzle (https://edpuzzle.com/) in class to answer questions posed on a brief video made by the teacher about an Essential Question designed for this lesson. This platform can be used on a laptop computer or on a smartphone via the Edpuzzle app. The Essential and Supporting Questions for this lesson plan can also be posted to the class website via the district's school page so that students' families can engage in the topic. The teacher can design an interview worksheet for students to optionally discuss these questions with their families.

Lesson Plan 2

Title of the Lesson: Environmental Health and Housing

Theme:
This topic is notable because of the prevalence of health-related issues that challenge access to and maintenance of resources such as water and housing. The NGSS standard that addresses "ecosystem services" is used broadly to apply ecological systems theory (Bronfenbrenner, 2005) as a framework to address interconnected issues of physiological effects of events and physiological interactions on people individually and across and within groups. Environmental health and its connection to housing is an element of the sociocultural ecosystem.

Grade Level:
This activity is best suited for students in grade levels: 6–8.

Essential and Supporting Questions:

- What is environmental health? (Knowledge)
- What is an example of the breakdown of health safety regulations affecting the environment and people's access to safe housing? (Health and Physiological Cognition)
- What are ways to protect people's housing and the environment near industrial sites? (Social Cognition and Civics)
- How is an understanding of civics important for fostering healthy environments? (Civics)

Time Required:
1 class period (block schedule) or 2 class periods on a shorter schedule.

Objectives: *Students will be able to*:

- define environmental health.
- identify an example of the breakdown of health safety regulations and the implications for why health regulations are important as a component of bioethics.
- explain a potential solution to protecting housing and the environment in a case where housing is near an industrial site.
- discuss an understanding of why civics is important for fostering healthy environments.

Using Socio-cultural STEM to Investigate Moral and Ethical Issues 185

Standards and Standards Integration:

- NCSS: D2.Civ.6.6-8. Describe the roles of political, civil, and economic organizations in shaping people's lives.
- NCSS: D3.1.6-8. Gather relevant information from multiple sources while using the origin, authority, structure, context, and corroborative value of the sources to guide the selection.
- NCSS: D2.His.12.6-8. Use questions generated about multiple historical sources to identify further areas of inquiry and additional sources.
- NGSS: MS-LS2-2. Construct an explanation that predicts patterns of interactions among organisms across multiple ecosystems.

Class Materials:
Computers with internet connectivity, presentation software, projector.

Socio-cultural Contexts:
There have been several major environmental disasters affecting drinking water and housing in the United States. For example, what became known as the "Flint Water Crisis" had critical adverse effects on the entire municipal drinking water system of Flint, Michigan, for years (Denchak, 2018; Green, 2019). The chemical spill from a train derailment in East Palestine, Ohio, caused an entire city to be evacuated and affected the region downwind from the explosion of the rail cars carrying toxic chemicals (Eavis et al., 2023). These are just two examples of what can happen when there is a breakdown in health and safety regulations or a lack of oversight to enforce regulations that are already technically in place. Complicating this issue, are suggestions that there were insufficient regulations and oversight of the regulations that did exist at the time of these events (Denchak, 2018; Eavis et al., 2023; Green, 2019).

These events highlight the importance of students learning about their potential roles as engaged citizens who can use evidence-based discussion skills to address health-related issues using science and social studies literacies. Practicing reading texts about these events as case studies and discussing them together with peers and their teachers can help students develop their ability to influence sociopolitical processes and discuss health issues related to the regulation of materials that potentially affect their environment.

Instructional Procedures:

1. Entry Task:
    a. Students watch a video on the topic of environmental health (e.g., https://youtu.be/I7STZsY_-Ps, "How the Environment Affects Our

Health," by the CDC) and answer these two questions for the Entry Task discussion: What is environmental health? What is one way the environment affects your health? (5 minutes)
   b. Think-pair-share activity. (5 minutes)
2. Main Activity:
   a. Teacher provides students with a copy of an article about environmental health as an ecological issue. The teacher can read aloud to the whole class if modification is necessary. Screen readers may be used for the digital version. (Source should be modified by the teacher to shorten it as necessary, "Water on Tap: What You Need to Know" by the EPA: bit.ly/48FgC6m.) Answer questions and cite the text at least once for evidence: How do the authors discuss environmental health as it relates to water? What patterns do you see in how civic policy affects environmental ecosystems? How is the protection of drinking water a bioethics issue? How can regulations and oversight be designed to address the protection of municipal drinking water to help establish and enforce bioethical conduct from companies and government agencies? (30 minutes)
   b. Introduce an example of state legislation regarding drinking water regulation, especially the case study of Flint, Michigan (e.g., reut.rs/4c0tbfq). The teacher reads this aloud with the article on the screen.
   c. Exit Task: What steps are needed to ensure safe drinking water for Flint, Michigan? Whole group discussion. (15 minutes)

Assessment:

Formative Assessment: Students write their responses to the Entry Task questions, the Main Activity questions, and the Exit Task question. These can be found in their paper or digital notebooks and reviewed by the teacher. Any of these tasks could also be considered part of summative assessment.

Socio-cultural Community Engagement:

An additional question could be posed in which students are asked to consider how their family or local community is affected by municipal water. A question could be posed that asks students to estimate how their local government regulates drinking water. Students can use Edpuzzle (https://edpuzzle.com/) in class to answer questions posed on a brief teacher-created video about the Essential Question for this lesson. This platform can be used on a laptop computer or on a smartphone via the Edpuzzle app. The Essential and Supporting Questions for this lesson plan can also be posted to the class website via the district's school page so that students' families can engage in this topic. An interview worksheet can be designed for students to optionally discuss these questions with their families.

Lesson Plan 3
Title of the Lesson: Public Health Policy

Theme:
Health-related issues and the need for access to health care are increasingly important topics. An NGSS standard notes that "ecosystem services" can be used broadly to apply ecological systems theory (Bronfenbrenner, 2005) as a framework to address interconnected issues of physiological effects of events (such as health care) and physiological interactions on individuals within groups. This importance is seen in Auld's 2020 notation that health policy-related education for K-12 students is a critical issue for the continued well-being of our nation.

Education, therefore, is essential for an individual's health, as education is itself an element of public health (Center on Society and Health, 2015). It is not surprising, then, that public health policy, as a macrosystem concept, affects an individual's microsystem.

Grade Level: This activity is best suited for students of the following grade levels: 6-8.

Essential and Supporting Questions:

- What is public health? (Knowledge)
- What is an example of access to health care? (Health and Physiological Cognition)
- What are ways to protect people's access to health care? (Social Cognition and Civics)
- How is an understanding of civics important for fostering effective public health policy? (Civics)

Time Required:
1 class period (block schedule) or 2 class periods on a shorter schedule.

Objectives: *Students will be able to:*

- define public health.
- explain an example of health care access.
- identify ways to protect access to health care as a component of bioethics.
- discuss how civics supports processes for establishing and reviewing public health policies.

Standards and Standards Integration:

- NCSS: D2.Civ.6.6-8. Describe the roles of political, civil, and economic organizations in shaping people's lives.
- NCSS: D3.1.6-8. Gather relevant information from multiple sources while using the origin, authority, structure, context, and corroborative value of the sources to guide the selection.
- NGSS: MS-LS2-5. Evaluate competing design solutions for maintaining biodiversity and ecosystem services.

Classroom Materials:
Computers with internet connectivity, presentation software, and a projector.

Socio-cultural Context:
Public health policy is part of social studies literacy, as it overlaps with medicine and related health civics. According to Columbia University Mailman School of Public Health (2021), "Public health policy is defined as the laws, regulations, actions, and decisions implemented within society in order to promote wellness and ensure that specific health goals are met" (p. 2). Numerous issues within a public health policy context affect education; example topics include dropout rates (Freudenberg & Ruglis, 2007) and the importance of physical education classes on cardiovascular health outcomes (Hills et al., 2015). Discussions about scientific issues associated with public policy are related to the power of social constructs and political ideology and their effect on local culture. These discussions suggest the crucial importance of social studies perspectives on how public policies are viewed and what cultural aspects influence decision-making related to governmental regulation of public health policies (Hahn & Inhorn, 2008). In a pluralistic society, there might not be a clear national consensus on public health policy, resulting in regional outlooks that require substantial diplomatic awareness of individual and group beliefs and the need for scientific literacy. It is important, therefore, to foster an understanding of civics in middle school in a manner that integrates social studies concepts with the sciences.

Instructional Procedures:

1. Entry Task
   a. Students watch a video on environmental health (e.g., https://youtu.be/t_eWESXTnic, "What is Public Health") and answer these three questions for the Entry Task discussion: What is public health? What is one way to describe or identify a public health policy? Why is public health policy a part of civics? (5 minutes)

b. Think-pair-share activity. (5 minutes)
2. Main Activity
   a. Teacher provides students a copy of an article about environmental health as an ecological issue. Screen readers may be used for the digital version. (Source should be modified by the teacher to shorten it as necessary, "School Health Guidelines" by the CDC: https://www.cdc.gov/healthyschools/npao/strategies.htm). Tell students to read only the first three Guidelines of "School Health Guidelines at a Glance": Healthy Eating and Physical Activity, School Environments, and Quality School Meal Program. Answer questions and cite the text at least once for evidence: How does the CDC identify and explain what it thinks is important public health policy for public schools? Why might there be disagreement about the CDC guidelines? How can issues related to public health affecting schools be examined as part of civics to develop guidelines? (30 minutes)
   b. The teacher introduces an example of a public health discussion from *The New York Times* (e.g., nyti.ms/3P0gZ4A). The teacher reads the text aloud with the article posted on a screen.
   c. Exit Task: What are two key takeaways you have about what is important about public health policy as a civic responsibility from the article? Whole group discussion. (15 minutes)

Assessment:
Formative Assessment: Students write their responses to the Entry Task questions, the Main Activity questions, and the Exit Task question in their paper or digital notebook for review by the teacher. These tasks could also be considered part of summative assessment.

Socio-cultural Community Engagement:
Additional questions could be posed in which students are asked to consider how public health policy affects their neighborhood. Questions such as: How far away is the nearest grocery store? Should the cafeteria offer foods high in refined sugar? Students will use Edpuzzle (https://edpuzzle.com/) in class to answer questions posed on a brief video made by the teacher about the Essential Question for this lesson. This platform is accessible at Edpuzzle and can be used on a laptop computer or on a smartphone via the Edpuzzle app. The Essential and Supporting Questions for this lesson plan can also be posted to the class website via the district's school page so that students' families can engage in class topics. The teacher can design an interview worksheet for students to optionally discuss these questions with their families.

Lesson Plan 4

Title of the Lesson: Access to Medicine for the Individual and the Community

Theme:

This topic highlights the importance of how knowledge about medical choice affects health access. Ecological systems theory links access to medical care to broader social constructs such as public health policy, environmental health, and individual and community sociocultural ecosystems.

Grade Level: This activity is best suited for students of the following grade levels: 7-8.

Essential and Supporting Questions:

- What is ethical medical practice? (Knowledge)
- What is an example of how medical practice functions in the United States? (Health and Physiological Cognition)
- What are ways to protect access to medical services? (Social Cognition and Civics)
- How is an understanding of civics important for understanding people's access to medical services? (Civics)

Times Required:
1 class period (block schedule) or 2 class periods on a shorter schedule.

Objectives: *Students will be able to:*

- define ethical medical practice.
- identify an example of how medical practice functions in the United States.
- explain how to protect access to medical services.
- discuss how civic responsibility is important for ensuring access to medical services.

Standards and Standards Integration:

- NCSS: D2.Civ.6.6-8. Describe the roles of political, civil, and economic organizations in shaping people's lives.

- NCSS: D3.1.6-8. Gather relevant information from multiple sources while using the origin, authority, structure, context, and corroborative value of the sources to guide the selection.
- NGSS: MS-LS2-5. Evaluate competing design solutions for maintaining biodiversity and ecosystem services.

Socio-cultural Context:
The practice of medicine typically operates within a cultural context that is predicated on the linearity of the scientific method. Intercultural communication or training can be an important component in physician effectiveness. Rosenberg et al. (2006) argue that there is a distinction between interpersonal and intercultural encounters in the physician-to-patient relationship. Some studies suggest the importance of intercultural literacy for clinicians to provide consistent and effective clinical practice, particularly in pluralistic societies.

For example, it can be important to cultivate active listening with a patient to gain an understanding of individual physiology (Malau-Aduli et al., 2019; Torri, 2012). Introducing multicultural literacy to middle school students is an important component of the C3 Framework and supports the premise of bioethics education. Cultural awareness and valuing multicultural competency are skills that should be fostered early in students' schooling and emphasized in middle school in preparation for civic responsibilities such as culturally responsive medical practice. The Pennsylvania State University College of Medicine (2023) notes the importance of including culturally responsive health care as a dimension of caring for patients from diverse populations. Medical education is adapting cultural responsiveness to clinical practice to enhance patient well-being (Brottman et al., 2020).

Instructional Procedures:

1. Entry Task:
    a. Students watch a video on medicine in a social context (e.g., https://youtu.be/6c8BCZd6GXU, "Relating Social Theories to Medicine" by the Khan Academy) and answer these two questions for the Entry Task discussion: What is medicine? What is one way medicine is affected by culture? (5 minutes)
    b. Think-pair-share activity. (5 minutes)
2. Main Activity:
    a. Teachers provide students with a copy of an article about environmental health as an ecological issue. The teacher might read aloud to the whole class if modification is necessary. Screen readers may

be used for a digital version. (The source could be modified by the teacher to shorten it as necessary, see, for example, "Is This Legit? Accessing Valid and Reliable Health Information" by the National Institute on Drug Abuse: bit.ly/3V1aq5Q.) Students may answer questions and cite the text at least once to provide evidence, including topics such as: How do the authors discuss health literacy? What are ways to identify legitimate health-related information? How can regulations and oversight be designed to address the protection of medical information in ways that remain culturally responsive? (30 minutes)
  b. Teachers introduce an example of culturally responsive health care using a story from *The New York Times* (e.g., nyti.ms/49qCnbr). The teacher reads this aloud along with the article on the screen.
  c. Exit Task: How is cultural responsiveness in health care demonstrated in this story? Write a culturally responsive statement that reflects a bioethics statement based on this story about how a patient should be consulted by the healthcare provider. Follow this writing with a whole-group discussion. (15 minutes)

Assessment:
Formative Assessment: Students write their responses to the Entry Task questions, the Main Activity questions, and the Exit Task question. These can be entered in their paper or digital notebooks and reviewed by the teacher. These tasks could also be considered part of summative assessment.

Socio-cultural Community Engagement:
An additional question could be posed in which students are asked to consider the location of the nearest hospital or clinic in their community. Students will use Edpuzzle (https://edpuzzle.com/) in class to answer questions posed on a brief video made by the teacher on the Essential Question for this lesson. This platform can be used on a laptop computer or on a smartphone via the Edpuzzle app. The Essential and Supporting Questions for this lesson plan can also be posted to the class website via the district's school page so that students' families can engage in these topics. The teacher can design an interview worksheet for students to optionally discuss these questions with their families.

EXPERT OPINIONS

The chapter authors asked several science teachers and teacher educators how the four lesson plans presented in this chapter might be received in school districts. Crystal Tebbe, science teacher and science club advisor at Fairbanks

High School in Milford Center, Ohio, explained the benefits and challenges that these lesson plans present. Jonathan Hall, assistant professor of science education at California State University, San Bernardino, explained the benefits and challenges of these plans from the perspective of science teacher educators. Insights were also discussed between the chapter co-authors in consideration of interdisciplinary approaches to bioethics.

Benefits of Socio-cultural STEM Curriculum

Authentic curriculum design is a major aspect of socio-cultural STEM teaching and learning; social diversity is a major consideration of biodiversity. Collaboration between science teachers and social studies teachers may additionally expand on these topics. Crystal Tebbe noted:

> Students participating in a socio-cultural STEM curriculum will have an added benefit of seeing STEM as cross curricular. Traditionally, subjects are separated into their individual silos and students, especially younger students, fail to connect them. Utilizing these real-life connections and specifying the connections between disciplines should help students better apply the content to life. For instance, in my current position, we are integrating Authentic Learning into our curriculum which is making teachers incorporate more real-life connections.

When we consider the correlation of STEM education with socio-cultural curriculum, we can begin to see the potential for in-depth and meaningful outcomes for learning experiences. If educators' training includes methods of incorporating students' socio-cultural perspectives and experiences, then a STEM curriculum can be framed as applicable and connected to a range of students. Tebbe notes the authenticity of an interdisciplinary curriculum as:

> I think this approach lends itself to creating more connections between content areas and allows for more context. The curriculum also makes the content more accessible by humanizing it. Both context and humanization give students more opportunities to internalize the material and see that it does, in fact, apply to them.

Both teacher educators and teachers have a considerable mission as they teach information literacy to their students. This mission prompts the question: What are the benefits of socio-cultural STEM education? Science is not a sterile or disconnected topic from an individual's daily life. Other questions about information literacy may emerge, for example, questions such as: (a) Is it possible to do science and ignore the socio-cultural context in which the science is being done? (b) What could possibly be the purpose of scientific efforts if not to better understand the tangible, universal principles that impact our species? and (c) How can we use socio-scientific understandings to better sustain the equitable welfare of our environment?

Foundational to this discussion of the benefits of socio-cultural STEM, then, is the pivotal role of diverse cultures in strengthening STEM education. We and others (e.g., Rudolph, 2020) note therefore that science education does have a moral purpose. Socio-cultural STEM education aims to equitably engage students in science-related social issues relevant to the diversity of their individual and communities' lives. Science concepts, perceived as complex, can become more understandable as they are grounded in the complexity of individual and personal meaning. Parents, always supportive of their children, and communities can change attitudes and actions when students engage in new and germane scientific understandings.

Challenges to Implementation

A STEM curriculum can sometimes appear to contrast with a socio-cultural curricular approach; therefore, careful planning is essential to ensure alignment across science and social studies learning standards. An overly rigid process of curriculum mapping with specifically timed outcomes may limit the successful implementation of a socio-cultural STEM curriculum. Best practices for accomplishing such a curriculum require an emphasis on critical thinking about the breadth of understanding central to an issue. Students can influence their own learning through experiencing personal and local problems and challenges.

One challenge to this curricular innovation, Tebbe writes is time: "The biggest challenge teachers face is TIME. There is no time built into the schedule that allows teachers to collaboratively plan out meaningful lessons that span content areas." Logistical tension in curricular implementation between what school districts can do within a very limited amount of time is an important consideration. The issue of how to empower teachers to innovate for their students is an additional challenge to implementation. In part, educator preparation programs (EPPs) can support teacher candidates and in-service teachers with curriculum design and implementation training; school administrators can seek ways to support teachers in incorporating socio-cultural STEM.

The social context of science could face political pressures. Teachers developing curriculum must navigate both district policy and local culture. Personal experience and the extant literature indicate that socio-cultural education can gain support and assistance from the larger community. Tebbe notes: "Many aspects of authentic learning and of a socio-cultural STEM curriculum land in this realm." Tebbe continues: "I do think this would be supported by teachers, so long as they are given proper support of time, flexibility, and compensation for developing the material." Jonathan Hall also notes:

> Teachers will need time to rehearse the lessons and receive feedback. They may want to work with educators who have implemented this type of curriculum. Since there are several social science standards, opportunities for collaboration should be facilitated.

Short (2009) suggests that an educator must try to present information objectively while balancing the "advocate" perspective as well as encouraging discussions sensitive to local culture and student perspectives. Hall notes that one of the challenges associated with the socio-cultural STEM curriculum is understanding how to lead lessons on sensitive issues that might deeply impact students. Teachers need to be aware of how students might respond to controversial issues. The lesson plans presented in this chapter provide insight into the topic of bioethics and quality of life. These lesson plans provide an initial basis for interdisciplinary collaboration between social studies and science.

CONCLUSION

The theme of bioethics is a topic underscored by teaching students to investigate moral and ethical issues. Interdisciplinary collaboration between social studies and science teachers is important in maximizing the effectiveness of teaching bioethics to middle school students. Online social media, housing, public health policy, and access to medicine and professional medical care are interrelated topics. Planning the curriculum with intentional interdisciplinary collaboration may present multiple benefits for student learning and encourage engagement in the topic of bioethics.

REFERENCES

Araújo, J., Gomes, C. C., Jácomo, A., & Pereira, S. M. (2017). Teaching bioethics in high schools. *Health Education Journal, 76*(4), 507–13. https://doi.org/10.1177/0017896917690566.

Asher-Schapiro, A. (2022, June 16). Analysis: U.S. states take center stage in battles for control over social media. *Reuters.* reut.rs/4bRjsIx.

Attwood, A. I. (2020). Changing social learning theory through reliance on the Internet of Things and artificial intelligence. *Journal of Social Change, 12,* 103–11. https://doi.org/10.5590/JOSC.2020.12.1.08.

Attwood, A. I. (2021). A perspective on the educational psychological value of *Jurassic Park* and similar films for bioethics discussions. *Frontiers in Education, 6*, 1–6. https://doi.org/10.3389/feduc.2021.618725.

Auld, M. E., Allen, M. P., Hampton, C., Montes, J. H., Sherry, C., Mickalide, A. D., Logan, R. A., Alvarado-Little, W., & Parson, K. (2020). Health literacy and health education in schools: Collaboration for action. *NAM Perspectives*, 1–13. https://doi.org/10.31478/202007b.

Bronfenbrenner, U. (2005). Ecological systems theory (1992). In U. Bronfenbrenner (Ed.), *Making human beings human: Bioecological perspectives on human development* (pp. 106–73). Sage.

Brottman, M. R., Char, D. M., Hattori, R. A., Heeb, R., & Taff, S. D. (2020). Toward cultural competency in health care: A scoping review of the diversity and inclusion education literature. *Academic Medicine, 95*(5), 803–13. https://doi.org/10.1097/ACM.0000000000002995.

Center on Society and Health. (2015, February 13). *Why education matters to health: Exploring the causes* [Issue Brief]. Virginia Commonwealth University. bit.ly/3V39eP8.

Columbia University Mailman School of Public Health. (2021, May 6). *Public health policy: Definition, examples, and more.* bit.ly/49Bnxii.

Denchak, M. (2018, November 8). *Flint water crisis: Everything you need to know.* Natural Resources Defense Council. on.nrdc.org/49BfUIJ.

Eavis, P., Walker, M., & Chokshi, N. (2023, March 7). Rail heat sensors, under scrutiny in Ohio crash, face few regulations. *The New York Times.* nyti.ms/3P2X70M.

Friesen, N., & Lowe, S. (2012). The questionable promise of social media for education: Connective learning and the commercial imperative. *Journal of Computer Assisted Learning, 28*(3),183–94. https://doi.org/10.1111/j.1365-2729.2011.00426.x.

Freudenberg, N., & Ruglis, J. (2007). Reframing school dropout as a public health issue. *Preventing Chronic Disease, 4*(4), A107. bit.ly/3P35pWw.

Green, E. L. (2019, November 6). Flint's children suffer in class after years of drinking the lead-poisoned water. *The New York Times.* nyti.ms/3UZW0Ta.

Gutierez, S. (2015). Integrating socio-scientific issues to enhance the bioethical decision-making skills of high school students. *International Education Studies, 8*(1), 142–51. https://doi.org/10.5539/ies.v8n1p142.

Hahn, R. A., & Inhorn, M. C. (Eds.). (2009). *Anthropology and public health: Bridging differences in culture and society* (2nd ed.). Oxford University Press.

Hills, A. P., Dengel, D. R., & Lubans, D. R. (2015). Supporting public health priorities: Recommendations for physical education and physical activity promotion in schools. *Progress in Cardiovascular Diseases, 57*(4), 368–74. https://doi.org/10.1016/j.pcad.2014.09.010.

Kern, R. (2022, July 1). Push to rein in social media sweeps the states. *Politico.* politi.co/3V6bYeR.

Malau-Aduli, B. S., Ross, S., & Adu, M. D. (2019). Perceptions of intercultural competence and institutional intercultural inclusiveness among first year medical students: A 4-year study. *BMC Medical Education, 19*, 346. https://doi.org/10.1186/s12909-019-1780-y.

National Center for Education Statistics. (2023). *Characteristics of public school teachers* [Report]. U.S. Department of Education, Institute of Education Sciences. https://nces.ed.gov/programs/coe/pdf/2023/clr_508.pdf.

National Council for the Social Studies [NCSS]. (n.d.a). *National curriculum standards for social studies: Introduction.* bit.ly/3wzdo7o.

National Council for the Social Studies (NCSS). (2013). *College, Career, & Civic Life, C3 Framework for Social Studies State Standards.*

NGSS Lead States. (2013). *Next Generation Science Standards: For States, By States.* The National Academies Press.

National Research Council of the National Academies. (2012). *A framework for K-12 science education: Practices, crosscutting concepts, and core ideas.* The National Academies Press. https://nap.nationalacademies.org/read/13165/chapter/1.

Pavarini, G., McMillan, R., Robinson, A., & Singh, I. (2021). Design bioethics: A theoretical framework and argument for innovation in bioethics research. *The American Journal of Bioethics, 21*(6), 37–50. https://doi.org/10.1080/15265161.2020.1863508.

Pennsylvania State University College of Medicine. (2023). *Office for Culturally Responsive Healthcare Education.* https://students.med.psu.edu/academics/culturally-responsive-health-care-education/.

Petersen, A. (2013). From bioethics to a sociology of bio-knowledge. *Social Science & Medicine, 98,* 264–70. https://doi.org/10.1016/j.socscimed.2012.12.030.

Reid, D., & Weigle, P. (2014). Social media use among adolescents: Benefits and risks. *Adolescent Psychiatry, 4*(2), 73–80. https://doi.org/10.2174/221067660402140709115810.

Rosenberg, E., Richard, C., Lussier, M.-T., & Abdool, S. N. (2006). Intercultural communication competence in family medicine: Lessons from the field. *Patient Education and Counseling, 61*(2), 236–45. https://doi.org/10.1016/j.pec.2005.04.002.

Rudolph, J. L. (2020). The lost moral purpose of science education. *Science Education, 104*(5), 895–906. https://doi.org/10.1002/sce.21590.

Short, P. C. (2009). Responsible environmental action: Its role and status in environmental education and environmental quality. *The Journal of Environmental Education, 41*(1), 7–21. https://doi.org/10.1080/00958960903206781.

Skloot, R. (2010). *The immortal life of Henrietta Lacks.* Crown.

Soderbergh, S. (Director), DeVito, D. (Producer), Shamberg, M. (Producer), Sher, S. (Producer), & Grant, S. (Writer). (2000). *Erin Brockovich.* Universal Pictures.

Stieger, S., & Wunderl, S. (2022). Associations between social media use and cognitive abilities: Results from a large-scale study of adolescents. *Computers in Human Behavior, 135.* https://doi.org/10.1016/j.chb.2022.107358.

Torri, M. C. (2012). Intercultural health practices: Towards an equal recognition between indigenous medicine and biomedicine? A case study from Chile. *Health Care Analysis, 20,* 31–49. https://doi.org/10.1007/s10728-011-0170-3.

Uhls, Y. T., Ellison, N. B., & Subrahmanyam, K. (2017). Benefits and costs of social media in adolescence. *Pediatrics, 140*(Supplement 2): S67–S70. https://doi.org/10.1542/peds.2016-1758E.

APPENDICES

Appendix A

Content Domain Learning Standards and Resources

Social Studies: National Council for the Social Studies (NCSS)
https://drive.google.com/file/d/1T7Z_JwpVjEmUeej2kYsaJtcqYMLoNSXS/view?usp=sharing

Science: Next Generation Science Standards (NGSS)
https://www.nextgenscience.org/

Math: National Council of Teachers of Mathematics (NCTM)/Common Core State Standards-Mathematics (CCSSM)
https://www.nctm.org/ccssm/

Engineering: American Society for Engineering Education (ASEE)
https://p12framework.asee.org/

Technology: The International Society for Technology in Education (ISTE)
https://www.iste.org/standards/iste-standards-for-students

Art: National Coalition for CORE ARTS Standards
https://www.nationalartsstandards.org/

Music: National Association for Music Education (NAME)
https://nafme.org/my-classroom/standards/core-music-standards/

English: National Council of Teachers of English (NCTE)
https://ncte.org/resources/standards/ncte-ira-standards-for-the-english-language-arts/

Appendix B

Lesson Plan Template

Title of Lesson	Title:
	Theme: Why did you choose this topic/event?
	What makes it important as a topic?
Grade Level	This activity is best suited for students of the following grade levels.
Essential and Supporting Question(s)	Pose an essential question(s) and supporting questions related to the lesson topic.
Time Required	Estimate the approximate length of time needed to complete this lesson.
Objective(s)	List one or more objectives specialized to this lesson (e.g., observation, identify different perspectives or viewpoints, map skills, make comparisons) Use the SWBAT language to identify your outcomes.
Standards **Standards Integration**	Your lesson should reference an integration of National Content Standards across domain areas: • Provide Social Studies Standards related to your Topic. • Provide STEM Standard(s) related to your Topic.
Classroom Materials	List classroom materials, equipment and technology used in this lesson.
Socio-cultural Context	Provide a 1-2 paragraph narrative about the socio-cultural and historical background of the lesson topic.
Instructional Procedures	Use this section to list the steps you will use as you teach this lesson: • List each *instructional procedure used in this lesson*. • Describe the implementation of each procedure using clear, direct language.

Appendix B

Student Inquiry	• Describe how this lesson will engage students in inquiry, developing knowledge, making interpretations, thinking critically, and becoming aware of challenges across Social Studies and STEM content areas.
	• Include strategies for students to communicate conclusions based on evidence and take action (if possible).
	NOTE: The following coding system is *only* a guide for the development of the instructional procedure description section. The codes are not needed in the plan.
	    o I = Inquiry
	    o K = Knowledge
	    o TC = Make interpretations or think critically
	    o A = Awareness of issues (local, global) or diverse perspectives
	    o C = Communication with small or whole group
	    o E = Use of evidence to support conclusions

Assessment	Describe how learning will be assessed. Provide information about formative and summative assessments about how you will evaluate student knowledge and understanding of lesson objectives.
Socio-cultural Community Engagement	How will you include socio-cultural perspectives of parents, colleagues, and students in this lesson?

Appendix C

Sample Letter to Parents/Caregivers and Community

Dear Community:

The teacher-teams at River Middle School are preparing a curriculum unit in which we will integrate STEM (Science, Technology, Engineering, & Mathematics) *along with* Social Studies and the Humanities to develop our unit topic: *Community Sustainability. Please join us* in the development of this unit by communicating your knowledge and cultural experiences to our teacher-teams.

What could you contribute? We are seeking your ideas about what we might need in order to sustain and expand our community as a vibrant and cost-effective place to live and work. Please contribute your suggestions, photos, stories, experiences, content knowledge, expectations, texts such as newspaper articles, book titles, websites and links.

Share your personal expertise and experiences. Do you have mechanical or technological experience? Do you have experience setting up websites or use of other platforms to disseminate information? Are you familiar with how machines work? Have you served on community finance or fundraising committees? Have you worked in human services such as nursing? Do you have hands-on experience with land, food, or animal management? Can you provide a description of a social or cultural community need such as food banks, transportation, or musical events?

Please use this online platform to send information and connect with us.

List platform link and instructions here.
Thank you for joining us in this collaborative effort!
The 7th grade teacher team
River Middle School

Index

action: informed, 87. *See also* taking action (lesson plan)
acupuncture, 113, 114
adolescence, 16
affinity map, 86
after-school model, 18
American Society for Engineering Education (ASEE), 11
AMLE. *See* Association for Middle Level Education
Analysis Tool, 167
ancient art, 122–26
ancient art (lesson plan): assessment of, 126; classroom materials for, 123; essential and supporting questions for, 122; instructional procedures for, 124–26; socio-cultural community engagement in, 126; socio-cultural context of, 123; standards integration in, 123
argumentation, scientific, 21
ASEE. *See* American Society for Engineering Education
assessment: of ancient art lesson plan, 126; of community pollution lesson plan, 169; of computers lesson plan, 88; of Eastern medicine lesson plan, 116; of environmental health lesson plan, 186; of e-textiles lesson plan, 143; of fashion robotics lesson plan, 135–36; of First Amendment Rights lesson plan, 139; of Hip Hop music lesson plan, 147; of Indigenous ways lesson plan, 121; of inquiry-based learning, 20–21; of local renewable energy lesson plan, 164; of medical access lesson plan, 192; of Polynesian voyages lesson plan, 110; of preservation lesson plan, 99; of public health policy lesson plan, 189; of renewable energy lesson plan, 66; of social media bioethics lesson plan, 183; of space collaboration lesson plan, 159; of taking action lesson plan, 173; of Typhoid Mary and disease lesson plan, 93; of water cycles lesson plan, 72; of watershed lesson plan, 76
Association for Middle Level Education (AMLE), 16
Atanasoff, John, 35
Ayurveda, 113

Beane, James, 15
bioethics, 180–81, 195
biofeedback, 115–16
blended learning, 149
Block, Herbert, 166
Bloom, Benjamin, 15
brainstorming, 5–6, 96

208 · Index

Career and Technical Education (CTE), 11, 148
case study: Māori and Language of Water, 72–73; Nile River, 75–76; Puebloan Cliff Dwellings, 65–67; Typhoid Mary, 91–92
CCSSM. *See* Common Core Standards in Mathematics
challenges: ancient art preservation, 125–26; global education, 59–60; identifying, 28–29; interdisciplinary team strategy, 17–19; socio-cultural STEM implementation, 79, 102–3, 149–51, 176, 194–95
chemical spills, 185
classroom level, 19–21
classroom materials: for ancient art lesson plan, 123; for community pollution lesson plan, 166; for computers lesson plan, 84; for Eastern medicine lesson plan, 112; for e-textiles lesson plan, 141–42; for fashion robotics lesson plan, 134; for First Amendment Rights lesson plan, 138; for Hip Hop music lesson plan, 146; for Indigenous ways lesson plan, 118; for local renewable energy lesson plan, 161; for Polynesian voyages lesson plan, 108; for preservation lesson plan, 96; for renewable energy lesson plan, 63; for social media bioethics lesson plan, 182; for space collaboration lesson plan, 156; for taking action lesson plan, 171–72; for water cycles lesson plan, 68–69; for watershed lesson plan, 74
Clean Air Act, 166
Clean Water Act, 166
climate change, 59
closure activity, 98–99
collaboration, xiii; in professional development, 18; space lesson plan, 155–60; technology linked with, 50–51

The College, Career, and Civic Life (C3) Framework for Social Studies State Standards, 178
Common Core Standards in Mathematics (CCSSM), 11, 19, 112, 118, 123
communities: contributions from, 49–50; needs determined for, 172–73; pollution in, 154; socio-cultural STEM at, 13–15; socio-cultural STEM for global, 22; STEM projects engaging, 15; sustainability concerns of, 28–29
community pollution (lesson plan), 164; assessment of, 169; classroom materials for, 166; essential and supporting questions for, 165; instructional procedures for, 166–69; modifications of, 169; resources for, 170; socio-cultural community engagement in, 169; socio-cultural context of, 166; standards integration in, 165–66
computer programming, 130
computers (lesson plan): assessment of, 88; classroom materials for, 84; instructional procedures in, 85–87; socio-cultural community engagement in, 88; socio-cultural context of, 84–85; standards integration in, 84; supporting questions in, 83
computer science (CS), 130
concept map, for investigations, 157–59
conferencing tools, 51
connection points, 35–36
connections, 44, 77–78
consolidation techniques, 124
content domain tools, 51
co-teaching, 16
counting machines, 83
COVID-19 pandemic, 141–43
creative communicator, 95
CS. *See* computer science

CTE. *See* Career and Technical Education
cultural funds of knowledge (FOK), 14
cultural heritage, 124
cultural knowledge, 3
curriculum: evaluating and revising, 42–43; implementing of, 41–42; input connections model for, 35–36; Node 5 implementing, *42*; Node 6 revising, 43, *43*; socio-cultural STEM benefits to, 101–2; socio-cultural STEM development of, 7, 13; socio-cultural STEM's integrative approach to, 6–7; socio-cultural STEM teaching of, 8; teacher's development of, 194–95; teacher teams goals for, 31–32; themes, 9, 30–32; units of study in, 34
curriculum development: content perspectives linked in, 39, *40*; definitions in, 27; feedback collected in, 39–40, *40*; Nodes in, 34–36; problems and questions in, 38–39, *39*

DaCast, 55
DCPS. *See* District of Columbia Public Schools
decision-making, scientific, 21
deep breathing exercises, 115
design project, of solar house, 64–65
Dewey, John, xiii, 15
disease, spreading, 82
dissemination, 44

EarSketch programming, 132, 144–48, 151
Earth: resources of, 63; water on surface of, 107
Earth Day, 166–67
Eastern medicine, 106; acupuncture, 114; classroom materials for, 112; herbal, 113–14; mind-body practices, 113–16; NGSS for, 112; overview of, 113
Eastern medicine (lesson plan): assessment of, 116; classroom materials for, 112; essential and supporting questions for, 111; instructional procedures in, 113; socio-cultural community engagement in, 116; socio-cultural context of, 113; standards integration in, 112
ecosystem services, 180–81, 184, 187
Edpuzzle app, 183, 186–87, 189
education, global challenges in, 59–60
educator preparation programs (EPPs), 194
Eduvision, 55
electrical inputs, 35
electric vehicles, 60
empathy, 167–68
energy transition, 60
engineering design process, 16–17
environmental health, 186
environmental health (lesson plan): assessment of, 186; essential and supporting questions for, 184; instructional procedures for, 185–86; socio-cultural community engagement in, 186–87; socio-cultural context of, 185; standards integration in, 185
Environmental Protection Agency (EPA), 166
EPPs. *See* educator preparation programs
Epstein, Joyce, 36
e-textiles, 130
e-textiles (lesson plan): assessment of, 143; classroom materials for, 141–42; essential and supporting questions for, 140; instructional procedures for, 142–43; socio-cultural community engagement in, 143; socio-cultural context of, 142; standards integration in, 141; student inquiries in, 143
ethical implications, 78–79
EthnoSTEM, 14
expert opinions, 192; ethical implications and, 78–79; on implementation

challenges, 102–3, 176, 194–95; on implementation considerations, 149–51; learning outcomes and, 78; real-world connections and, 77–78; on social sciences STEM curriculum, 175–76; on STEM, 126–28; on STEM curriculum benefits, 101–2, 148–49, 193–94

fashion, robotics in, 131
FashionBots, 131, 135
fashion robotics (lesson plan): assessment of, 135–36; classroom materials for, 134; essential and supporting questions for, 132–33; instructional procedures for, 134–35; socio-cultural community engagement in, 136; socio-cultural context of, 134; standards integration for, 133–34
feedback, 39–40, *40*
finalization, 45
First Amendment rights, 138
First Amendment Rights (lesson plan), 136; assessment of, 139; classroom materials for, 138; essential and supporting questions for, 137; instructional procedures for, 138–39; socio-cultural community engagement in, 139–40; socio-cultural context of, 138; standards integration in, 137–38; student inquires in, 139
5-3-1 discussion, 87
five-stage design thinking model, 20
flexible space, 38
Flint water crisis, 185
Flipgrid, 55
FOK. *See* cultural funds of knowledge
fossil fuels, 60
A Framework for K-12 Science Education, 178

gallery walk, 87
Gameplay, 136

Gardner, Howard, 15
gathering space, Nodes as, xiv, 8, 35–36
Gay, G., 14
genetically modified organisms (GMOs), 12
global communities, 22
global warming, 60
GMOs. *See* genetically modified organisms
Gordon, W. R., II, 27, 31, 38
Grant, S. G., 57
guided imagery, 115

health-related issues, 185, 187, 191–92
herbal medicine, 113–14
higher-order thinking, 19
Hip Hop music (lesson plan): assessment of, 147; classroom materials for, 146; essential and supporting questions for, 144; instructional procedures for, 146–47; socio-cultural community engagement in, 147–48; socio-cultural context of, 146; standards integration in, 145–46; student inquires in, 147
historical facts, 157
historical maps, 49
historical preservation investigation, 97
Hollerith Machine, 83

implementation, of socio-cultural STEM, 79, 102–3, 149–51, 176, 194–95
Indigenous ways, 106; introduction to, 118–19; technologies used in, 121; understanding of, 120; values of, 119–20
Indigenous ways (lesson plan): assessment of, 121; classroom materials for, 118; essential and supporting questions for, 117; instructional procedures for, 118–21; socio-cultural community

engagement in, 121; standards integration in, 117–18
information, collection of, 38
informed action, 87
initial development, 44
inquiry-based learning, 20–21
inquiry-based teaching, 19
Inquiry Design Model (Grant, Lee and Swan), 57
inquiry project, 97–98
instructional procedures: for ancient art lesson plan, 124–26; for community pollution lesson plan, 166–69; for computers lesson plan, 85–87; for environmental health lesson plan, 185–86; for e-textiles lesson plan, 142–43; for fashion robotics lesson plan, 134–35; for First Amendment Rights lesson plan, 138–39; for Hip Hop music lesson plan, 146–47; for Indigenous ways lesson plan, 118–21; for local renewable energy lesson plan, 162–63; for medical access lesson plan, 191–92; for Polynesian voyages lesson plan, 109–10; for preservation lesson plan, 96–97; for public health policy lesson plan, 188–89; for social media bioethics lesson plan, 182–83; for space collaboration lesson plan, 156–57; for taking action lesson plan, 172–73; for Typhoid Mary and disease lesson plan, 90–91
integration, 45
intelligent face mask, 132, 140–44
interactive platforms, 55
intercultural pedagogy, 105
interdisciplinary approach, 149
interdisciplinary project-based learning, 17
interdisciplinary team planning, 17–19
International Society for Technology in Education (ISTE), 54, 137–38, 141, 145; Eastern Medicine lesson plan and, 112; fashion robotics lesson plan and, 133; Indigenous ways lesson plan and, 118; as knowledge constructor, 89–90, 95
International Space Station (ISS), 154, 155–59
International Technology Education Association, 123
investigation, concept map for, 157–59
ISS. *See* International Space Station
ISTE. *See* International Society for Technology in Education
ITEEA STEL standards, 96

justice, 59

Keep America Beautiful, 166
Kennedy, John F., 81
Kilpatrick, William Heard, 15
knowledge constructor, 89–90, 95

Lafayette Park World (educational game), 131, 136–40
language development strategies, 153
learning: blended, 149; cultural knowledge and, 3; inquiry-based, 20–21; interdisciplinary project-based, 17; problem-based, 18, 20–21; project-based, xiii, 6–7, 17, 20–21, 28; teacher outcomes for, 78
lesson plans, 7, 57
Library of Congress (LOC), 53, 167
life experience, 29
LOC. *See* Library of Congress
local culture, 188, 194–95
local renewable energy (lesson plan): assessment of, 164; classroom materials for, 161; essential and supporting questions for, 160; instructional procedures for, 162–63; resources for, 164; socio-cultural community engagement in, 164; socio-cultural context of, 162; standards integration in, 161
Loom platform, 55

Mallon, Mary, 90, 92–93
The Man Who Invented the Computer (Smiley), 35
Māori and Language of Water case study, 72–73
maps, historical, 49
math data, 15–16
math-e-dol-ogy series, 50
mathematics, teachers of, 17, 49
McTighe, Jay, 30–31
medical access (lesson plan): assessment of, 192; essential and supporting questions for, 190instructional procedures for, 191–92; socio-cultural community engagement in, 192; socio-cultural context of, 191; standards integration in, 190–91
meditation, 115
middle school, xiii, 5
middle school students, 15–16; multi-cultural literacy for, 191; socio-cultural theory for, 176–77; water cycles and, 60–61
mind-body practices, 113–16
mindfulness, 115
Minecraft programming, 136–40, 151
modifications, 159, 169
multi-classroom model, 18
multi-cultural literacy, 191
muscle relaxation, 115
Music Standards (2014), 145–46
music therapy, 116

National Core Arts Standards, 133–34, 141
National Council for the Social Studies (NCSS), 81, 178; standards integration and, 83, 108, 134, 155–56, 161, 165–66, 171; thematic strands in, 89
National Council of Teachers of Mathematics (NCTM), 11, 54–55
National Curriculum Standards for Social Studies, 123, 138, 141, 145; Eastern Medicine and, 112; Indigenous ways and, 118; Polynesian voyages and, 107–8
National Defense Education Act, 81
National Endowment for the Arts (NEA), 54
National Endowment for the Humanities (NEH), 53
National Research Council (NRC), 11–12
National Research Council of the National Academies, 178
National Science Foundation (NSF), 54
NCSS. *See* National Council for the Social Studies
NCTM. *See* National Council of Teachers of Mathematics
NEA. *See* National Endowment for the Arts
NEH. *See* National Endowment for the Humanities
Nelson, Gaylord, 166
Next Generation Science Standards (NGSS), 11; bioethics and, 180; core ideas and concepts from, 19; on Earth's resources, 63; for Eastern medicine studies, 112; standards integration from, 107, 117, 123, 156, 161, 166, 171
Nile river case study, 75–76
Node 1, problems identified, *39*
Node 2, perspectives linked in, *40*
Node 3, feedback collected in, *40*
Node 4, participant responses analyzed in, *41*
Node 5, curriculum implemented in, *42*
Node 6, curriculum revisions, 43, *43*
Nodes: in curriculum development, 34–36; as gathering space, xiv, 8, 35–36; inputs to, 8–9; participant inputs into, 37; Pryor-Kang Model function of, 38; resource collection in, 47; socio-cultural STEM using, 36; video inputs in, 48–49
non-invasive techniques, 124
NRC. *See* National Research Council

NSF. *See* National Science Foundation
Nuthall, G., 4

Oliva, P. F., 38

Panopto platform, 55
parents, contributions from, 49–50
participant responses, 41
PBL. *See* Project-based Learning
phases, of Pryor-Kang Model, *37*, 37–43, 47–48
physical evidence, 29
physical preservation, 97
physical space, 19
POE. *See* Predict, Observe, and Experiment model
pollution, in communities, 154
Polynesian voyages, 106, 109–10
Polynesian voyages (lesson plan), 106; assessment of, 110; classroom materials for, 108; essential and supporting questions for, 107; instructional procedures for, 109–10; presentations and discussion of, 110; socio-cultural community engagement in, 111; socio-cultural context of, 108–9; standards integration in, 107–8
Predict, Observe, and Experiment (POE) model, 135, 139, 143
pre-recorded videos, 48
preservation (lesson plan): assessment of, 99; classroom materials for, 96; instructional procedures for, 96–97; resources for, 100–101; socio-cultural community engagement in, 99; socio-cultural context of, 96; standards integration in, 95–96; supporting questions for, 94
preservation, of ancient art, 124–26
problem-based learning, 18, 20–21
problems, in curriculum development, 38–39, *39*
problem-solving, 4–5, 28
professional development, 18

project-based learning (PBL), xiii, 6–7, 20–21; interdisciplinary, 17; problem-solving from, 28
Pryor-Kang Model, 57; input and output evaluation in, 43; model phase discussions of, 44–45; Nodes function in, 38; phase 1 of, 38–39; phase 2 of, 39; phase 3 of, 39–40; phase 4 of, 40; phase 5 of, 41–42; phase 6 of, 42–43; phases of, *37*, 37–43, 47–48; Socio-cultural STEM Curriculum Development Model and, xiv, 34–35; socio-cultural STEM impacted by, 36–38; team discussions on, 44–45
Pryor-Kang Socio-cultural Curriculum Development Model, 8
public health policy, 188–89
public health policy (lesson plan): assessment of, 189; essential and supporting questions for, 187 instructional procedures for, 188–89; socio-cultural community engagement in, 189; socio-cultural context of, 188; standards integration in, 188
Puebloan Cliff Dwellings case study, 65–67

Qi Gong, 115
questions: for ancient art lesson plan, 122; for community pollution lesson plan, 165; for computer lesson plan, 83; curriculum development with problems and, 38–39, *39*; curriculum theme developed with, 9, 30–32; for Eastern medicine lesson plan, 111; essential, 29; for e-textiles lesson plan, 140; for fashion robotics lesson plan, 132–33; for First Amendment Rights lesson plan, 137; for Hip Hop music lesson plan, 144; for Indigenous ways lesson plan, 117; for local renewable energy lesson plan, 160; for medical access lesson

plan, 190; for Polynesian voyages lesson plan, 107; for preservation lesson plan, 94; in problem-solving, 4–5; for public health policy lesson plan, 187; for renewable energy lesson plan, 62; for social media bioethics lesson plan, 181; for space collaboration lesson plan, 155; supporting, 184; about sustainability, 30–31; for taking action lesson plan, 171; teacher's response to, 5–6; for Typhoid Mary and disease lesson plan, 89; for water cycles lesson plan, 67; for watershed, 73

real-world connections, 77–78
reconfiguration, 45
recycling resources, 174
Reed, 50
Reflections on Big Science (Weinberg), 11
renewable energy, 60–62, 154
renewable energy (lesson plan), 61; assessment of, 66; case study in, 65–67; classroom materials in, 63; questions for, 62; resources for, 67; socio-cultural community engagement in, 66–67; socio-cultural context of, 63; solar house instructions in, 63–65; standards integration in, 62–63
resources: for community pollution lesson plan, 170; for computers lesson plan, 88; of Earth, 63; for local renewable energy lesson plan, 164; Nodes collection of, 47; for preservation lesson plan, 100–101; recycling, 174; for renewable energy lesson plan, 67; for space collaboration lesson plan, 160; for taking action lesson plan, 174–75; types of, 51–55; for Typhoid Mary and disease lesson plan, 94; for water cycles lesson plan, 73; for watershed lesson plan, 76

Reynolds, Michael, 166
robotics, 130–31, 151

school level STEM, 15–19
Science, Technology, Engineering and Mathematics (STEM), 3, 81; classroom level, 19–21; communities engaged by, 15; community level, 13–15; curriculum benefits of, 101–2, 148–49, 193–94; EthnoSTEM in, 14; school level, 15–19; social sciences curriculum with, 175–76; social studies and, 11–13; socio-cultural environment for, 4–5; socio-cultural environment integration with, 5–6; teachers devoting time to, 18–19
science-based design thinking protocol, 153
science-related careers, xiii
scientific argumentation, 21
screencastify, 55
Smiley, Jane, 35
Smithsonian Museums and Zoo, 53
social media, 182
social media bioethics (lesson plan), 180; assessment of, 183; essential and supporting questions for, 181; instructional procedures for, 182–83; socio-cultural community engagement in, 183; socio-cultural context of, 182; standards integration in, 181
social studies, 11–13
socio-cultural community engagement, 66–67; in ancient art lesson plan, 126; in community pollution lesson plan, 169; in computers lesson plan, 88; in Eastern medicine lesson plan, 116; in environmental health lesson plan, 186–87; in e-textiles lesson plan, 143; in fashion robotics lesson plan, 136; in First Amendment Rights lesson plan, 139–40; in Hip Hop music lesson plan, 147–48; in

Indigenous ways lesson plan, 121; in local renewable energy lesson plan, 164; in medical access lesson plan, 192; in Polynesian voyages lesson plan, 111; in preservation lesson plan, 99; in public health policy lesson plan, 189; in social media bioethics lesson plan, 183; in taking action lesson plan, 174; in water cycles lesson plan, 72; in watershed lesson plan, 76

socio-cultural context: of ancient art lesson plan, 123; of community pollution lesson plan, 166; of computers lesson plan, 84–85; of Eastern medicine lesson plan, 113; of environmental health lesson plan, 185; of e-textiles lesson plan, 142; of fashion robotics lesson plan, 134; of First Amendment Rights lesson plan, 138; of Hip Hop music lesson plan, 146; of local renewable energy lesson plan, 162; of medical access lesson plan, 191; of Polynesian voyages lesson plan, 108–9; of preservation lesson plan, 96; of public health policy lesson plan, 188; of renewable energy lesson plan, 63; of social media bioethics lesson plan, 182; of space collaboration lesson plan, 156; of taking action lesson plan, 172; of Typhoid Mary and disease lesson plan, 90; of water cycles lesson plan, 69; of watershed lesson plan, 74

socio-cultural environment, 4–6
socio-cultural participatory model, xiv
socio-cultural STEM: adolescent responsiveness of, 16; benefits of, 148–49, 193–94; at classroom level, 19–21; at community level, 13–15; curriculum benefits of, 101–2; curriculum development for, 7, 13; curriculum's integrative approach with, 6–7; expert opinions on, 77–79, 101–3, 126–28, 148–51, 175–76, 192–95; framework for, *12*; global communities and, 22; implementation challenges of, 79, 102–3, 149–51, 176, 194–95; inquiry-based teaching of, 19; interdisciplinary approach to, 149; lesson plans, 57; Nodes used in, 36; Pryor-Kang Model impacting, 36–38; at school level, 15–19; teaching curriculum of, 8

Socio-cultural STEM Curriculum Development Model, xiv, 34–35
socio-cultural theory, 176–77
socio-scientific issues (SSI), 12–14
solar house instructions, 63–65
Soper, George, 90
space collaboration (lesson plan): assessment of, 159; classroom materials for, 156; essential and supporting questions for, 155; instructional procedures for, 156–57; investigation concept map for, 157–58; modifications of, 159; resources for, 160; socio-cultural context of, 156; standards integration in, 155–56; student inquiries of, 157–58

SSI. *See* socio-scientific issues
standards integration: in ancient art lesson plan, 123; in community pollution lesson plan, 165–66; in computers lesson plan, 84; in Eastern medicine lesson plan, 112; in environmental health lesson plan, 185; in e-textiles lesson plan, 141; in fashion robotics lesson plan, 133–34; in First Amendment Rights lesson plan, 137–38; in Hip Hop music lesson plan, 145–46; in Indigenous ways lesson plan, 117–18; in local renewable energy lesson plan, 161; in medical access lesson plan, 190–91; from NGSS, 107, 117, 123, 155–56, 161, 166, 171; in Polynesian voyages lesson plan, 107–8; in preservation

lesson plan, 95–96; in public health policy lesson plan, 188; in renewable energy lesson plan, 62–63; in social media bioethics lesson plan, 181; in space collaboration lesson plan, 155–56; in taking action lesson plan, 171; in Typhoid Mary and disease lesson plan, 89–90; in water cycles lesson plan, 68; in watershed lesson plan, 73–74

STEM. *See* Science, Technology, Engineering and Mathematics

STEM-Social Studies (STEM-SS), 6

storage capacity, 35

student choice, 99

student inquiries, 85–86; to e-textiles lesson plan, 143; to First Amendment Rights lesson plan, 139; to Hip Hop music lesson plan, 147; to space collaboration lesson plan, 157–58

students: brainstorming by, 5–6; contributions from, 49–50; FOK for, 14; health-related issues of, 185; interactive platforms for, 55; in middle school, 15–16, 60–61, 176–77, 191; questions from, 4–5; scientific argumentation for, 21; socio-cultural participatory model for, xiv

sustainability: communities concerns for, 28–29; intergenerational justice related to, 59; physical evident for, 29; questions about, 30–31

Sustainable Development Goals, 67

Tai Chi, 115

taking action (lesson plan), 170; assessment of, 173; classroom materials for, 171–72; essential and supporting questions for, 171; instructional procedures for, 172–73; resources for, 174–75; socio-cultural community engagement in, 174; socio-cultural context of, 172; standards integration in, 171

TCM. *See* Traditional Chinese Medicine

teachers: beliefs of, 6; co-teaching of, 16; curriculum development by, 194–95; curriculum themes shared by, 31; on environmental health, 186; ethical implications considered by, 78–79; health care and, 192; inquiry-based learning and, 20–21; interactive platforms for, 55; interdisciplinary team planning of, 17; learning outcomes by, 78; of mathematics, 17, 49; question response of, 5–6; real-world connection goals of, 77–78; socio-cultural STEM curriculum from, 8; STEM curriculum time devoted by, 18–19; of weather science, 5

teacher teams, 16–17; curriculum goals stated by, 31–32; curriculum implemented by, 41–42; inputs and outputs, *39–40* ; participant perspectives integrated with, 27

teams, Pryor-Kang Model discussions by, 44–45

technology, 50–51, 121

thematic strands, NCSS and, 89

Think-Puzzle-Explore VTS, 162

This We Believe (AMLE), 16

timeline project, 86–87

Traditional Chinese Medicine (TCM), 106, 111, 113

Transforming Our World (United Nations), 59

Twin Forks simulation, 90–91

Tyler, R. W., 38

Typhoid Mary, 82, 91–92

Typhoid Mary and disease (lesson plan): accommodations and modifications to, 93–94; assessment of, 93; instructional procedures for, 90–91; Mallon's own works in, 92–93; resources for, 94; socio-cultural context for, 90; standards integration in, 89–90; supporting questions for, 89; Typhoid Mary case in, 91–92

typhoid outbreak, 90

United Nations, 59
United States (U.S.), school systems of, 130
units of study, in curriculum, 34
U.S. *See* United States

videos: input-outputs of, 48–49; pre-recorded, 48; production sites of, 55; as technological tool, 50–51; water cycle, 68
visible thinking strategies (VTS), 153, 162
visual vocabulary, 97
VTS. *See* visible thinking strategies
Vygotsky, L. S., 3, 153

warm-up activities, 96–98
water, on Earth's surface, 107
watercolors, preservation of, 126
water cycles, 60–61; model instructions, 69–70; video, 68
water cycles (lesson plan): assessment of, 72; case study in, 72–73; classroom materials for, 68–69; essential and supporting questions for, 67; objectives of, 67–68; resources for, 73; socio-cultural community engagement in, 72; socio-cultural context of, 69; standards integration in, 68; water cycle model instructions in, 69–70; water filter test in, 70–71
water filter test, 70–71
Water is Life theme, 61
watershed (lesson plan): assessment of, 76; case study in, 75–76; classroom materials for, 74; essential and supporting questions for, 73; resources for, 76; socio-cultural community engagement in, 76; socio-cultural context of, 74; standards integration in, 73–74; watershed model instructions in, 74–75
watershed model instructions, 74–75
watersheds, 73–76
watershed-scale processes, 61
weather science, 5
Weinberg, Alvin W., 11
Wiggins, Grant, 30–31
Wilhelm, Jeffrey, 30
Wilson, Woodrow, 138

yoga, 115

About the Contributors

CHAPTER 6

Dr. Sharon Locke is the Director of the Center for STEM Research, Education, and Outreach and a Professor of Environmental Sciences and Education at Southern Illinois University Edwardsville. She studies how innovative curricula and programs can increase the participation of traditionally underrepresented groups and has led several projects that integrate STEM and humanities, including the middle school program Digital East St. Louis.

Dr. Georgia Bracey is a Research Assistant Professor at the Center for STEM Research, Education, and Outreach at Southern Illinois University Edwardsville and an experienced K-12 teacher. She studies STEM teaching and learning in formal and informal settings, including authentic science experiences and citizen/participatory science.

INTERVIEWEES

Dr. Jessica Krim is a former professor of science education and Chair of the Department of Teaching and Learning at Southern Illinois University Edwardsville and is currently a STEM education evaluation specialist with Goshen Education Consulting.

Mr. Ben Scamihorn is a science teacher at Roxana Senior High School in Roxana, Illinois.

CHAPTER 7

Dr. Whitney Blankenship is Assistant Professor of History, San Antonio College, former high school social studies teacher, and a member of the Editorial Advisory Board of the *Teaching Critical Themes in American History* series.

Dr. Anne Aydinian-Perry is Assistant Professor of Secondary Social Studies Education, University of Wyoming, a National Board-Certified Teacher, and co-Director of Publications for the Social Science Education Consortium.

Dr. Dean P. Vesperman is Associate Professor of Education, University of Wisconsin-River Falls and editor of the *Iowa Journal for the Social Studies*.

Dr. Matthew T. Missias is a School Support Specialist and Adjunct Faculty at Grand Valley State University and a research portfolio program evaluation examiner.

INTERVIEWEES

Dr. Tonia Dousay is the Dean of the College of Education at the University of Alaska. Her area of expertise is learning, design, and technology.

Dr. Katherine McGaha has taught English language arts, science, and social studies as an elementary teacher in the Houston Independent School District and is a teacher educator at the University of Houston.

Ms. Rachelle Haroldson is an Instructional Designer at the University of Wisconsin-River Falls.

CHAPTER 8

Dr. Matthew Lindquist is the Director of Educator Preparation at Alaska Bible College and District Core Math Specialist for the Matanuska-Susitna Borough School District.

Dr. Joseph Peters is Dean of Education at Georgia College & State University, Milledgeville, Georgia.

INTERVIEWEES

Dr. Suzanna Roman-Oliver is Assistant Professor of Science Education, Georgia College & State University.

Dr. Rebecca Cooper is Professor of Curriculum and Instruction, Science Education, Georgia Gwinnett College.

Dr. Anthony Stawiery is Assistant Professor of Science Education, Augusta University.

Dr. Lacey D. Huffling is Associate Professor of Science Education, Georgia Southern University.

CHAPTER 9

Dr. Lily R. Liang is Professor of Computer Science at the University of the District of Columbia in Washington, DC. She conducts research in computer science education, cybersecurity, artificial intelligence, and digital image processing.

Dr. Rui Kang is Professor of Education at Georgia College & State University. She conducts research in mathematics education, STEM education, and teacher preparation and professional development.

Dr. Briana Wellman is Associate Professor and Chair of the Department of Computer Science and Information Technology, University of the District of Columbia, Washington, DC. She conducts research on artificial intelligence, cybersecurity, robotics, and computer science.

INTERVIEWEES

Dr. George Dimitoglou is Associate Professor of Computer Science and Information Technology at Hood College in the state of Maryland. His areas of expertise include software engineering and cybersecurity.

Ms. Onyinye Ukeneru-Steve is a high school Career and Technology Education (CTE) teacher in the District of Columbia Public Schools (DCPS), specializing in information technology.

Mr. Daniel Scott is a high school Career and Technology Education (CTE) teacher in the District of Columbia Public Schools (DCPS), specializing in information technology.

CHAPTER 10

Dr. Barbara O'Donnell is Professor of Teacher Education at Southern Illinois University Edwardsville. Her research focuses on social studies, STEM education, and creativity.

INTERVIEWEES

Dr. Michael Karpyn teaches social science courses at Marple Newtown Senior High School, Pennsylvania, and is the editor of *Teaching the Causes of the American Civil War, 1850–1861*.

Mr. Nicholas Simmons teaches social science courses at Mount Olive High School and Lincoln Land Community College, Illinois.

CHAPTER 11

Dr. Adam I. Attwood is an assistant professor in the Eriksson College of Education at Austin Peay State University. He was previously a social studies teacher and department chair (grades 6–12).

Dr. Donna F. Short has 16 years of teaching experience in middle school science, holds an MAEd in K-8 science, teaches science methods courses, and is Co-Director of the Jack Hunt STEM Center at Austin Peay State University.

Dr. Philip C. Short has been a science educator for over four decades and is currently a professor of science education and co-director of the Jack Hunt STEM Center at Austin Peay State University.

INTERVIEWEES

Dr. Jonathan Hall is an assistant professor of science education at California State University, San Bernardino.

Ms. Crystal Tebbe is a science teacher and science club advisor at Fairbanks High School, Ohio.

About the Authors

Caroline R. Pryor is Professor of Curriculum and Instruction in the School of Education, Health, and Human Behavior at Southern Illinois University Edwardsville. She joined SIUE in 2005 after serving five years as an Assistant Professor/Regents Fellow at Texas A&M University. Pryor teaches graduate courses in Analysis of Instruction, Curriculum Models, Adult Education, and Grant Writing. Pryor's teaching and research focus is STEM-Social Studies curriculum integration. She is the immediate past chair of the Special Interest Group (SIG) Democratic Citizenship in Education of the American Educational Research Association (AERA) and serves on the SIUE Museum Advisory Council.

Research Profile: Dr. Pryor is Senior Editor of the fifteen volume book series *Teaching Critical Themes in American History,* Peter Lang Publishers. She is the past editor of the international journal *Learning for Democracy: An International Journal of Thought and Practice*, a 2019 SIUE STEM Center Community Impact Scholar, and a Wye Fellow of the Aspen Institute. She is the author of over fifty publications, including *Teaching Lincoln: Legacies and Classroom Struggles* (with S. Hansen). Pryor received the 1998 Best Paper Award from the Arizona Educational Research Organization, an affiliate of AERA.

Her research has generated award-nominated publications for the National Council of the Social Studies, AERA, and the Association of Teacher Educators. She has received six National Endowment for the Humanities grant awards for her workshops for school teachers on Abraham Lincoln, as well as an award from the American Library Association with the National

Endowment for the Humanities to bring the Smithsonian exhibit *Lincoln and the Constitution* to SIUE.

Rui Kang is Professor of Secondary Education (grades 6-12) at Georgia College & State University (GCSU). She teaches graduate courses in numerous areas, including math pedagogy, assessment, educational research, and learner development. She holds two Ph.D. degrees: one in Curriculum and Instruction from Texas A&M University (2007) and one in Mathematics Education from the University of Georgia (2022). Her scholarship focuses on mathematics teaching and learning, STEM education, and teacher preparation and professional development. Her publications include articles that appear in journals such as the *International Journal of Science and Mathematics Education*, *Journal of Social Studies Research*, *School Science and Mathematics*, and *Mathematics Teacher*. She served as the Program Chair of the Special Interest Group (SIG) Democratic Citizenship in Education of the American Educational Research Association (AERA) from 2016 to 2018. She has taught high school mathematics and holds a clear, renewable teaching certificate in mathematics in the state of Georgia. She currently serves as a Co-Principal Investigator (Co-PI) of several grants funded by the National Science Foundation (NSF), the Georgia Foundation for Public Education (GFPE), and the Partnership for Inclusive Innovation (PIN), Georgia Smart Communities Challenge, 2023.

www.ingramcontent.com/pod-product-compliance
Lightning Source LLC
Chambersburg PA
CBHW061441300426
44114CB00014B/1790